But Little Dust

But Little Dust

Life Amongst the 'Ex-Untouchable' Buddhists of India

Padmasuri

WINDHORSE PUBLICATIONS

Published by Windhorse Publications
11 Park Road
Birmingham
B13 8AB

First published by Allborough Press 1990
First Windhorse edition 1997
© Hilary Blakiston (Padmasuri) 1990
Cover photograph © Dhammarati
Photograph of Dr Ambedkar © Clear Vision Trust Picture Archive
Other photographs courtesy of Dhammarati, Karuna Trust,
Padmasuri, Virabhadra, and Nagabodhi

Design Dhammarati
Photo layout Graham Parker

Printed by Biddles Ltd
Guildford, Surrey

British Library Cataloguing in Publication Data
A catalogue record for this book is available from the British Library

ISBN 0 904766 85 3

The publishers acknowledge with gratitude permission to quote extracts
from the following:
Mrs Winifred Binster for the quotation from E.A. Burtt (ed.), *Teachings of the
Compassionate Buddha*, New American Library, 1955, on page 51.
Dharma Publishing for extracts from *The Life and Liberation of Padmasambhava*, on page 74.
Eleanor Zelliot, for the poem on page 107.

For all those participating in the Peaceful Dharma Revolution

about the author

Padmasuri was born Hilary Blakiston in Aylesbury, Buckinghamshire, in 1951. In her mid-twenties, a desire to travel took her to India, a country which was later to become an important part of her life. She moved to Cornwall in 1976 to further her nursing training as a midwife, and came across the Friends of the Western Buddhist Order (FWBO). Four years on she was ordained into the Western Buddhist Order itself and given the name Padmasuri.

In 1982 she left London, where she had set up a vegetarian restaurant run by a team of Buddhist women, and moved to Poona in India to help establish a medical project among the ex-Untouchables. Eventually she decided to put her energy into teaching meditation and Buddhism to the ex-Untouchable Buddhist women. In 1987, on behalf of her teacher, Sangharakshita, Padmasuri helped to conduct the ordination of one of the first women in India to join the Western Buddhist Order.

Now back in England, Padmasuri lives with other Buddhists in a residential women's community in Cambridge, and spends most of her time helping women to transform themselves in the light of their Buddhist ideals.

contents

acknowledgements

I should like to thank the many friends who have helped, advised, and spurred me on to write this book.

In particular I should like to mention Vajrapushpa, who has been a constant source of encouragement. Reading and re-reading the book at various stages of its development, she inspired me with confidence to speak out, to keep going, assuring me that what I was writing would be of interest to others when I began to doubt.

Secondly, Jinananda, who, with extraordinary patience and good humour, put hours of time into juggling around and tightening up my unruly manuscript. I am indebted to his consistently skilful and enjoyable editing.

For this second edition, further thanks go to all the Windhorse Publications team, also to Dhammarati for his sensitive design work. Finally a special mention to Hannah Manasse who persevered with further editing on the book during a time of sudden affliction in her own life.

The poem beginning 'Ah the married life …' was composed by Bahinabai Chaudhari, an illiterate village woman of Maharashtra. Her many songs were written by her son who became a well-known poet. This English translation is by Philip Emblom and Jayant Karve, and first appeared in the *Journal of South Asian Literature: a Marathi Sampler* in winter–spring 1982. My gratitude to its editor, Eleanor Zelliot, for giving me permission to quote from the poem called 'Samsar'.

Padmasuri
Cambridge
January 1997

a c t i o n

Shortly after he gained Enlightenment, the Buddha considered what he should do. It occurred to him that the Truth he had discovered was hard to see and to understand, and he inclined towards solitude, reluctant to teach what he had discovered.

Seeing this thought in the Buddha's mind, the god Brahma Sahampati appeared before him and said: 'Lord, let the Sublime One teach. There are men and women with but little dust on their eyes who are wasting their lives through not hearing the Dharma. Some of them will gain final knowledge if the Master teaches.'

Hearing this the Buddha surveyed the world with the compassionate eye of an Enlightened being, and saw beings with little dust on their eyes and others with much dust on their eyes, some with keen faculties and others with dull faculties, with good qualities and bad qualities, some who would be easy to teach and some who would be hard to teach, and some who dwelt seeing fear in the world.

He resolved to go out into the world to teach people what he had discovered, for the well-being and happiness of men and women everywhere.

ADAPTED FROM A STORY IN THE PALI CANON

Miss Bennet's Bangles

Bhaja village is an insignificant hamlet in western India. Above and to the east of its cluster of mud-built huts, around which chickens scrabble and peck in the parched earth, where water buffalo amble gracefully along its single dusty track, and men, women, and children live toil-worn lives in a fashion little changed over the centuries, stand the majestic ancient rock-cut caves of Bhaja. A place of pilgrimage for Buddhists from all over the world, it is where some of the earliest Buddhist monks once lived and practised, following a spiritual tradition that is still developing today, of unparalleled richness and penetration.

In the valley below the caves and to the west, an unobtrusive collection of one-storey buildings has been built, within which, on the evening of 18 January 1987, two ex-Untouchable women were ordained into that same tradition. By taking this step they moved away for ever from a religious culture which labelled them subhuman and denied them any hope of dignity and freedom, and committed themselves instead to the sublime and transforming ideals and practice of Buddhism.

This book describes my part in the coals-to-Newcastle enterprise that led to their ordination; it is the story of an Englishwoman helping to bring the teaching of the Buddha back to India. It also provides close glimpses of life in an ex-Untouchable community today, seen through my eyes as I worked as a nurse and midwife in a shanty-town on the outskirts of Poona in the early 1980s.

The long threads of my journey to Bhaja must be traced back some two and a half decades, however, to Wroxall Abbey Boarding School for Girls, in Warwickshire. The twenty or so girls of Miss Bennet's second form are unalluringly dressed in classic St Trinian's style, from the Clarks brown sandals to the striped tie coming well adrift from the collar of a sky-blue Viyella shirt, under a navy blue tunic. The room is heavily scented with ink and chalk, the desks are deeply pitted, the linoleum scuffed and scored. It requires a strong imagination to feel warmth from the radiator. Outside, a misty drizzle hangs in the air, half obscuring the chapel tower in the distance across the lawns. I am already dreading the grim sequel to the currant-bun-and-cold-milk break, when I'll have to change into my pleated shorts and run the straight drive to the bleak games pitch, stick in hand, for an agonizing hour of hockey.

My form-mistress is Miss Bennet, diminutive, bespectacled, her iron-grey hair cropped. This morning, as a special treat, she has brought in some slides of Africa, where she worked after the war. Her blue eyes light up as we pull down the blinds and huddle together, avid as birds, around the central desks, while the whirr of the projector fan gains momentum. Soon I am spellbound by gorgeous images. Elemental warriors, armed and plumed, stamp out tribal dances, women carry pots from the river, proud as royalty, and shining, naked black children laugh, all against a backdrop of mud huts with straw roofs, palm trees, brilliant foliage, and a cloudless blue sky. It dawns on me that I could plunge into this brilliant and sensuous world, and perhaps be able to help those who live in such conditions. A seed is planted which will lie dormant for many years. At the end of the show, as the strip lights flicker on and the blinds are drawn up, Miss Bennet reverently gives each of her pupils a brightly-coloured plastic bangle from Africa. I still have that bangle today.

I was born in 1951 into a loving and secure family, the daughter of a kind, middle-class Anglican clergyman of slowly developing eccentricity, and a capable and outspoken nurse. I am the youngest of three children. My father is the last in a long line of Reverend Blakistons. My brother Roger, while inheriting the eccentric streak that is the essential hallmark of a Church of England clergyman, broke with tradition to become a professional magician and illusionist. My petite but resolute and self-possessed sister, Philippa, took up Anthroposophy in her early twenties, and today works mainly with disabled children in Rudolf Steiner schools.

When I was still a baby, the family moved from rural Buckinghamshire to the urban Midlands so that my father could secure a better-paid living in order to feed and clothe his growing family. At the age of eleven I was sent to boarding school on a clergyman's daughter's bursary and with some financial help from my very generous great-aunt Nancy. She drank tumblers full of sweet sherry before lunch and pink gins before dinner, and could be seen most days of the week either striding through Windsor Great Park with a snuffling pug in tow, or playing a round of golf at Sunningdale before an evening of bridge. I was very fond of her, and not only because her maid brought me breakfast in bed.

When I left school I maintained a strong though largely unexpressed interest in the developing world. There was a time when the organization Voluntary Service Overseas (VSO) sent school leavers to help as general workers on their projects, but by the time I applied they required only trained people such as doctors, nurses, teachers, and agriculturalists. At that stage in my life I was not prepared to knuckle down to any kind of serious training, and some contrary spirit drew me to take a short course in cordon bleu cookery, and then to work for some of the wealthiest and most privileged people in Europe. It was not long before this world of gracious living lost its attraction for me and, following a sad love affair while working for a countess in a Palladian villa in northern Italy, I decided to train as a nurse. I was twenty-one.

Three years later I qualified as a nurse at London's Middlesex Hospital and applied to do VSO. Again the requirements had changed. A general nursing qualification was no longer enough; they wanted specialists, which for me would mean a minimum of a year's postgraduate training. A little despondent, but not deterred, I took six months off work and travelled overland to India. Returning to England, I moved from London to Cornwall and plunged into a year's course in midwifery. It was there, during the hot summer of 1976, in a stuffy little upstairs room in a partly derelict building in Truro, that I made my first contact with living Buddhism.

I had given up formal Christianity a number of years earlier and perhaps my trip to the East had been an unconscious search for an alternative, though I had never been a hippie and was not looking for a guru or enlightened master to initiate me into the meaning of life. Knowing nothing of Buddhism before my first meditation class, I surprised and even shocked not only my family and some of my friends but also myself by declaring after only a few months that I was definitely not a Christian but a Buddhist. This was not an attraction to the exotic or the mysterious. What first struck me about Buddhism was how it simply made sense.

One of the fundamental differences between Christianity and Buddhism is that in the former Jesus Christ is understood to have claimed to be the son of God. Those who wish to gain salvation must recognize him as such, since otherwise they have no hope of doing so. The Buddha, on the other hand, was born an ordinary human being, and through his own efforts gained a state of human perfection that Buddhists call Enlightenment. Jesus Christ was the bringer of salvation, whereas the Buddha was only the one who showed the way to salvation, discovering a path which every man and woman can, if they choose, follow by their own human effort. Since in Buddhism there is no God, it is, unlike Christianity, Islam, or Hinduism, a non-theistic religion. Many Buddhists even prefer not to describe Buddhism as a religion, as the word connotes a belief in God. Theistic religions teach that God is infallible, and therefore that his word cannot be questioned. What the Buddha taught was based on his own reason and experience, and, as he himself urged, should not be followed unquestioningly or regarded as dogma. In fact the Buddha emphasized that one should think for oneself, questioning everything and testing it out as a goldsmith tests his gold in the heat of a fire.

In Cornwall I attended some lectures on the Buddha's Noble Eightfold Path, which comprises a Path of Vision and a Path of Transformation. I learned that, once we have a glimpse of Perfect Vision, then through practising the other stages of the Path other elements of our lives can gradually be brought into alignment with that Vision. Developing and refining our emotions, speech, actions, livelihood, effort, and concentration, and ultimately developing perfect meditation, we can transform our lives in accordance with our vision. I learned that though we can realize that life as we know it is essentially unfulfilling, we soon forget our realization and cover it up, not allowing it to motivate us to do something about it. Perfect Vision is not just an intellectual understanding, but a direct experience that impels us towards an inconceivable emancipation.

Looking back, it is hard to recall exactly what it was in those lectures that spoke so strongly to me, but I felt as though I had come home; as though someone was speaking a language that resonated so strongly within me that I just couldn't ignore it. Buddhism seemed to offer a path that Christianity did not, and its discovery was very exciting to me. Never having deeply questioned my own beliefs in God as a child or adolescent, it came as quite a surprise that I could so easily give him up, but I did, and I never looked back.

During this time I continued to study pelvic anatomy and physiology, and delivered numerous babies. I too was undergoing a kind of birth, and it was not to be without complications. A year later and almost qualified as a midwife, I re-applied to VSO. This time I seemed a suitable candidate: not too young, quite mature, single, well-travelled, having good life experience, keen, stable, adaptable.... In due course I received a letter of acceptance: 'We would like to post you to Malawi for two years.'

I thought of Africa, of Miss Bennet, and of glossy black babies. Had my dream come true? Far from feeling delight and excitement I felt my heart sink. After so many years of trying to get what I thought I wanted, I wrote and told the organization that I was unable to accept the post in Malawi. Understandably, they were not pleased and I received a stern letter suggesting that I was breaking a contract, and asking me to return the train fare they had provided for the interview. It hurt a little; I knew they would be extremely cautious about any further application I made, but I also had a strong conviction that the course of action I was taking was the right one. I had an unknown, uncharted future ahead of me and what I felt was a sense of freedom.

The Buddhists I met in Cornwall were members of a movement called the Friends of the Western Buddhist Order (FWBO), which was founded by Sangharakshita, an Englishman. Born Dennis Lingwood in Tooting, London, in 1925, he became a Buddhist as a young man, and having been conscripted to India he remained there after the war and was ordained a Buddhist monk. He travelled, studied, and taught in the East for twenty years. It was a time when the age-old verities of Hindu society were being shaken up by the drive to form a unified and democratic state after independence had been won in 1947. Among the most dramatic events of this period was one in which Sangharakshita himself took a major role: the mass conversion to Buddhism of hundreds of thousands of ex-Untouchables along with their leader, Dr Ambedkar.

Untouchability is part of the Hindu caste system, a system of graded inequality backed by the authority of the Hindu scriptures. Right at the bottom of the caste system are those both called and treated as Untouchables – considered to be so inherently inferior as to pollute others. Forced to live outside villages in the most unhealthy quarters, they were allowed to do only the most menial and degrading of work, often having to beg in order to survive. They were not allowed to wear new clothes or to own property, and were denied any form of secular or religious education.

Though in 1950 it was declared illegal to treat anyone as 'untouchable', chains forged over centuries, and embedded in the religious fabric of a culture, take more than laws to break.

Only someone of the most extraordinary spirit, persistence, and courage could hope to overcome the disadvantage of being treated as a spiritual pollutant wherever he went. Bhimrao Ramji Ambedkar was such a man. By the 1920s, he had succeeded in becoming the first Untouchable to matriculate, and then, helped by two socially-minded Indian rulers, he completed his education in Britain and the USA. Eventually he became the first Law Minister of free India and played a leading part in drafting the Indian constitution.

Ambedkar began his work for the Untouchables by working politically to try and reform the caste system from within. By 1935, however, he had reached the conclusion that the only way to eradicate Untouchability was to break away completely from the caste system that created it. None the less, he saw the need for spiritual guidance and inspiration and, not wishing to leave his followers with no religion, he considered at length alternative religions to which he might turn. He studied the major world religions, evaluating them against four criteria he had devised, and came to the conclusion that Buddhism was the only one that fulfilled all four.

The first criterion was that a religion should uphold the highest ideals for both humankind and society; it should advocate a natural morality. He recognized that without the sanction of law or morality, society would disintegrate. Law, he felt, actually plays a very small part in society, and is intended to keep the minority within the range of social discipline. The majority has to be left to sustain its social life by the observance of morality. Morality, based on such ideals as generosity, non-violence, and truthfulness, must therefore remain the governing principle in every society. Buddhism not only encourages the observance of ethical precepts, but also upholds the highest ideals of wisdom and compassion, giving practical ways in which to develop these qualities. Disciplines such as meditation, which is the cultivation of positive, higher, more refined states of mind and consciousness, help to lead the practitioner to higher realms of being.

Secondly, Ambedkar believed that any religion or philosophy should be in accord with reason. He had experienced the extreme suffering created by the irrational beliefs of both Caste Hindus and his own Untouchable people – for example the misery caused by the belief that an Untouchable, by merely touching a Caste Hindu, would automatically pollute him or her. He had seen the suffering caused by superstitions that could be damaging to health and even fatal, and by the unquestioning worship of 'holy men' and gurus which led people to abdicate all responsibility for themselves. The Buddha, on the contrary, always taught that one should believe nothing without examining it for oneself and testing it against one's own reason and experience.

Ambedkar's third criterion was that a religion should encourage equality, liberty, and fraternity. In Buddhism there is no caste, class, colour, or gender prejudice. The Buddha's teachings are for all who wish to use them. His Dharma is a path of self-transcendence to be understood personally by those who follow it, leading them to higher states of experience, where body, speech, and mind are free from greed, hatred, and ignorance.

His fourth criterion was that a religion should not sanctify or ennoble poverty: 'Renunciation of wealth by those who have it may be a blessed state. Poverty never can be. To declare poverty to be a blessed state is to pervert religion, perpetuate vice and crime, and consent to make earth a living hell.' Hundreds of thousands of Untouchables earned, and still earn, their living by begging or scavenging in rubbish heaps, living without a roof over their heads in dire and inhuman conditions. To Ambedkar, the idea that a religion should sanctify such poverty was perverse and unacceptable. The Buddha taught a middle path between self-denial and self-indulgence.

Thus it was that at a historic ceremony in Nagpur in the centre of India on 14 October 1956, Dr Ambedkar and some 500,000 followers recited the three Refuges – committing themselves to the Buddha, the Dharma (his teaching), and the Sangha (the spiritual community) – and the traditional five ethical precepts, thereby becoming Buddhists. Dr Ambedkar knew that if the conversion was to be a success, it had to be followed by proper teaching, and he emphasized above all that Buddhism was a religion to be practised. Tragically, only six weeks after the conversion he died, leaving his new Buddhist movement leaderless and in a state of shock.

Sangharakshita had been a close adviser to Ambedkar, and at once stepped into the breach, spending the winter months of the next seven years addressing mass rallies of the new Buddhists, teaching them the basic principles of their faith, and converting thousands more ex-Untouchables. By the mid-sixties, however, after a visit to England at the invitation of the English Buddhist establishment, he decided that he wanted to contribute to the spread of the Dharma in the West. He believed that Buddhism would take root in the West only when the vital core of the Dharma could be understood by and manifested in people who were living a Western Buddhist life. He sought out Western cultural models and Western language through which to communicate the universal principles of the Buddha's teachings, and in 1967 he drew up the constitution of an entirely new kind of Buddhist movement: the FWBO. A year later he ordained twelve men and women as Dharmacharis/Dharmacharinis ('Dharma-farers'), bringing into being the Western Buddhist Order (WBO) itself, the spiritual community of fully committed individuals that would become the heart of the movement.

Over the years the movement has expanded into other parts of Europe, Australasia, and the USA. There are now nearly 600 Order members worldwide, plus thousands of Friends of the Order, teaching Buddhism and meditation in cities, running country retreat centres, and setting up businesses based on Buddhist principles. These are all separate, self-governing projects, connected by a worldwide network of friendships.

In 1979 the wheel came full circle, and Jeremy Goody, having been ordained and given the name Lokamitra in 1973, arrived in India to spearhead a new development of the great work begun by Dr Ambedkar in 1956. Warmly received by many people who had known Sangharakshita, he very quickly started giving lectures, running courses in Buddhism, leading retreats, and publishing a newsletter. Within a couple of years, several ex-Untouchables had been ordained into the WBO (known in India as Trailokya Bauddha Mahasangha – TBM).

Meanwhile, I had moved from Cornwall to London's East End, where I helped to establish and manage a vegetarian restaurant next to the London Buddhist Centre. In 1978 I had my first personal conversation with Sangharakshita, during which we discussed the possibility of setting up a medical project amongst the ex-Untouchables of Maharashtra in western India. At once I felt I would soon be able to slot in a jigsaw piece that I had been puzzling over for years. In 1980 I was ordained and given the name Padmasuri, which means 'Lotus Heroine'. I was pleased with the way my new name combined the traditionally feminine qualities of the lotus flower – receptivity and unfoldment – with the more traditionally masculine qualities of heroism – being pioneering and adventurous.

In 1982, with financial backing from Aid For India, a charity set up by the FWBO, I set out with another member of the Order, a doctor called Virabhadra, to establish a medical project in Maharashtra. I was working most closely with Lokamitra and Virabhadra, but there was also Vajraketu who had been recruited to oversee the building work of the medical centre. He and I had fallen for each other while he was reconstructing the restaurant where I was working in London, and we were already lovers when we flew out to India for the first time.

For three years I worked primarily on the medical and social project. But then visa restrictions were imposed and foreigners doing social work were no longer allowed to stay in India, which meant that first Vajraketu and then Virabhadra had to leave the country and were not allowed to return. When my time was up I left quietly, but managed to return during the next four years on a six-monthly basis. I no longer did medical and social work, however; this was rather prematurely handed over to Indian people to run. Instead I turned to more specifically Buddhist work, focusing especially on the needs of Indian women. After an initial hiccup the social projects soon gained strength and momentum, and they are now being effectively run and expanded.

Lokamitra married an Indian woman shortly before the visa restrictions had come into force, and was thus able to stay in India. He was the chairman and overall administrator, and had been very actively involved in all the work on both social and more specifically Buddhist projects; it would have been something of a catastrophe if he had been forced to leave along with Vajraketu and Virabhadra.

Welcome to Poona

I first flew out to India in January 1982. On the morning of my flight London was looking bleak. Snow had fallen the previous day, partly melted, and frozen again overnight, making the first part of the journey from Hackney to Heathrow somewhat treacherous. I was travelling to India with Vajraketu, he to oversee the building construction work, and I to spend three months getting a feel for what it might be like to work as a nurse in the slums in India before finally committing myself. Friends saw us off from Heathrow, and after a couple of stops in the Middle East we arrived in Bombay before the dawn of the next day had broken.

Even at that hour, the heat and humidity were unbearable. We had thought we might be met but nobody had come. Hot, jet-lagged, and tired, we had the first row of what was by then a six-month-long relationship; we argued over whether we should take a train or a taxi to Poona. I had been informed that the former was slow but easier and more dependable while he had heard that the latter was easier and faster, though perhaps less dependable. In a country as chaotic and punishing as India, such tips can mean the difference between heaven and hell, so one comes to believe in the reliability of one's sources with the faith of a fanatic.

Vajraketu won. Either way we would have to take a local taxi from the airport into the heart of Bombay. Not understanding the queueing system, we somehow managed to skip the queue and hail a passing taxi. The sun was up. Having come straight from the snowy wastes of Hackney, I thought it seemed preposterously hot. We were bad-tempered and very tired, but luck was on our side, or so we thought. The taxi screeched to a halt. Relieved, we climbed in, slammed the doors shut, and as we headed out of the airport complex, confidently began to explain our destination to the driver in arm-waving language.

We had gone a few hundred yards when the taxi huffed, puffed, spluttered, and expired. The driver got out. He hit the bonnet. He hit the engine. He tried to start it again from the ignition. He cranked it. Finally, digging deep into his knowledge of the ways of engines, he kicked it. But even this was to no avail. Chastened, we carried our luggage, which included a small library for Lokamitra, back to the taxi-rank we had started from, and sheepishly queued up with scores of other disorientated-looking people.

Eventually we did get out of the airport, and within minutes were engulfed in the teeming cacophony of the city. The wide noisy roads heading towards the city centre were lined with hutments, mile upon mile of dismal shanties propping each other up. For the inhabitants it must be like living in a goldfish bowl: squatting outside to do their washing, comb their hair, or clean their teeth, the children playing in the stinking open gutters, ignoring the trucks, buses, and taxis, the aeroplanes thundering overhead, and us, the thousands of gaping foreigners who are whisked down those roads every day.

In the centre of Bombay we changed taxis and got a shared long-distance one up to Poona, some four hours' journey out of the city up the

Western Ghats (literally 'steps'). We took the journey at breakneck speed, squealing around hairpin bends, the driver paying no heed to the sobering view of overturned trucks halfway down the mountainside, and little more to trucks still on the road and coming in the opposite direction. Up we hurtled, through the pleasant leafy hill station of Lonavala, which at that time of year was ablaze with magenta bougainvillea, then across a plateau to come at last to the industrial suburbs of Poona. It was a much larger city than I had imagined. Once in the centre of Poona we exchanged our taxi for a black and yellow three-wheeled auto-rickshaw and, via a rather circuitous route, reached our destination: Ambedkar Society, the home of many Buddhists and the housing colony where Lokamitra had been living for the past three years and establishing Buddhist activities.

Although I had travelled in India before, it was a very different matter learning to live there instead of simply viewing it through the eyes of a tourist. My three-month trial period was, for a number of reasons, rather fraught but also very useful. Though I enjoyed the familiarity of being in the company of English friends, they were all men, whereas in London I had been used to living and working with women. Lokamitra and I had very little communication, mainly because he was constantly busy and under considerable pressure. Virabhadra, arriving some ten weeks after me, was still stunned by culture shock and prolonged jet lag when it was time for me to return to England, so we were not able to spend a very constructive time together to make plans for the work ahead. And my relationship with Vajraketu was put under a lot of strain, partly because he had little stomach for India at that stage, and partly because we had been advised to keep our relationship under wraps. Generally, Indian Buddhists accord respect most readily to someone in the robes of an *anagarika*, a celibate monk. A sexual relationship between unmarried committed Buddhists, while quite respectable in England, does not fit into Indian ideas of morally acceptable behaviour.

Fortunately I had enough to do in those months just adapting to the heat, the culture, and the food, looking around, taking things in, and meeting people. I was excited by what I saw of Lokamitra's work, but the real eye-opener was when my teacher Sangharakshita visited India to give a lecture tour. I was used to seeing him in England, addressing the psychological problems of perhaps a few dozen wary and sceptical disciples. In India he was equally affable and unruffled as he received the unreserved acclamation of thousands of people at a time, all hungry for the taste of freedom that Dr Ambedkar had offered them through Buddhism. I saw him speaking to thousands of his old friends and acquaintances from twenty-five years previously as well as to people who had only heard of him through the work that Lokamitra had been doing but who already revered him as their teacher.

Returning to England in April of the same year, I spent ten weeks joining in the work of fund-raising for the Karuna Trust (as Aid For India was now called; Karuna means 'compassionate action based on wisdom'). This involved knocking on people's doors and asking them to consider signing covenants to support our work. The aim is that through being kept in touch with progress through a newsletter, supporters of the charity will develop a positive and close interest in its work.

By October I had sorted out my affairs and was ready to leave England. The inevitable pre-departure anxiety was allayed by a surprise party the night before my flight to India. I was given presents, and my friend Judy Child performed a wonderful parody of 'This is Your Life' for my benefit. Early the next morning two car-loads of friends came to see me off from Heathrow. As we drove down the deserted streets of London's East End, three magnificent rainbows arched overhead and continued to hover until we reached the airport. I had no idea how long I would be out of the country and I walked through the security check choking back tears, and sat alone in the departure lounge where I felt sudden waves of panic. I desperately wanted to turn back. But I knew underneath that all would be well; the triple rainbow seemed to promise as much.

Vajraketu met me in Bombay, and escorted me up to Poona, this time by train. He had been close to giving up; sorting out who exactly owned the land on which the first buildings for the social work were to be constructed, and getting planning permission, required the patience of Job. In fact it was to be another three years before the building work was started, and as the overseeing of this work was to be Vajraketu's prime project he was left temporarily redundant and floundering. Meanwhile, he took on a far more difficult task. Despite his hatred for Bombay, he bravely decided to move there and establish activities among the thousands of Buddhists who live in some of the worst slums in Asia. Having no permanent base, he camped with friends or slept in the corridors of crumbling tenement blocks, and was to become, over the next two years, an excellent and inspiring Buddhist teacher. Long after his sudden enforced departure his name still reverberated around the tenements and shanties of Bombay.

Lokamitra, who had been strictly celibate for three years, was thinking about getting married, which was causing him a considerable amount of conflict, and Virabhadra, who I thought had got things rolling on the medical project in my absence, was experiencing the frustrations that are inevitable in India in any effort to start a new project. He was delighted that I had returned and was even happy to humour me in my fastidious desire for a room of my own. He, on the other hand, had submitted with admirable good humour to the free-for-all turmoil of life with a Buddhist family in Ambedkar Society. He slept alone in his room, but during the rest of the day it was used by various members of the ten-strong household for sewing clothes, sifting stones from rice, eating when there were guests, and mending bicycles, among other things. Neighbours walked in and out, children played games in it, yet the only times Virabhadra truly appeared to suffer from this invasion was when the eldest son played Abba or warbling Hindi film music on his tape recorder while he was trying to work. I rarely heard him complain, but as soon as the tape had finished Virabhadra would leap up and replace Abba with the strains of Janet Baker or a Mozart violin concerto, which wafted out of doors and windows to compete with clanking pots, snorting pigs, bicycle bells, and children's laughter. He enjoyed the family atmosphere, picked up the local language far quicker than any of the rest of us, and was treated and respected not only as one of the family, but as an important member of the local community.

Lokamitra lived in another small house in Ambedkar Society which was at that time the office headquarters for all our social and Buddhist activities. He slept in the kitchen, which was a walk-through room leading to the veranda, the meditation room, and the latrine. The enormous wooden bed, big enough for a well-fed family of five, totally dominated the room (it was a condition of the rental that the bed should not be moved). During the day, with mattress rolled up, the bed served as a writing table, a typing table, or a cyclostyling table, and at other times it served as a meeting platform for up to six people. Beneath the bed Lokamitra stored his clothes, his briefcase, books, a mosquito net, and our medical stocks and equipment, including several thousand government-supplied condoms. Lokamitra at that time being in robes and strictly celibate, this last item beneath his imperial-sized bed was a piquant reminder of his state in life, and the occasion of a good deal of facile merriment from time to time.

I had baulked at this, as I saw it, heroic lifestyle, and before I returned Virabhadra had kindly put an advertisement in the local newspaper: 'English nurse looking for self-contained accommodation in central Poona.' A flurry of replies greeted my arrival back in India, and within a couple of days I was on my bike following them up. The advertisement seemed to attract replies of a certain type – from middle-class Anglo-Indians and Parsees. I discovered on further investigation that what the respondents really wanted was a nice young English nurse to look after some elderly member of their family, in exchange, or part exchange, for the rent. But I did eventually find a suitable room in the servants' quarters of a large and crumbling bungalow in the leafy cantonment area of the city, which became my home for the next three years. It was self-contained and allowed me privacy, which is probably what enabled me to survive my first years in India.

The focus of the medical work was a large slum area in a suburb of Poona called Dapodi. From where I lived it was a bus or train ride away, and I usually took one or other of these. Occasionally, however, I would make my way to Dapodi via Virabhadra's house. I would cycle through the Poona cantonment and down a wide but dangerous tree-lined avenue which ran past the large and fashionable Blue Diamond Hotel. Crossing a bridge over the river, and dodging other cyclists, bullock carts, scooters, buses, rickshaws, and pedestrians, I would reach the Yerawada district. From here I would cycle alongside the river, where young boys jumped naked on the backs of water buffalo, submerged like whales in the muddy waters. The boys scrubbed the hides of the buffalo, while just a few yards away women beat their washing on stone slabs, laying it out to dry in the sun. Across the river stood the exclusive 'members only' Poona Boat Club. Taking a right turn away from the river and up a gentle incline, I would pass through a Sikh slum locality, permeated by the nauseating, acrid smell of illicit liquor. A small, garishly-painted Hindu temple at the top of the hill emitted the rhythmic, hypnotizing chants of devotees, accompanied by clanking of bells, and sometimes an accordion, most hours of the day every day of the week and, at the times of the frequent special festivals, all night as well. The end of my bike ride took me across an open piece of wasteland sometimes 'squatted' by nomadic tribes. It was from here that I got my first glimpse of the ochre-painted single-storey buildings of Ambedkar Society.

For much of my journey children waved at me, rickshaws, scooters, and buses honked at me, women laughed at me, boys and young men shouted out to me, and elderly folk stared bemused from doorways, shops, and street corners. Rarely were their attentions aggressive, but many were the times when I wished I could walk down a street quite unnoticed. At first I always wore Punjabi dress: a long top over baggy trousers which is extremely comfortable, but is usually only worn by unmarried girls, although Punjabis and very 'modern' women also wear them. Everyone was delighted at my first attempt to wear a sari, and told me that from now on I was always to wear one: though not married, someone of my age and status should wear a sari. To begin with I felt as though I were dressing up to go to a fancy-dress party rather than getting ready to work in the slums, but by dressing appropriately I was accepted, and became more 'one of them', even though I could never hope to fade into the background.

Finally I would turn off the tarmac roads and enter the lanes of the Society, where I began to be recognized as a friend rather than as an alien, and make my way to Virabhadra's house. From there I would ride pillion, demurely side-saddle in my sari, on his scooter, through further outskirts of Poona to Dapodi.

Namaste, Sister!

Starting the medical project wasn't easy. We had financial backing, skills, and enthusiasm, but we had no building from which to work, and had to discover through trial and error how best to establish our presence in the community. Although many foreigners, especially Europeans, visited Poona, it was usually either to study a course in hatha yoga with the world-renowned Iyengar or to stay at the even more famous Rajneesh ashram. I doubt if any Westerners had ever visited Dapodi before we started to work there. More recently, since the various social projects have got under way, the charity has expanded, and the more specifically Buddhist aspects of our work have become better known, visitors have come from all over the world.

Dapodi is a large, sprawling, predominantly slum area which, when I first went there, had greatly expanded over the previous decade as a result of a continuous migration from the villages to the cities of people in search of work. Whereas in the villages people live in large extended families, in the slums they tend to live in small family units. Dapodi is close to the main industrial area of the city, so employment opportunities there are better than in other areas; but unskilled manual labour still predominates, and most of the work is temporary. There are far fewer women workers than men and they also find work as unskilled labourers. All the settlements are built on private land, the inhabitants either renting the space on which to build their own hut or renting the hut itself. No area is officially designated a slum area.

Many of the slum dwellers, thirty per cent of males and sixty-five per cent of females, have had no formal education, and most live in severely overcrowded conditions. Well over half the people of Dapodi are Buddhists, followers of Dr Ambedkar. The rest are either Hindu or Muslim, and there are a few Christians. One great advantage of working in rural areas is that these different groups live in separate districts, but shanty towns like Dapodi cannot be mapped in this way. We were fortunate in that, as Buddhists, we were able to turn to the Mahila Mandalas (literally 'women's circles'), groups of Buddhist women who met weekly. With their help we quickly set up mother and child clinics and gradually established a presence in all the various localities. They would call a group of women together, tell them about our proposed work, get them to organize a venue, and invite all the mothers and children under five to attend at the appointed time.

Our first clinics were mainly run in the open air, weighing and measuring babies to detect malnutrition in its early stages, and giving advice accordingly. We emphasized preventive medicine, particularly trying to teach and encourage oral rehydration therapy. It is thought that in India alone 1,500,000 lives are lost every year through dehydration caused by diarrhoea. A simple solution of sugar, salt, and water in specific quantities prevents dehydration; this very basic rehydration formula has been described as one of the biggest medical breakthroughs of this century, as even the poorest of people will have these ingredients in their homes. Thus much of our work was in the field of preventive medicine, but we did do curative work as well, carrying around a metal trunk full of medicines on the back of Virabhadra's scooter from one locality to another. Before long we were known and trusted – and we began to see the results of our efforts.

Over the first three years we slowly expanded our activities, extending the medical work and moving into other areas such as kindergartens and hostels for children who lived too far away from a school or where conditions at home prevented them from studying. We set up adult literacy classes, free expression groups, informal education for scavenger children, a small library, tuition classes (after-school sessions in which homework was done), and much more. As we had originally intended, all these projects are now run by Indians, and the Poona project at last runs from a large purpose-built resource centre in Dapodi – the one Vajraketu initially came to India to build. Many of the social projects have also extended to other cities in the states of Maharashtra, Gujerat, and Andhra Pradesh.

Nothing in India seemed to be straightforward or direct. Even leaving my home in the morning involved slipping over the garden wall at the side in order to avoid menacing overtures from three guard dogs. On the days when I did not cycle, a ten-minute stroll took me to Poona central train station. The 8 o'clock local was packed full of commuters to the industrial areas on the outskirts of the city. Poona Junction being the starting point of the journey, I always managed to get a seat in one of the two Ladies Only compartments, which I shared with bright young office girls wearing strongly-scented white jasmine flowers in their hair, and talking incessantly about clothes, food, and film stars. We were also joined by gaggles of schoolchildren, dwarfed by their bulging satchels, and swinging their legs as they committed pages of their textbooks to memory; older, more sedate women doing their knitting; schoolteachers marking papers as the train swayed along; and babies, sitting on their mother's lap attached to a breast, standing looking out of the window, or being passed from one stranger's lap to another to make space for more people to squash into the narrow aisles. There were also weather-beaten women laden with baskets of fruit or vegetables sitting on the floor in the open doorways. Sometimes they were joined by a group of transvestites, who form a sub-caste of their own, who cracked coarse jokes, coyly played with their bangles, and shouted aggressively at any men – that is, any men actually dressed as such – who might try to enter the compartment.

To any sum of Indian humanity must be added a good number of beggars: a blind man warbling to the strum of a one-stringed instrument; a half-naked little girl with a rather gruesome portrait of a Hindu goddess hung in a frame around her neck doing a few steps of a dance with castanets, then holding out a hopeful palm; a leper exhibiting the stump of his arm in front of my face, eyes imploring. There was a woman selling hairpins and earrings from crumbling cardboard boxes, and a boy selling segments of guava smeared with salt and chilli powder. Many of these characters became familiar faces to me as we wedged ourselves like sardines on the wooden benches. By the second station we were almost sitting on each other's laps and treading on each other's feet; even the most demure had lost some of their composure, and large moons of perspiration glowed under the arms of their tight-fitting blouses.

To the amusement, and perhaps concern, of the more sophisticated and prim commuters, I befriended some weaver women who always travelled on the same train. They boarded with piles of rush mats in bundles on their heads, long- and short-handled brooms, and sometimes baskets. There were about six of them, all young, and at least two (one of whom couldn't have been more than fourteen years old) carrying babies in cloth slings across their sides. They were usually accompanied by three or four toddlers and they were travelling beyond Dapodi station to Pimpri bazaar, where they would sit all day selling their wares. They never carried train tickets and on at least three occasions the inspector came and found them without. He swore and cursed at them, threatened them, but never fined them: there would hardly have been any point.

They were amused and delighted that I entered into conversation with them, though their colloquialisms and guttural voices were so dense I found it hard to understand much of what they said. They lived, they told me, in tents of sackcloth not far from Poona station. The older women made the mats and brooms while the younger ones went out to sell them. I never discovered what the men who accompanied them did; usually they would have one or two male companions, and an ongoing banter of flirtation and abuse would ensue when the men dashed round to the women's compartment at each station to check out the women, before jumping back into their own carriage as the train started to move off. Without exception both men and women were earthy, tough, full of vigour and life, and they exuded a great sense of camaraderie. Their skins were very dark, their clothing tatty, and their feet bare. They mimicked some of the stuffier travellers with pitiless accuracy, employing a natural theatrical gift that often had me in stitches with laughter.

Many was the time they would plonk a wet baby on my lap and say, 'Have him (or her). We've got too many. Let him live with a white auntie!' Sometimes I was tempted. At other times they offered me scraps of food, which made me heave even to look at them. They cajoled me into buying one of their brooms, at a grossly inflated price, and once in the rainy season they stole my umbrella, but in a way I didn't mind. They wanted to show me where they lived, and I rather regret that I never went. Once when an English friend was with me they saw her camera, pushed their matted hair under the ends of their saris, held their babies next to their cheeks and smiled innocently. She clicked. 'Now we will become famous in your country!' they said. Much to the amusement of the other passengers they always waved me goodbye, and told me to take care, when I pushed my way out of the train at Dapodi to wend my way through the alleys to the Khandagales' house.

The Khandagale family was a great help in the early days of our work in Dapodi. At the beginning of each day Virabhadra and I would meet at their hut. Entering it was like walking into a Wendy house: it was only ten feet long and five feet wide, and just tall enough to stand up in. I would duck my head low through the doorway and go down two steps. Apart from a tiny barred window next to the open door, there was no natural light source, but it contained all the requirements of basic living. To the left of the door and under the window was a small area for washing surrounded by a waist-high wall, on top of which stood six shining brass water pots and a large black earthenware pot for cool drinking water, which was collected each morning from a communal tap. A metal bed stood alongside the left-hand wall with blankets and patchwork spreads neatly piled up at one end. The far end of the hut served as the kitchen area where Mrs Khandagale, squatting in a space three feet square, chopped vegetables, kneaded and rolled out chapattis, pounded spices, and cooked on a one-burner kerosene stove on the floor. Along the wall at the far end of the room were wooden shelves on which were arranged shining metal plates and canisters for dry food.

We would sit on the floor along the right-hand wall or perch on the bed opposite. On the wall hung a small browned mirror below which was a small ledge supporting a wireless, the family comb, and a tin of coconut hair oil. On either side of the mirror hung pictures, one of Dr Ambedkar and the other of the Buddha; and two or three hooks jutting from the wall held Mr Khandagale's spare trousers and shirt. Underneath the bed were a couple of metal trunks holding all the rest of the family possessions, together with six or eight chickens underneath an upturned woven straw basket. The cow-dung floor was renewed every six weeks by Mrs Khandagale and her daughter, the brick walls were coated with mud and painted sky blue, and the roof was made of sheets of corrugated metal which made the room an intolerable furnace in the hot season. Mr and Mrs Khandagale lived here along with their three fast-growing teenage sons and 'Baby', their eight-year-old daughter. Whenever I called it was spotlessly clean, neat, and tidy. It had no electricity, no running water, and of course no latrine.

For me it became a second home, as not only did Virabhadra and I meet here every morning, but here every lunchtime, sitting on the floor, we ate with our fingers excruciatingly hot, chillied food. A warm welcome greeted my arrival each morning and a cup of sweet tea was thrust into my hands as I sat on the bed to wait for Virabhadra. One of the sons might be squatting behind the low brick wall taking his morning 'bath', Mrs Khandagale would be making chapattis on the kerosene stove, while Baby might be scrubbing the pots and pans with ash in the alley outside the door, or stringing together white *mogra* flowers to wear as a garland in her hair. I was frequently filled in on some piece of local gossip, and had a chance to practise my Marathi with Mrs Khandagale, or Baby would practise her English with me before getting herself ready for mid-morning school. Often she would sit on the bed beside me so that I could plait her hair, before grabbing her satchel laden with books, swinging it over her shoulder, and rushing out into the bright sunlight. The other sons, if they were not already at school, would be sitting on the floor doing their homework. Everyone knew how to work around one another and I rarely, if ever, heard an argument.

When Virabhadra arrived on his scooter we would leave the Khandagales' and pick our way through the alleys, jumping over open drains and avoiding human excrement, to reach wherever was the venue for the clinic that day. It was not long before our faces were familiar, and we were hailed as we went, especially by children, 'Namaste, Doctor! Namaste, Sister!' If they were Buddhists they would also call out 'Jai Bhim!' (literally 'Victory to Bhim', a shortened version of Ambedkar's first name, Bhimrao). And like the Pied Piper of Hamelin, we would very often have a group of little children running along in our wake.

To begin with we held the clinics in the shade of a solitary tree in an alley, or in someone's home. Later we had our own huts in each locality, which at other times would be used as kindergartens, or for adult literacy, sewing, and tuition classes. Wherever we were, cloths would be laid on the ground, a weighing scale hung from a beam or a branch, and a large wooden hand-painted measuring board propped against a wall or tree trunk. As well as malnutrition, we treated common ailments such as worm infestation, scabies, night blindness due to vitamin A deficiency, chronic coughs, ear and eye infections, and skin rashes of various types. Everything was done sitting on the ground with the medicine chest by our side, as well as a small briefcase of paperwork, two or three small pieces of portable medical equipment, and a gaggle of onlookers.

After an initial wave of enthusiasm from the Mahila Mandala we were left on our own, but by then we had made enough progress to be able to employ a health worker for each locality. Most of these were illiterate women who lived in the area and so knew their neighbours far better than we did. They were well-respected members of the local community, having been recommended and voted in by their neighbours. With a little practical training they were able to become key workers in the medical project, offering vital guidance on nutrition in the home, recognizing and advising on common illnesses, and making suggestions on family planning. Now that we have left they are an indispensable link between the woman doctor who has taken our place, and the locality.

We aimed to see each child once a month, though until we had carried out a house-to-house survey, which we did in our second year, we didn't know how many under-fives actually lived in the area. As confidence built up and we became more organized the mothers hardly needed to be called and they would come and queue with their children to see us. Working as we were with a predominantly Buddhist population, being Buddhists ourselves was a great asset; we could never have made the progress we did if we had not had this immediate point of contact with so many thousands of people. Naturally we tried to treat all, without discrimination, though some members of other religious communities probably looked upon us with suspicion.

For the first year or so we were largely groping in the dark. Although in India there are many such projects run either by charities or by government-sponsored organizations, some of which are very effective, most of them are based in rural areas. Doing such work in the slums posed many unforeseen difficulties, one of the greatest being the fluctuation of the population. We had no blueprint for such a project, so we had gradually to create our own.

One obvious difficulty we both faced was the tremendous heat which persisted for three months of the year and was severely aggravated by urban life. I have strong memories of eating lunch at Mrs Khandagale's house with the heat beating down on the tin roof, eating food that made my mouth and fingers burn, my nose run, and my eyes water. Then I would walk under the shade of my umbrella to the bus stop on the main Bombay–Poona highway with the incessant traffic roaring past, belching out black exhaust fumes. At the bus stop I would climb into a crowded bus and have to stand squashed against other hot sweating bodies for the twenty-minute journey home. There, with enormous relief, I would tear off my sari and douse myself with a bucket of cold water. Perhaps it was not surprising that I lost a lot of weight and, until I contracted hepatitis in my third year there (which had the remarkable side-effect of curing many of my gut problems), I frequently suffered from diarrhoea. For another four months of the year we had the dubious blessing of the monsoon, when open gutters overflowed, alleys turned to sludge, and sewage brought infection and disease.

For three years my main work was with the mother and baby clinics, though I gradually started to help set up other social projects as the need and possibility arose. Many of the ideas that Virabhadra and I had explored before going to India we soon realized were inappropriate when we were faced with the realities of life in the slums, and we had to drop them. For instance, we had planned to build a small hospital with in-patient beds, but we could see that health work based in the localities and a central clinic was providing far greater benefits than a hospital could have done, and anyway Poona has reasonable government-run hospitals to which we could refer patients if necessary.

Our work inevitably brought successes and failures. It was rewarding to see a malnourished child put on weight and come off the danger list merely as a result of quite simple but appropriate guidance, but sometimes we were notified too late. That, combined in certain cases with harmful superstition, was frustrating and sad. Traditional beliefs and practices were often contrary to the kind of health care we were trying to give. Cow-dung, for example, is regarded as essentially pure and cleansing, and is often plastered on the umbilical cord of a newborn baby, which can easily lead to sepsis and sudden death. If during a clinic session we discovered a child who was very ill or severely malnourished, we would make a home visit. This was an aspect of the work that I particularly enjoyed, working closely with an Indian woman who interpreted for me. In this way I came to understand something about the lives of the Indian women rather than just what was wrong with their children. It was not long before I was well known in Dapodi, as well as knowing a great many of its inhabitants.

One Hindu couple I looked after were the Kolis, from the fisherman caste, who eventually, after many years of marriage, had produced a daughter. In gratitude to the priests for helping to give them a child, they had promised that their first daughter would be offered to the temple once she had reached puberty, to be 'given to the gods' – in effect to become a temple prostitute. Their daughter turned out to be deaf. I left Dapodi before she reached puberty, but her parents had great faith, and I was sure they would keep their promise. There was a little boy with a heart murmur who became one of the noisiest and most active children in his locality, and there was a man whom Virabhadra diagnosed and cured of leprosy in its very early stages. There was a child who died of malnutrition while she had measles because intervention during measles is believed to bring bad luck. There was a woman whom I watched deliver her baby in a hut no bigger than a dog kennel. The following day I was horrified to see great burns around the child's navel, which I discovered were the result of the common practice of placing a caustic seed on the stomach of a male child to bring good luck. And there were hundreds of children whom I saw just growing up healthy and remark-ably robust amid the toil and sweat of India's notorious slums.

Life is Frail

The cases I remember most vividly are the ones where I seemed able to do nothing very useful and could only watch helplessly. One slum hut I visited was bigger than many, covering an area about ten feet square. It had three sides made of corrugated iron and a tin roof. The fourth wall divided it from the house next door and was made of broken pieces of plywood boxes. Through it you could hear the family next door: every sound, every word, every argument, every time a baby cried. Life in India is like that; privacy and physical aloneness are not understood and the idea of personal space a totally incomprehensible and even undesirable concept. To get to this hut I walked down one of the lanes from the bazaar past a terrace of about eight single-roomed brick huts, with an open concrete gutter running right in front of their doorways. The lane had been concreted, but was too narrow for any vehicle bigger than a three-wheeled auto-rickshaw. During the cold season the families occupying these 'highly desirable' brick huts lived mainly outside in the lane as it caught the early morning sun.

One morning as I took this route I passed two groups of women making colourful patchwork bedspreads out of brightly printed pieces of cloth from children's dresses, old saris, men's shirts, and petticoats. There were three women working on one bedspread and two women and two girls on another, gossiping, laughing, and joking together. I had passed them before; sometimes they would sing; sometimes they worked in silence. A number of children played around them and a baby lay asleep in the middle of one of the bedspreads while the women stitched around the edges. Smoke billowed up to the clear blue sky from a couple of newly-lit *shegadi* stoves. (Shegadi is a mixture of coal dust and earth kneaded together with water to make little balls which are laid in the sun to dry. It is used like coal, usually in a bucket with a little window in the side to let in a draught; the coal dust maintains the flames, and the earth keeps the heat strong.) An occasional puff of wind would change the course of the smoke and blow the grey clouds in through doorways and windows. Nobody minded, nobody even noticed.

A little further down the lane women were still queueing at the communal water pipes; by now only a miserable trickle dribbled out from one of three pipes, sluggishly filling just one pot at a time. Highly polished brass and copper water pots stood piled up one on top of another, waiting their turn to be filled. Most people would have collected their water earlier than this when the water pressure was higher and when three trickles came out of the three pipes. Within half an hour the water would be turned off altogether, and would not be on again for another eight hours.

Outside one hut, a couple of old men squatted on their haunches, deep in conversation, rubbing their white stubbled chins, and nodding their heads knowingly. From another hut Hindi film music drifted out and a little girl mimed the words and danced in circles in the lane while a doting grandmother clapped her hands in delight. Three youths, one with a bike, leaned against the opposite wall smiling at the uninhibited child; one of them began to sing along to the words of the song, swooping down and lifting the giggling girl up in the air. He sat her on the crossbar of his bike, and continued singing, looking into her eyes, while his comrades smiled and clapped. They nodded to me in recognition and as I passed children ran up to me shouting 'Namaste, namaste,' before fleeing in fits of giggles as I said 'Namaste' back to them.

At the end of the row a squatting woman was energetically polishing her brass pots in ash and leaving them upside down in the sun to dry. Opposite her, against the wall, sat another woman, gripping her teenage daughter between her legs while she picked lice out of her long, black, coconut-oiled hair, and squashed them between her fingernails. A mangy dog rooted for sustenance in the gutter until two children, who were running up and down the lane rolling along a metal hoop with sticks, started throwing stones, making the dog yelp, cringe, then scurry away. All around was the noise of clanking pots and pans, babies crying, people shouting, music playing, distant trucks and trains revving and hooting, and occasionally the roar of an aeroplane overhead. The early morning sun shone impartially on it all.

As I turned the corner the concrete lane abruptly finished, and now I had to pick my way from left to right over an unformed, uncemented gutter which wound its course through the alleys, sometimes widening to form a stagnant pool. Every so often a stone had been thoughtfully placed in the middle of the gutter to aid crossing from one side to the other. In this area the huts had little uniformity, for they were simply made out of any old scrap materials – tin cans beaten out and flattened, polythene sheeting, broken wooden boxes, sackcloth; anything that people could lay their hands on to form some sort of shelter. A large rat scurried stealthily past one of the huts and disappeared down a foot-wide alley too narrow for any human to walk along.

A woman was beating her washing on a stone slab in front of her hut with a bucket of water beside her; others were making their way through the shanty town, past the public latrines and over a stretch of wasteland to the river, climbing over a barbed wire fence with their dirty washing in bundles on their heads. Two small children were defecating next to the gutter, an expectant black pig snorting in the shadows waiting for them to finish. A drunken man lay spreadeagled beside a pile of rubble and a group of schoolchildren, dressed in blue and white uniforms and carrying satchels laden with books, fluttered by, laughing and shouting as they nimbly jumped from one side of the gutter to the other.

Opposite the hut towards which I was heading stood a shop, a wooden box on stilts, in which an elderly man sat cross-legged, selling tea powder, sugar, sweets, cigarettes, matches, bidis (a kind of minute cigar made from one neatly folded tobacco leaf), and biscuits. He raised his hand to his head in recognition and said 'Jai Bhim!' As I crossed the alley to enter the hut that was my destination a man sitting in the doorway ushered me in. I had never seen him before, but it appeared that he not only knew who I was but was expecting me. Inside, the hut was dark and gloomy, and felt cold in comparison to the bright sunshine outside. I looked around me. Even the poorest huts I'd been into had had some sort of rickety shelves to hold pots, pans, and plates, but this hut had none; a few aluminium plates and a couple of pots stood piled in a corner. There was no furniture at all, not even a metal bed frame or charpoy (a string web stretched on a basic wooden frame). As my eyes became accustomed to the dark I could see a rusty trunk standing in one corner which must have held all the family possessions, though six people lived here. A shirt and pair of trousers hung from a nail in the wooden wall.

I had come because I had been told that there was a newborn baby living here, that he wasn't feeding, and that neighbours thought he would not live. Luckily India has not been perverted by propaganda advocating powdered milk instead of the mother's own, and it is very rare for Indian mothers to have feeding problems, so I naturally wondered what the problem might be. It was simple enough; the mother had none of her own milk to give. She sat huddled in a dark corner, squatting over the shegadi stove on which she was heating a pot of water to make black unsweetened tea. Most Indians, except the very poor indeed, put milk in their tea; to drink it with neither milk nor sugar is a refreshment only for paupers. While the tea was brewing the woman kneaded *bakeri*, a bread made from gram flour and water, beating the dough into flat cakes with the palms of her hands. I asked her what she would be eating with the bakeri which was to be for both breakfast and lunch; in response she pointed to a basket of dried chillies. 'There's no money to buy any other food,' she explained. As she crouched over the fire her sunken eyes looked me up and down. Beside her, lying on a ragged piece of cloth, lay the baby, half covered in an even tattier piece of cloth.

'He's five weeks old,' she said dully, 'but he never settles. He's always crying.'

An older boy ran into the house, and stood leaning against his mother's back for a few minutes, staring at me. Then while his mother wasn't looking he pinched a chilli and fled out of the house.

'He's my eldest son. He works in the café in the bazaar. He gets three rupees a day for cleaning the cups and washing under the tables. It doesn't go far but at least he gets fed there, and he tries to steal scraps to bring home for the rest of the family. He was very clever at school, but had to drop out last year so that he could work to help keep the family. It's my wish that one day he'll be able to return to school.'

Her husband, she told me, was a labourer, working on the roads, but he was also a drinker. Almost everything he earned got spent on drink, and often he did not bother to go to work even when it was available.

'I'm his second wife; the other four children are not mine. Rumour has it that his first wife was found drowned at the bottom of the village well. He never talks about her and I never ask questions.'

A young girl came in carrying a pot of water on her head and another in the crook of her arm. Setting them on the floor, she came and sat beside her stepmother and helped to make the bakeri, all the time staring at me, just as her brother had done.

'My parents married me to him even though he is twenty years older than I am. We are from neighbouring villages. My parents are very poor landless labourers, with five daughters – I'm the second – and just one son, the youngest of the family. His family were prepared to take me without any dowry, so my parents didn't have much choice. I can't blame them; they still don't know how they are going to marry off my three younger sisters.'

I looked around the walls. There weren't even any family photographs, just a calendar attached to a garish representation of the Hindu god Shiva, he who presides over personal destinies and is known as 'the Destroyer'.

'I started getting ill soon after we moved here. He had lived in this hut with his first wife; the neighbours tell me he didn't treat her well and kept coming home drunk. He beat the children and sometimes his wife too, shouting and swearing. He's never beaten me, and I think the neighbours would try to stop him if he did. His two elder daughters are out rag-picking at the moment. I was lucky as a girl – I worked in the fields. The hours were long and the work was very hard, but it was better than working in the gutters. They're good girls and they help me in the home in the evenings, but they too are weak. None of us eats properly.'

I thought of the man, her husband, whom I had seen sitting in the doorway, and of the many rag-picking girls I knew in the area. They carried large sacks on their backs which they filled with any broken bottles, scraps of metal, and pieces of rag or paper that they could scavenge. In the evening they would take their sacks to a depot so that their pickings could be weighed and sorted, in exchange for a few rupees. Some of these girls could hardly be more than six years old. I leant forward to pick up the baby. He was lying in his own urine. I asked his mother if she had a clean cloth; opening the trunk she handed me a worn faded sari in which I wrapped the shivering baby. His tiny body felt cold and his eyes were staring and sunken; for months afterwards they haunted me. Every rib was showing, and his skin was frail and shrivelled, with broken sores on his buttocks. He made little jerking movements with his arms and legs then fell silent. I held him close to my warm body; he made no noise but just opened and closed his mouth like a fish looking for food. His mother's eyes too were hollow and glazed, her body so weak she could hardly keep it upright, and yet she continued to beat out the bakeri. Without doubt both mother and child were grossly mal-nourished. She had no food to speak of to eat herself, and not a drop of milk was in her shrivelled, sagging breasts. It seemed hard to believe that the baby had managed to survive five weeks in such conditions. It was one of the many times that I wished I could have known sooner.

With a lot of persuasion I got them to the Municipal Hospital, where my suspicion that they both had TB was confirmed. The doctors wanted to keep the baby in hospital for intravenous feeding because he was too weak to take a bottle, but his mother refused to let him stay. Maybe she was frightened, or perhaps her husband put pressure on her not to stay. It was often hard to know what was really going on. So, against all advice, she brought him home again. Perhaps she knew better than all of us that there was little hope of his survival. Within two days the baby had died. I saw the mother a few days later in the bazaar buying fish. She told me the news, broke down in tears and walked away. Who had given her the money for fish I don't know. The following day, in the early hours of the morning, she was found dead. She had died in her sleep, curled up beside the tin trunk. Her body was cremated the same morning. She and her son were soon forgotten and her husband and the other children moved back to their native village. The older boy now studies in one of our hostels.

A Woman's Place

To get to the clinic we held in the most squalid locality of Dapodi, I walked down the Bombay–Poona road from Dapodi station, and cut into the hutments past a notice stuck high up on a lamp-post which read:

Wanted: snakes poisonous or other to be used for charming.

Jumping over the gutters which ran like rivulets through the alleys, I passed the butcher's shop and slaughterhouse, a partitioned hut in which on one side a variety of animals being fattened awaited their fate, while on the other those which had gone before hung as fresh carcasses, a mecca for a host of droning flies. Coming into this part of town I always felt it to be an area of darkness, embracing an obsessive, almost frightening reverence for the charms and omens that governed people's lives. Having made a few *faux pas* in the past, I had been cautioned in this neighbour-hood in particular not to pay compliments such as 'Hasn't this baby got beautiful eyes,' for the evil ones might make it blind, or 'What lovely soft skin this child has,' for he or she might develop smallpox.

The clinic was to be held in the Kambles' house. They were one of the few Buddhist families living in the area. The Buddhists who did live there had divided into different factions, so the response to our work here was not altogether favourable. Local leaders were suspicious of anyone ap-pearing to muscle in on their patch. At least half the population were told not to come near our clinics because we were only doing the work to gain political power. People did not seem able to judge for themselves, and our efforts to work effectively in this locality were largely in vain.

There was a measles epidemic. Although measles is a relatively mild disease for children in the West, it can be a killer for children who are undernourished. There is a widely-held traditional belief in India that children with measles should be kept indoors and not taken to see a doctor. We therefore rarely had a child with the disease brought to our clinics, but we sometimes managed to visit them in their homes. Even that was not easy, and our work was hindered by many other traditional beliefs and customs concerning a child with measles, such as the belief that someone coming into the house from outside should not touch the child, nor should a woman with her period. Frankly, on occasion, I lied.

There were other, less harmful, customs concerning measles: a metal charm should be tied on a thread around the child's neck to ward off evil spirits; ash should be smeared on the child's forehead; mother and child should bathe and perform a puja (a religious devotional practice); earth from the threshold of the house should be applied to the child's body; lemon-tree leaves should be brought and stored in the house; and the floor should not be covered with new cow-dung for the duration of the disease. Though none of these were harmful in themselves, the child might have got better more quickly if the mother had paid attention to good nutrition rather than relying solely on the intervention of the gods.

Although most of our work was with children, we also treated women. Being rather inquisitive, I asked a lot of questions and in this way I began to build up a clearer picture of the way Indian women, especially the poor ones, live their lives, the way they express themselves, and how they think and feel. In subsequent years this gradual accumulation of knowledge and first-hand experience helped me in the more specifically Buddhist work that I began to do, enabling me to teach in a manner that made Buddhist theory relevant and practical. Having learned about Buddhism myself in a Western context, I had to look at it in a completely different culture, a culture which is far closer to the Buddha's own experience, having changed relatively little in the last 2,500 years.

Terrible social conditions are prevalent in the slums: poverty, drinking, caste prejudice, and, by no means least, gender prejudice. These hardships can start from the moment of birth. '*Mulga zhala!* – a son has been born!' Sheer delight spreads over the faces of parents, relatives, friends, and acquaintances. Much rejoicing and festivity follows the birth, expensive sweets are passed around, the status of the child's mother is raised several notches in the family hierarchy, while his father proudly gains an heir, someone to light his funeral pyre when death comes to take him at last. '*Mulgi zhali* – a daughter has been born.' Faces drop, and few words are spoken. There is little festivity or rejoicing, an inferior confectionery is handed around, and life continues as normal.

Thus the great majority of Indian girls are greeted into the world. This common response to the birth of a daughter is not only that of poor village folk; it is prevalent across a broad spectrum of Indian society. A son can earn his living, whereas a daughter is seen as a financial burden, as money must be saved for her dowry. A woman is expected to carry on producing offspring until at least one son has been born, causing her much anxiety, especially when the outcome of nine months of pregnancy ends in the birth of a third, fourth, or fifth daughter. She will often have to carry the blame for not producing sons; it is quite common to hear of husbands finding second wives to give them sons. Within the family, men of whatever generation hold the highest status, so that once the father and grandfather have died the eldest son rules the family even if his mother and grandmother are still alive.

Although in the cities today there is the possibility of education for all, many more girls than boys do not attend school, or drop out at an early age to help with household chores and look after younger siblings. In villages very few girls go to school at all. Boys are much more likely to be encouraged in education, particularly at college and university level, while their sisters stay at home to look after the house. When girls are encouraged to take higher education this is often not so that they can get a good job or consider a career, but to enhance status: the more letters you have after your name, the more educated a husband you are likely to get. Caste apart, more education means more money and greater social standing. Once married, if the new bride is to live with her extended family, she will join her husband's family on the lowest rung in the family hierarchy, her status being raised only when she produces a son or when a younger brother-in-law brings a new bride into the house, the latter then taking the lowest place. If she has a job, her husband or in-laws will decide whether she should continue working or give up work and stay in the home. More and more educated women are working after marriage, but such women are often accused of not looking after their husbands properly.

A woman who remains in the home is soon under the thumb of her mother-in-law. For a new bride in an extended family her relationship with her mother-in-law is more important than that with her husband, because it is with her mother-in-law that she will spend the day, whereas she will spend little time alone with her husband. I have heard numerous stories of atrocities inflicted on a new bride coming into her husband's home, in particular cruelty on the part of her mother-in-law, which the husband seemed to know nothing about, and in these situations the usual pattern of victims becoming the worst offenders appears to operate. I also used to read in the newspapers that suttee – the burning of a dead man's wife on his funeral pyre, sometimes by self-immolation, sometimes murdered by family members – was on the increase.

One particular morning when a clinic held at Mrs Kamble's had finished, Mrs Kamble sat Virabhadra and me down with a cup of tea and told us how a cousin of hers, who was staying with her for a while, had been married for two years, and had not yet conceived. Frustrated and angry, her husband and mother-in-law were getting desperate. Could we give her some potion to make her pregnant? She'd been to other doctors, she'd taken pills and injections (we wondered what), she'd seen holy men and magicians, but nothing had worked. We talked in the back room with the girl and her husband, explaining the most fertile times for conception. This had been explained to them before, but still she had not conceived. Virabhadra suggested he do a proper internal examination, and she agreed. When her husband left the house, with the encouragement of Mrs Kamble the girl confided that before her marriage she had become pregnant and had resorted to a back-street abortion. None of her family knew about this apart from Mrs Kamble. Could this, she asked us, be the reason why she had not conceived?

Virabhadra examined her. Horrified at the anatomical misshapenness he found, he was convinced that this indeed was the cause of her inability to conceive. She would probably need surgery. She couldn't possibly have an operation, retorted Mrs Kamble: not just because of the expense, but also because it would make her husband suspicious. There was nothing we could do. A few days later the woman returned to her village, and we lost contact with her. I imagine that it wasn't long before her husband took a second wife to produce heirs. His first wife may stay in that family, or she may be thrown out, but in either case she will have to live the rest of her barren life with this closely-guarded secret.

The following week we were back at the Kambles' house. A neighbour came in: 'Mhaskebai is in labour, I think the baby will come any moment.' Very few women in the slums have their babies at home; the majority go back to their mothers' homes in the villages; others deliver in local municipal hospitals which, though overcrowded, are relatively cheap, while the facilities, archaic by Western standards, are adequate. When first working in the slums I had imagined myself rushing out to huts at all hours of the day or night, aiding numerous home deliveries. Here at last was my chance at least to witness, if not help with, a home delivery. I left Virabhadra to carry on the clinic while I went round to Mhaskebai's house. She lived in a wooden hut about seven feet square with polythene and sackcloth roofing which was not high enough for me to stand up in. It stood in a row of similar huts, each one propping up the next. The space allotted for the alley dividing the rows of huts was so narrow that I could touch the walls on either side, and had to duck most of the way along to avoid knocking my head on overhanging roofs.

As I stooped through the open doorway, moving from the glaring sun outside into the gloomy, stiflingly hot interior, I could just perceive Mhaskebai, semi-draped in a dark green sari, sitting in the middle of the room. She was holding on to a vertical wooden prop which held up the roof. Beside her sat a wizened, toothless old woman, a relation from the village who had come to aid the delivery. Mhaskebai's husband was sitting in the doorway, but he went and squatted outside the house when I entered. A pot of steaming water simmered over a shegadi stove, filling the darkness with steam and smoke. It took a few minutes for my eyes to adjust to the scene. A kitchen knife lay on the floor beside the stove.

'How long has she been in labour?' I enquired.

'Since first light,' replied the old woman.

Mhaskebai started to moan. She squatted on her haunches and held tightly to the pole, pushing down with all her might as beads of perspiration formed and dripped from her forehead. I looked around me. There was no furniture in the hut, only the cloth on which she sat and a few cooking pots. Her hair was matted and dishevelled; her eyes and teeth flashed white against the deep colour of her skin. When the contraction was over, she flopped back on to the cloth and her head sank down on to her knees. She did not speak. I only stayed about five minutes: the old woman appeared to be in control and I didn't want to interfere unnecessarily. The contractions were not yet frequent, and they were the only criterion by which I could judge how long she might be, for she had not wanted me to examine her internally. Thinking it would still be some time before the birth I returned to Virabhadra and the clinic, intending to go back to Mhaskebai's at the end of the morning.

About thirty minutes later the same neighbour came round: '*Mulga zhala!*' Mhaskebai had delivered a son. Virabhadra raised a quizzical eyebrow at me. 'But … but …' I stammered. I grabbed some cotton wool and gauze, some sterile scissors and antiseptic, and returned to Mhaskebai's house. There was the baby, all pink, smeared in white vernix and streaks of drying blood, lying on the cloth beside his mother. The placental cord had already been cut with the kitchen knife, and a length of cotton used for tying up packages of grain had been tied round the stump. The mother lay there looking exhausted, while the father still squatted in the lane, occasionally poking his head through the doorway. The placenta lay on the floor near the stove, and the old woman covered it with ash. Later she would bury it on the threshold of the house. She gave me a toothless grin.

'It's a son – a son, and he's fit and strong,' she whispered in glee. It was true, he did look healthy, though he couldn't have weighed much more than four pounds. But then most Indian babies are small compared with Western babies. I lifted the baby on to my lap and tied a second loop around the cord. The old woman wanted to wash the child. Taking some of the water off the stove she poured it into a second pot and took the baby from me. Just as she was about to plunge the whimpering baby into the pot I put my finger into the water and leapt at the scalding temperature.

'It's far too hot!' I almost shouted, adding a little more calmly, 'You must add some cold water.'

The old woman looked surprised. She stuck her hand into the hot water and kept it there. To her hardened hands, which for years on end had scrubbed pots and pans with mud, dunged floors, worked in the fields, ground spices and kneaded dough, the heat did not penetrate. Before she had the chance to reply, I added some cold water, took the baby from her, and lightly washed him down.

Concerned that she might smear cow-dung on the baby's navel, I covered it with sterile gauze, something I would not do in England where it is considered better to expose it to the air, but definitely the lesser of two evils in this case. The old woman looked on in surprise and wonder at this little square of pristine white gauze. She smiled, perhaps thinking that it was a magic charm, or that I was crazy. I wrapped the baby in a piece of clean rag and handed him to his mother who, though it was her first child, looked as though she had always held a baby in her arms. I visited him every day for a week, and subsequently at less frequent intervals. The child survived; in fact he thrived. The old woman returned to her village, and within six months Mhaskebai was pregnant again.

'The Backward Half-Look...'

Like the Khandagales, the Sonowanes, also of Dapodi, helped Virabhadra and me a great deal in the early days. Mrs Sonowane was a member of the Mahila Mandala. A short, rotund woman, she appeared homely and cuddly on the rare occasions when she smiled, but much of the time wore a sour expression upon her chubby face which gave her a grumpy, angry look. Mr Sonowane always dressed in the politician's garb of white Nehru cap, and long, white, high-collared Nehru shirt, over white pyjamas (Indian pyjamas consist of the bottom half only). Many politicians favoured this vamped-up version of proletarian attire to make a show of solidarity with the workers. He worked in the local ammunition factory and without a doubt he was boss in the home: though he spoke little, the rest of the family stood in fear of him. They had three grown-up offspring and a school-going son. Sushila, their only daughter, was the eldest: tall, slim, and rather beautiful. When I first got to know the family Sushila ran tuition classes for young children in their front room, lasting a couple of hours daily; the rest of the time she helped her mother and grandmother with household chores. Raju, the eldest son, had surprisingly coarse features compared with his siblings. He was a policeman on the beat somewhere outside Poona, so I rarely met him, though he did occasionally appear unannounced in uniform carrying his lathi (a double-sized truncheon); I would not like to have crossed him when he was on duty.

Kailas, the next son, was obviously the apple of his parents' eye. He was in his second year at Wadia Further Education College, studying for a Bachelor of Commerce degree. He was good-looking and knew it. Immaculately dressed and groomed, he always wore tight-fitting trousers or jeans, a tight brilliant white neatly-pressed shirt, opened at the neck just a button more than necessary to show off the gold chain around his neck, and a flashy wristwatch. Not a hair on his head was ever out of place. Despite his rather foppish appearance, which often struck a note of incongruity in the slums, he was gentle and soft-spoken. He rarely seemed to attend college lectures, and I seldom saw him studying, though he went on to become a lecturer in commerce within a year of qualifying. Much of the time he hung around street corners with groups of friends, leaning on his bicycle and watching the girls go by. Mahesh, the youngest son and about fifteen, was also extremely good-looking and beginning to follow in the sartorial footsteps of Kailas, though he seemed rather more studious.

They lived in a two-roomed brick house near Dapodi station, with a flagstone floor, a roof of corrugated asbestos, and walls painted a pastel aquamarine. The front door opened off a large open space between other slum dwellings, while the back door led out through the kitchen to a dust lane with open cemented gutters running a few inches away. By Dapodi standards it was definitely a 'pukka' house, and stood on the edge of the real slum area. For the first year of our work in India, Virabhadra and I ran a weekly mother and baby clinic from their front room. Mrs Sonowane soon lost interest, but Sushila grew quite keen, and for a while became a key worker, going around the locality collecting the children we needed to see. The front room had a metal bed on which Virabhadra and I sat and on which we laid the babies to examine them. The scales were strung up from a beam and the trunk of medicines balanced on a stool. Within minutes the small room would be filled with crying babies, chatting mothers, and usually a crowd of onlookers: men, women, and children of all ages standing in the open doorway and peering through the barred windows, blocking out the daylight. Sushila had a loud voice and would attempt to order the mothers into some sort of queueing system and shoo away the voyeurs from the door and window, but she rarely succeeded. Anyway, a lot of the mothers didn't much mind if their child wasn't seen until after a later arrival: initially it was such a novelty for them that the opportunity to get away from the home and socialize was as important to them as any clinical work we could do.

Kailas often hung around the clinics, seeming at a bit of a loose end. Later he became very helpful to us, acting as interpreter and hoisting babies into slings to be lifted on to the scales. Later still he helped establish sports for older boys, and tuition classes for secondary schoolchildren. Even doing the more physical work he somehow still managed to remain irreproachably groomed and unruffled.

There were of course disadvantages to using people's homes for our clinics. For many it boosted their status in the locality, but in the case of the Sonawanes we discovered, after several months of working at their house, that they were not popular in the area, and a significant number of their neighbours would not deign to cross their threshold. It was therefore a great improvement when we had our own hut in each locality in which to run the clinics.

One day I walked into the Sonowanes' house and could not help noticing a very large new calendar hanging on the wall next to a picture of the Buddha and Dr Ambedkar. It featured a well-endowed, fair-skinned, thickly mascara'd woman, in a baby-pink plunge-neckline negligée, lying on a deep pile carpet, stroking a long-haired kitten. Along the bottom was written 'Courtesy of Indian Oil'. Kailas stood combing his moustache in the mirror and I sat on the bed to await Virabhadra's arrival.

'Do you like our new calendar?' asked Kailas.

I hesitated. 'It's very large,' I replied, glancing up at it quickly and trying to think of something to say.

'It looks like you. That's why I bought it,' he continued. Apart from the fair skin I could see no resemblance whatever.

'Oh!' I said awkwardly.

'Yes, we all think it looks like you, Sushila, my father, everyone....'

When friends of Kailas then came into the house and also began to say with great pleasure and a twinkle in the eye that the picture was 'just like Padmasuri' I became a little more concerned. Slowly it began to dawn on me that perhaps the frequency of coincidental meetings with Kailas in the street, and the number of occasions when he just happened to be loitering around Dapodi station when I arrived there in the mornings from Poona, were beyond the bounds of statistical probability. Furthermore, whenever we did meet he inevitably just happened to be walking in the same direction as me. There was little I could do about it, however, except keep distantly cool when in his company, and later I began to suspect it was more a question of getting kudos out of being seen in the company of a white woman than of any serious amorous intentions.

There were so many conventions I had to learn and respect. For instance, a lot of people thought it strange that I should ride on the back of Virabhadra's scooter, something a 'decent' woman would never do unless the driver were a relative. When I discovered this I understood why Mrs Khandagale and Mrs Sonowane insisted on telling people in Dapodi that Virabhadra and I were brother and sister; then no more questions were asked. I suspect I violated social customs every day without even knowing it, but people like Sushila, and later a woman social worker with whom I worked closely, were very good at pointing things out, saving me future embarrassment and preventing me from causing offence.

One day Sushila told me that the whole family were going to their native village for a few days, and asked if I would like to join them. I jumped at the chance. A special fair was being held in the village, and they always visited at this time of year. The family would be staying several days but it wasn't far from Poona so I could, if I liked, just go for a day. We met early in the morning at Poona bus stand; the whole family was there apart from Raju.

'Why are you wearing that sari?' asked Sushila in greeting. It was a cool, cotton, handloom one in dark green with a subtle red stripe: one of my favourites.

'It's cool and I like it,' I replied.

'You should have worn your new polyester one.' It was true I had purchased a new polyester one to wear on more formal occasions, as it didn't crease, but I did not much like wearing it for long as my body could not breathe in it.

'It's very hot to wear,' I said.

'Yes, but today is a special day. You shouldn't have worn this cotton one; it's the one you wear for work. The other would have been more suitable.'

It was too late; there was nothing much I could do now. Already the heat was building up and secretly I was still glad to be wearing cotton.

There were extra buses going on to Gurunagar, the nearest town to the fair; obviously the fair was going to be a big one. Each bus was positively bulging with humanity, but eventually Mr Sonowane and Kailas managed to insert themselves into one and even get us seats. We pushed our way down inside the bus and plonked ourselves down. Kailas, fresh and dainty as always, stood in the gangway. I wondered how he did it as I dragged the end of my sari through a crush of bodies and pushed a damp strand of hair from my eyes. An hour and a half later we arrived in Gurunagar where swarms of people choked the bus station and surrounding streets. We jostled into a local bus, this time having to stand in the gangway, and emerged half an hour or so later at Latpur.

Along the whole route from Gurunagar to Latpur we passed bullock carts in a long caravan. Each wooden cart held at least a dozen people, all colourfully dressed. Some of the carts had dome-shaped awnings, reminding me of Hollywood Westerns, while others were open to the elements. Cooking pots and water pots clattered at their railings. The large white bullocks had their horns painted orange, blue, or green and some had bells or tassels attached to the tips of their horns, while others had vermilion powder sprinkled over their rumps. As we overtook them in the bus, children jumped up and waved to us. Others ran along beside the bus, clinging to open doorways or climbing up the ladder at the back to sit on the luggage rack on top. Other people we overtook were walking or riding bicycles. Some were lame or maimed and lurched along on crutches, while others, having no legs and sometimes no arms either, were pulled along on small skateboard-like contraptions.

After about six miles we arrived in Latpur village.

'Look! There's the Shankar temple,' said Kailas, pointing out the local Hindu place of worship. I assumed he was simply being idly informative, in the spirit of a tourist guide. The landscape was barren, with just a few trees lining the road and arching overhead to provide shade. In the distance, like a great dune rising out of the earth's crust, loomed a steep hill, and, sure enough, on top of the hill was a massive, grey stone Hindu temple. In retrospect, it seems strange that I had not realized that a 'fair' would be held around a place of Hindu pilgrimage. After all, the Sono-wanes were only going because it was being held in their native village. However, I was momentarily taken aback at finding myself being es-corted by my Buddhist friends, not to a sort of village fete, but to a Hindu festival. It was clear to me now why there were so many visible signs of physical handicap among the crowds: these were pilgrims, going to get the god's blessing. Some had probably travelled for days to get here, full of faith.

The bus dropped us on a kind of ledge at the foot of the temple hill; over the side of the ledge, as far as the eye could see, down a gentle slope and then spreading out across the flat desert plains, were hundreds of thousands of people, bullock carts, and stalls selling sliced watermelon, tea, sugar cane, samosas, bhajis, sweetmeats, and all manner of other edibles. There were also stalls laid out with gaudily saccharine plaster images of Hindu gods, and shoeshine boys and bicycle repair boys hovered, awaiting custom. Bullock carts had been parked in designated areas, and some people had obviously established themselves in their 'park' for several days, setting up awnings for shade. The women were cooking on dung fuel fires beside their carts; the bullocks provided the ready-made fuel which only had to be made into pancakes and laid in the sun to dry before it could be used.

A long dust track ran straight through the middle of it all. We started the descent. I was the only white person to be seen and everyone seemed to stare at me. As we walked down between stalls away from the temple, people approached to ask who I was. The Sonowanes, clearly gratified at being able to show off their exotic friend, did all the replying. Eventually we left the crowds behind us and walked in a dense haze of heat through the main part of the mud-built village, and out beyond the furthest houses to a separate quarter: the Maharwaddha, the place where the Untouchables had always lived, with their separate well, on the rocky land at the outskirts of the village. Some eight or ten houses huddled together. One of these belonged to the Sonowanes and out of it came various relations to greet us. We were given cool water in which to wash our hands, faces, and dusty feet, standing on a stone slab in the middle of a courtyard. We were then offered water to drink; I knew that it had been drawn from the open well, and that it would be foolish to drink it, but parched as I was I gulped it down.

Sushila and I sat in the corner of a darkened room while various female cousins, aunts, a grandmother, and others gathered round talking.

'Who is she? Where is she from? Where is her family? Does she have children? Doesn't she look beautiful in a sari! Why is her hair so short? Doesn't she use coconut oil on it? Does she speak Marathi?' The questions were all directed at Sushila, so I let her answer them.

Before long a meal was spread before us on the floor. The men had gone off to another house to eat. I had little appetite but, as I was a special guest, they insisted I eat more and more, and piled mounds of hot chillied food on my plate. Sushila knew my ways and managed to prevent the embarrassment of my having to leave a portion on my plate – which would have been considered extremely rude – by transferring the food to her own plate and eating it when nobody was looking. After the meal we lay down on a mat in the cool darkness of the house and tried to doze off as flies buzzed around our faces. Apart from the buzzing of the flies and a crying baby in another house, it was quiet, and I drifted into sleep.

Before long I was brought back from my reverie by raised voices in the courtyard outside. All the women were gathering in the doorway, not wanting to miss a moment of high drama. Centre-stage in the courtyard were Mr Sonowane and his brother, exchanging abuse. Each appeared to listen carefully to the other's string of invective, think for a moment, and then release a suitably caustic and venomous reply. But there was in fact nothing civilized, or even human, about this duel. The air was thick with brutish malevolence as, teeth bared, the two men bristled, hissed, snapped and snarled. The women huddled together, and Kailas tried to intervene but was pushed to one side. Mr Sonowane upped the stakes sickeningly by picking up a rock. Sushila rushed out, blabbering with fear, 'Don't, don't, leave him alone!' She was dragged away by Kailas, and came sobbing into the house. As his brother suddenly lunged forward and grabbed him by the collar, Mr Sonowane let the rock drop to the ground and slapped him hard on the cheek, drawing blood. Physical violence only seemed to refresh their vocabulary, and the mutual cursing was renewed. A crowd of neighbours, adults, and children now stood in the shade of one of the huts and looked on; nobody said a word.

I had no idea what the fight was about and I felt very scared, for the rock could easily kill. Mr Sonowane's brother darted forward again and this time grabbed him around the neck by the crook of his arm, swivelling him round to dig a knee into his back. Kailas and another youth rushed forward and separated them. They spat at one another and kicked the ground, sending up showers of dust. Mr Sonowane picked up the rock again. The women and I drew in a deep breath and cowered further inside the doorway. We need not have worried. He had merely decided that his exit line, yet another colourful oath, would sound more menacing if he hurled the rock down by his brother's foot. Having done so he turned on his heel and strode out of the courtyard, pursued by one last imprecation from his brother, who exited in the opposite direction.

'Come on,' said Sushila, 'let's go and visit some friends.' I did not wait for any curtain calls. Kailas caught up with us. Little was said about the fight; only that there was some conflict over the dowry for Sushila's forthcoming marriage. Astounded at their detached attitude, I found that I was still quaking at the knees. Perhaps fights like this were a common occurrence in their family but it was certainly a long way from the home life of the Rev. and Mrs Patrick Blakiston.

The friends we went to visit were, surprisingly, a Hindu family, who owned a pair of enormous prize white bullocks. The usual introductions were made, and although we did not stay long, it was long enough for a variety of photos to be taken by me, and then of me, accompanied by various members of the family standing beside the sturdy bullocks. Slowly it dawned on me that Sushila and Kailas were showing me off in the same way that this family were showing off their handsome bovine couple; no wonder Sushila was rather annoyed I had not worn my best sari. After a cup of sweet hot tea served as we sat beneath rows of framed Hindu gods, we made our way back to the fair. As we walked over the rocky terrain I noticed splatters of blood at regular intervals, dotting the ground like a paper-chase. Just for a moment my mind flashed back to the fight, and I felt my heart pounding in my throat. But then ahead of us I saw two men, one of whom was swinging a freshly severed goat's head. I felt slightly relieved. 'That will be a holy sacrifice for the gods,' said Kailas, cheerfully. For me the day was taking on the qualities of a nightmare.

Back at the top of the slope we watched bullock cart races, as exciting and fearful as the chariot race in *Ben-Hur*, with whips cracking, bullocks sweating, dust rising, and intoxicated crowds leaping up and down. The tremendous heat and the sense of barbaric atavism in the air made me feel slightly faint. But before leaving I wanted to look inside the temple itself. Kailas and Sushila said I wouldn't like it, and wondered why I wanted to bother to see a Hindu temple anyway when I was a Buddhist. I said I'd never yet been inside one, and considered it part of my education. They laughed, but said they would wait outside; I could go in on my own. We climbed the steep steps up the hill and went through a stone gateway into a forecourt. The other two went to wait in a corner where I would meet them after my visit to the gods. Thousands of people milled around; bells were clanking, people were shouting, and I thought I could hear wailing.

In trepidation I pushed my way forward until I became part of the flow of humanity entering the temple and could no longer turn back. Inside, it was murky and forbidding. Walls and floor had been splashed with vermilion powder, and the air was suffocating. Around me people had lowered their voices, but from an inner chamber I heard wailing and groaning. By the smoky light of oil lamps I could discern a woman, her unbraided tangled hair streaming down to her waist, in a frenzy before an image of Shankar, apparently possessed by the god. I was treading on a pulp of squashed garlands, coconut milk, and red and yellow powder, and was hardly able to breathe for the smell, and the smoke rising from sticks of incense. Before people entered the inner sanctum, the most holy of holies, they sounded a bell which echoed back and forth in the narrow chambers. I had seen enough, and managed to squeeze my way out through a side entrance into the blinding light of day. Kailas and Sushila laughed at my appalled report. I was extremely happy to return down the steps and back to the bus queue.

They waved me off, and after a rather arduous and very cramped journey, I felt a great relief to be back in Poona and civilization. Immediately after my visit to Latpur I became ill with a high fever, probably due to a combination of the unboiled well-water and sunstroke.

Holy Matrimony

A few weeks after my visit to Latpur, Sushila's wedding was officially announced. Some time before this our first woman interpreter had become pregnant, and wanted to give up work. Sushila, who had for several months been working voluntarily with us, had stepped into her place, and although her English was minimal her attitude and contacts within the community made her an excellent addition to the team. So for purely selfish reasons Virabhadra and I were a little upset when her marriage was arranged so soon; when she married she would move away from the locality.

The arrangement of Sushila's marriage was an affair for the whole community as well as for the family. The future husband's family was known by other people in Dapodi, so that when the two families met to discuss dowry details, it was in the company of several other match-makers. Although the dowry system often becomes a source of exploitation and even blackmail, and was therefore strongly opposed by Dr Ambedkar, many of the Buddhist community still regard it as the only way to find suitable husbands for their daughters. Almost daily in the newspapers I would read about 'dowry deaths'. In a typical scenario a new wife would be put under so much pressure to extract more money from her family – money which they did not have, or which they would go into terrible debt to borrow – that she would pour kerosene over herself and light a match.

After four hours of discussion the sum of 5,000 rupees (£315 at the exchange rate of the time, 1983) – a lot of money for the Sonowanes – was agreed upon, and two days later the date of the wedding was fixed. Between this day and the wedding Sushila met her husband only once. When I asked her how she felt about it, she rather non-committally shrugged her shoulders, complained that he was too dark-skinned (the personal columns in newspapers always ask for 'fair-skinned' partners as this is considered a sign of beauty and good caste), but said she hadn't actually spoken to him. She did, however, admit to crying all night after it had been arranged.

During the six weeks leading up to the big day, Sushila went out visiting relatives in the city and in villages, becoming more and more twitchy as the time neared. Shopping expeditions were made into Poona city for jewellery (part of the dowry comes in the form of jewellery): bangles, nose rings set in gold, and a wrist watch for her future husband. There were new saris to be bought: three for the wedding itself, one for the engagement, plus cotton saris for all the female relations and Nehru caps and towels for all the male relations – about thirty-five of each. The main wedding sari was of cream-coloured thick satin, with a royal blue and gold border, costing about £60 and not included in the dowry. Though the Sonowanes were not desperately poor, they were not at all rich either, and I suspected that they must have taken out vast loans to pay for all this. Perhaps they thought they would easily regain the money from a daughter-in-law when Kailas got married. If so, they were to be disappointed. Kailas ran off with an 'unsuitable' girl from a different community and got married secretly. He was disowned by his family and he and his bride were refused entry into the house. The next I heard of him was that he had taken to drink, though he continued to work as a college lecturer. It was a sad and disturbing story.

One day when I arrived at the house, a ceremony was being performed over all the gift saris, caps, and towels, which were wrapped in a big white cloth. In turn, each friend of the family in the room, both men and women, put a smear of turmeric powder around the tie. When the last of the powder had been smeared, the bundle was opened up and the contents displayed and admired. During the weeks that followed, special dishes were prepared for the wedding feast, and special poppadoms and sweets were dried out in the sun and strung in bags from ceiling beams to protect them from ants, cockroaches, and rats. All the women of the Mahila Mandala joined in with the preparation; it was obviously going to be Dapodi's wedding of the year.

The engagement ceremony was held the night before the wedding. About fifty relatives and close friends were invited. Virabhadra and I were unable to attend the ceremony itself but arrived in time for the food. At this point the men and women separated and Sushila had still not spoken to her husband. I don't know what the men were doing, but the women were painting intricate designs on each other's hands and feet with henna powder made into a thick paste. I had my palms and nails painted. It took five weeks for my hands to return to their normal colour, and three months later my thumb nail still had a crescent moon of orange henna, like a nicotine stain, on its tip. The following morning we had clinics, so I didn't join the women for the turmeric bathing, in the course of which they smeared the exposed parts of each other's bodies with an infusion of turmeric powder (which symbolizes purification in Hindu ritual), giving their skins a golden glow. Sushila had to give green and gold bangles to all her well-wishers, and they were expected to return the compliment, so she was soon bangled from wrist to elbow. During the afternoon I remained with Sushila and about half a dozen female cousins in the 'beauty parlour', a one-roomed hut where the excitement and nervousness seemed to add to the already stifling heat. Glasses of water were continuously handed round as the sweat trickled down and the sun boiled us under the tin roof. A slightly intoxicated light-headed-ness made me wonder if this wasn't all a dream. At least an hour was spent combing and oiling her thick, waist-length hair, before it was piled into a bun and decorated with numerous garlands of sickly sweet-scented flowers which dangled around her ears. A design of red and white dots was painted in arches over her eyebrows; to my mind the overall effect would have looked better on a clown than a beauty. Just as this notion was amusing me, some girls insisted on doing the same to me, as well as garlanding my hair, affording much amusement to Virabhadra when he saw me later on in the evening. Sushila's nails were filed and polished, then she was bedecked with jewellery, and finally she was swathed in a silver-bordered pure white sari, meticulously pleated into place.

Meanwhile a stage had been set up on the open space in front of their house, neatly placed away from the open gutters. Bunting and fairy lights were strung across the surrounding buildings – no expense had been spared – and loudspeakers blared out a mixture of disco music and songs dedicated to Dr Ambedkar. On the stage a Buddhist shrine had been erected, with a Buddha image in the centre.

While the final perfumed oils were being smoothed around Sushila's neck and wrists, the distant sound of drums and brass band, high pitched whistles, and general halloos, was nearing the stage. The bridegroom was borne aloft on the shoulders of his male friends and caparisoned with garlands hanging around head and ears. He looked nervous, childlike, and bewildered. Sushila was twenty-eight. Her husband looked little more than twenty-four. As it is not considered correct for a man to marry a woman older than himself Virabhadra suspected that the Sonowanes had lied about Sushila's age to her new in-laws.

As the band gathered in the open space, and the groom sat waiting on a throne-like chair on the stage, people flocked to watch the event: some 300 guests sat on the ground, while others stood watching round the edges. The ceremony itself was over in a flash. The Buddhist Refuges and Precepts were inaudibly rattled off at high speed while the spectators were still in a general state of commotion, finding space to sit down and chattering. The bride, who by now sat on a second throne, was asked by the Master of Ceremonies to stand facing her betrothed. They made promises: he to keep her in clothing and jewellery, she to look after his house and family. Neither looked at the other. He put around her neck a black-beaded mangala sutta (literally 'Blessings Discourse' – a short Buddhist text listing the true blessings to be looked for in human life), with two gold charms dangling from it – the recognized badge of all married women – and placed silver rings on her toes. She gave him a ruby ring and a watch. A few lines were spoken by the MC and then members of the audience threw flower petals over the couple. Finally verses of blessing were gabbled unintelligibly and the loudspeakers came on bellowing out scratched recordings of more Ambedkar songs, while Sushila was whisked back into the beauty parlour to change into her exquisite satin sari so that she could be paraded around and admired.

I followed and found her in tears; she couldn't get the silver rings to fit properly on her toes. She shook all over while the cousins swathed her in the next sari but within minutes she was back on the platform. One by one a number of the guests, including Virabhadra and me, were called up to the stage to be presented with flower garlands and coconuts. A great array of wedding gifts was put on display – mostly stainless steel pots, pans, beakers, and plates – and the name of each person presenting a gift was read out over the loudspeaker, together with the precise nature of their gift. At this point Virabhadra and I escaped, just before a meal was served on banana-leaf plates to the 300 guests.

Immediately after her marriage Sushila went to live with her husband and in-laws in a Poona suburb not far from Dapodi. During this time she continued to work for us, but before long her husband took her off to his native village where she lived with other relatives. During her first few weeks of marriage she was obviously not happy, but gratified that at least she had a good mother-in-law. She did her duty and produced a son within a year, returning to her mother's house for the delivery. But the child died when he was only two. She produced a second son, and they all moved back to Dapodi, living next door to her parents' house. As the child got older Sushila came back and worked on our social projects, helping to run a crêche for babies whose mothers worked on building sites. She started meditating, she came on Buddhist retreats, and she became involved in a free expression group doing songs, music, and drama with some of the very poor children in the area. I have not met her husband since her wedding day.

reflection

The human body, at peace with itself, is more precious than the rarest gem.
Cherish your body, it is yours this one time only.
The human form is won with difficulty – it is easy to lose.
All worldly things are brief, like lightning in the sky.
This life you must know as the tiny splash of a raindrop; a thing of beauty
that disappears even as it comes into being.
Therefore set your goal. Make use of every day and night to achieve it.

TSONGKHAPA, *Principal Teachings of Buddhism*

The Lucky Hotel

There were times in India when I became particularly aware of my Western roots and my English conditioning. Sometimes I strongly identified with being English; at other times I rebelled against it. I wanted to absorb India, and by so doing overcome the sharp distinctions between 'me' and 'them'. When I was alone with Indian people I did to a degree achieve this kind of absorption. I remember Virabhadra saying once as we travelled on a local Poona train that despite our looks, our fair skin, and my height, we were beginning to blend into the background in a way that tourists rarely do. It wasn't just due to knowing what was going on and what to do; it was more the degree to which we had imbibed India on a deeper level. But when visitors came from England, without realizing it was happening I would start to feel unsettled. It is rare for anyone to have a neutral response to India; there are some aspects people love, others they hate. I had and still have some quite powerful reactions to India, but working there I began to accept a lot of aspects of Indian life which in the beginning thoroughly frustrated me. It seemed that visitors tended to irritate me by awakening the itch of my own European conditioning.

On many levels life among the ex-Untouchable Buddhist community was straightforward. People were on the whole very honest, and they got on with their daily lives in a routine way. Many lived from hand to mouth. It seemed to me that whereas Indians have their sufferings thrust upon them Westerners create their own. My English friends needed both physical and psychic space, which is hard to acquire in India. They wanted quiet and couldn't tolerate the dirt, noise, and heat, or being pestered in the street. This was very understandable; it was only out of necessity that I had learned to cope with the conditions in India myself. Yet their reactions still threatened me, if only by highlighting the conditions under which I lived. If I was to stay in India I had to block out some of these irritants; it was the only way to cope. To a degree I had to bury my sensitivity to the atrocities I saw around me, grit my teeth, even allow myself to be quite cold and hard. My visitors' responses expressed feelings which I could not allow myself to be sucked into; sometimes I must have appeared rather aloof. The longer I lived in India the more I experienced this split. Both worlds belonged to me. I had found a way of functioning effectively in both the West and the East, but I was not the same person in each world.

The down-to-earth, sometimes over-simplistic outlook of many Indians stands in stark contrast to the contortions of the sophisticated Western mind. Yet, at the risk of over-generalizing, I would say that despite their dire living conditions many Indians I knew tended to be happier, or at least more contented and certainly more positive, than many Westerners who materially and educationally had so much more. None the less, despite the occasional conflicts, I loved having friends from England to stay. Through them, and through letter writing, I was able to maintain the strong links I had built up with friends in England, and this helped me to bridge the troublesome gap between my past roots and my present life. One such friend was Judy. The daughter of a Methodist missionary, she was born in India and had spent the first seven years of her life in southern India until the family moved back to live in England. Rachel, a mutual friend who was also Lokamitra's half-sister, had come with her, and decided to stay and work in India for a short while. They were both Buddhists I had met in London. I had worked with Judy in the vegetarian restaurant in Bethnal Green, and we had been on Buddhist retreats and in study groups together. We also, of course, shared the experience of being preachers' daughters.

I no longer recall which one of us suggested that we should visit Goa, but Rachel stayed in Poona helping Lokamitra out with some administrative work while Judy and I set off for a three-day break to the beaches. Judy had adjusted well to India. Many of the Indian customs felt familiar to her, although she was so young when her family returned to the West. She was therefore an excellent companion.

A train journey of a day and a night took us to our destination. Around 9 p.m. we changed trains at Miraj Junction from broad gauge to narrow-gauge sleeper, and trundled through the dark night lying on wooden benches. At about 5 a.m. I awoke to discover that dawn had broken, and that we had left behind the arid plains of Maharashtra and were now in the depths of the jungle. Through the bars of my window I could see glossy, dust-covered leaves, and tree trunks reaching high above the train, while roots hung from their branches like a Middle-Eastern bead curtain. Verdant undergrowth carpeted the ground and monkeys swung acrobatically through the forest while brilliant green parrots swooped from tree to tree. We stopped at many small stations where the Goanese people were already up and working. The women waiting to board the train wore Gauguin-coloured saris hoisted above the knees, and they carried great baskets on their heads. The men wore equally vivid lungis also tied above the knee. As we passed through villages I saw white painted churches standing in forest clearings, with large wooden crosses perched on top. This was a very different India from Maharashtra. Not only were the scenery and buildings different to look at; the people were too, broader in the face and thicker-lipped. I could not understand their Goanese language; fortunately, many of them spoke English.

Goa lies on the west coast of India, just south of Maharashtra. It belonged to the Portuguese from 1510 until it was annexed by India in 1961, becoming India's smallest state. Its Portuguese flavour is still very strong, and at times I had the feeling that I was in Europe. Christianity is still Goa's major religion, with churches and wayside Christian shrines replacing the Hindu temples and lingam shrines of other parts of India. Over the last thirty years or so Goa has become the hippies' Happy Land, with both marijuana and harder, chemically-produced drugs cheaply available. At Christmas thousands of Europeans, Antipodeans, and Americans flock to Goa's miles of white sandy beaches and bliss out for days, weeks, or even months on end. The local people have cashed in on the ever-increasing influx of a new kind of tourist: the ten-day break package tourist, coming for the white sand, the warm sea, the sunshine, and the palm trees. Pukka hotels, discos, restaurants, and 'genuine ethnic art and craft work' have been hastily assembled, and Rajasthanis and Tibetans journey south to sell their wares on the beaches. Beach umbrellas decorate the shores and prices are rising – while at the same time young boys scale coconut palms for fruit in a manner unchanged for thousands of years. But the natural unspoilt charm will perhaps remain only a little longer.

Judy and I made our way by local transport to Colva beach, and put up at the Lucky Hotel. This was one of several such constructions comprising an open-air café-bar attached to a concrete bungalow block which housed a row of cheap rooms to let. Situated amid palm trees right on the beach, with the distant lapping of waves, and the breeze gently wafting through the coconut palms, one could hardly wish for a more idyllic setting. This primitive beach complex was owned by a very large Goanese man who always dressed in a white T-shirt, stretched taut across a spectacular paunch. He was an unattractive-looking character; but apart from nonchalantly offering some best-quality dope, which we declined equally nonchalantly, he seemed innocuous, and spent most of the day leaning on the bar-counter staring into space.

For three days we did very little. Getting up around 6.30, Judy went round to the café and brought back a couple of glasses of hot sweet tea. Then we meditated before the reggae music started. Much of the rest of the day we spent getting horribly sunburnt: somehow an essential part of the 'holiday experience'. In India I usually avoided the sun but here, because few Indians ever walked far from Colva itself, the white sun-lovers who ventured beyond went naked, and Judy and I followed suit. In the early morning we would walk along the beach and watch the fishermen bringing in their catch. They were met by women and children who shouted and laughed at the water's edge and helped to sort the fish. Some they laid out to dry in lines on the sand, while other women piled their baskets high with the rest, swung them up on their heads, and transported them by bus into the local town to sell. At dusk we would watch the small rowing boats with their lanterns swinging in the breeze, being pulled and pushed into the high waves by sinewy fishermen starting their night's work.

During the day the local women could be seen splashing into the waves wearing baggy vests and bloomers which billowed out in a comical fashion, bringing to mind old prints of Regency ladies plunging into the sea at Brighton. The women laughed and sang as they tumbled over the broken waves near the shore and scrubbed down their fish-smelling bodies, using pumice stones as I would use a sponge. They shouted and waved to us as we passed, inviting us to join them. During the first day as we lazed on the beach, reading and talking, there emerged on the shimmering horizon, like a mirage, a tall, very dark-skinned woman in a sari. Slowly and gracefully she swayed towards us, carrying on her head a basket laden with tropical fruit: bananas, *chikku*, pineapple, guava, papaya, grapes, and mangoes. Arriving where we lay, she put down her basket, wiped the perspiration from her brow with the end of her sari and sat beside us, her wide grin displaying a brilliant white set of teeth. She spoke a few words of broken English.

'Sea beautiful,' she said huskily, nodding her head from side to side. We agreed.

'You like the pineapple?' she asked, cupping one in her hands, admiring it, then rolling it temptingly from one palm to the other before our wide eyes.

'Much juice in my pineapple,' she continued, cutting off the top so that the juice burst in mouth-watering droplets from the fleshy fruit. Her sales pitch was too strong for us.

'You try some … just try. See the juice….'

We watched, our resistance crumbling.

'Only ten rupees, whole fruit, very cheap!'

Judy and I looked at one another. We would die hard.

'That's too much money,' I protested. 'Five rupees is the most I'd pay for a pineapple.' We pretended not to look very interested.

'I walk l–o–n–g way,' she said, pointing back to where we had first spotted her on the horizon. 'Sun very hot, basket very heavy.'

I could hardly disagree. 'OK, I'll give six rupees,' I replied. She put the fruit back in the basket, shrugged her shoulders, and waved her hands around in the air. There was a pause as she looked down at us.

'We Indians cover our bodies, don't like going naked. You foreigners strange peoples,' she said. I must admit I did feel rather strange, lying there like a boiled lobster, as she sat beside us in her dark green sari, looking remarkably vital and beautiful.

'You take this for eight rupees … last price!'

We handed her the money and she smiled, once again showing her brilliant white teeth. Awkwardly I helped her lift the basket on her head, and off she walked. In the far distance sat two other sun-lovers and she headed towards them. Her swaying regal figure held our attention until it was just a speck on the horizon. The pineapple was delicious. She visited us every day after that.

After our siesta we would sometimes wander into Colva village. Indian tourists came to Colva too, but rarely ventured far from where the luxury coaches dropped them. The city women, wearing their best silk or nylon saris, would paddle at the water's edge, squealing as the waves splashed them and preferring to get the bottoms of their saris wet rather then lift the material to show a forbidden knee. Doting fathers built sand-castles with their little darlings. Staying for little more than an hour, with just enough time for a cup of tea or a drink of coconut milk, they would pick up a few shells and then clamber back into their luxury coach to be taken to another beach. These tourists never walked far enough along the beach to find the nudists, and the nudists clothed themselves when walking into Colva.

After three days of living such a lifestyle I felt deeply refreshed, but I also felt I'd had enough of hedonism. It was time to turn away from the bland siren-song of the beachcomber. Judy tried to prescribe such a break for me every three months or so, but I was not sure that it would fit in appropriately with my work in Poona. 'Grossing out' in Goa on a regular basis would not nourish me as I needed to be nourished in order to throw myself wholeheartedly into what was very often a draining situation. A spell in heaven is not the best preparation for a stretch in hell. In fact, I never returned.

Instead of the long train journey back to Poona we decided to take the boat from Panjim, the Goan capital, to Bombay. From there I would take a train up the Western Ghats to Poona. Relaxed, salty, and peeling, we left the Lucky Hotel with its fat proprietor, took a taxi to the nearest town, and from there caught a bus to Panjim, alighting en route to walk over a bridge which was too weak to support a fully-loaded bus. Buying strings of cashew nuts at the small port to munch on our journey, we boarded a steamer which was carrying as many foreigners as Indians. The Western-ers sat outside, strumming guitars and smoking dope, while the Indians sat in the shade of canopies, playing cards and drinking toddy (a liquor made from the sap of palm trees). Amusing themselves thus, everyone minded their own business as the boat chugged along the deserted coastline of the Kokan region, past sandy bays and inlets, through a deep azure sea, under a paler blue sky. A couple of times we stopped near harbours where a fleet of six-oared rowing boats came out to meet our steamer, depositing new passengers and carrying others away.

Like most of the passengers, we slept out on deck. By 7 a.m. we had docked. Rachel was there to meet us on the quay. She had come to stay in Bombay with a wealthy Parsee family, friends of her family, and having been chauffeur-driven to the docks, she was dressed for the part. Just off a steamer as deck-passengers, we were covered in soot; our grimy beach clothes were crumpled, our hair matted, and our skin peeling off in paper-thin strips. It was the first time I'd ridden in a private car in India, let alone a chauffeur-driven one. I tried to imagine what it would be like always to travel that way. Through the darkened windows the scenes were all too familiar: street dwellers in their thousands, beggars, seething masses hurrying hither and thither; yet within the car I felt strangely protected and distanced from it all. Even the noise and heat were kept at bay from within our limousine capsule. There must be hundreds, if not thousands, of Indians, as well as foreign businessmen and dignitaries, who only ever see India in this way.

Rachel's friends lived in a luxury apartment in one of the smartest areas of Bombay, overlooking the sea. Here we were able to shower and change, wander through the cool, air-conditioned, marble-floored rooms, and enjoy a full-scale English breakfast, before our hostess joined us. Later in the morning I left Judy and Rachel, who had the use of car and chauffeur for the day to visit the antique markets, and took the train back to Poona.

Woman on the Wall

I lived and worked in the knowledge that I could escape at any time, whether to my room in Poona, or even to England. What separated me from the vast majority of people I saw every day was the palpable fact that for them there seemed to be no escape at all. One such was the woman on the wall.

She occupied a space on a wall on one corner of a large, chaotic road junction, the intersection of four roads. On one corner stood the Alanka Talkies cinema, on the next a large semi-luxury hotel-cum-restaurant. A jumble of small shops stood on the third corner. There was a photographic studio which displayed behind a scratched glass window a random selection of faded pictures: film stars, weddings, babies, and stiff-looking family groups. Next door was a typewriter repair shop with dingy blackened windows exhibiting even dingier blackened typewriter keyboards of monstrous proportions. And last in the row was a general food store mainly frequented by Iranian students.

Then, on the fourth corner, which was the one most dangerous for a pedestrian, for it had not even the semblance of a pavement, stood a crumbling stone wall behind which lay a small municipal garden. The only parts of the garden which could be seen from the road were a few dusty palm trees and a profusion of magenta bougainvillea which cascaded over rusty barbed wire to droop down the street side of the wall. Revving trucks, honking rickshaws, bell-ringing bicycles, roaring buses, pert little scooters carrying a family of four or more, nippy mopeds, hand-drawn carts, bullock carts, horse-drawn tongas, and a constant river of colourful pedestrians shunted their way around this corner. Weaving in and out of each other like dodgems, the drivers sometimes shouted and joked, or sometimes swore irately at each other.

It was on this corner that the woman sat. Every morning for three years I passed her, sometimes walking round the corner on her side, sometimes round the corner on the other side of the road. Come cold, rain, or heat she was always there, wearing her once-colourful nylon sari, now faded to a dull grey, with a bundle of belongings wrapped in a piece of cloth by her side. In the cold season she sat shivering, wrapped in a rag over her sari. In the hot season she moved along the wall a few feet to the shade of a palm tree. In the rains she covered herself in a torn piece of polythene sheeting. Black exhaust fumes belched towards her from the passing traffic as if from some seething, raging dragon. The sun beat down and the grit and dust sprayed up, clogging her pores, cementing her oiled hair, and reddening her eyes. A passing train going under the railway bridge fifty yards up the road made the wall vibrate, loosening a trickle of sandy mortar which fell to the ground from between the stones. Yet she appeared oblivious to all: the noise, the heat, the dust and pollution. She sat with a smile permanently on her pock-marked face, sometimes talking to herself, sometimes just staring around her, only occasionally making eye contact with a passer-by. It was difficult to determine her age; her cratered skin gave her an ageless look, but she was probably somewhere between twenty-five and thirty-five. She was slim but not malnourished. She never begged or interfered with anyone. Occasionally she walked up and down alongside the wall with an uncannily confident bearing, straightening her sari and combing and plaiting her long black hair. She was always alone.

I would pass her again at around 3 p.m. during the afternoon lull. At this time of day in the hot season, most of the street vendors cover their wares and sleep beside them in the shade. It is the calm before the evening storm when every type of conveyance screeches or grinds around the corner, carrying their passengers back from city schools, offices, labouring sites, and colleges, to their family homes in slums, colonies, apartment blocks, or bungalows. And in the other direction, housewives and children will be transported into the city, dressed in their best clothes, to the enticing shopping arcades of Mahatma Gandhi Road and the cloth stores in the heart of the city, or to the fruit and vegetable bazaar around the corner from the Ganpatti temple. But at three in the afternoon it was relatively quiet, and very hot. Unlike the street vendors the woman on the wall would be wide awake. She might be sitting with her legs dangling down over the wall, her sari neatly covering her ankles, or she might be sitting with her legs crossed as though in meditation, looking down or looking out, bright-eyed, not bored, in a world of her own which nobody shared. At night she would lie down on top of the wall, a cloth covering her body from head to toe; a nondescript, unnoticed, unloved, unwanted bundle of humanity.

Occasionally I saw her eating scraps of food out of newspaper and wondered who had brought it and who had cooked it. Unlike the Bombay street dwellers who live, cook, eat, and sleep on the pavements, rigging up pieces of sackcloth or polythene sheeting under which to do their cooking, she had no cooking pots, no shegadi bucket or kerosene stove on which to cook the basic meal of rice and dal. On two occasions I gave her some food. She looked into my eyes and, seeming rather bemused, took it and put it to one side. I never knew if she ate it or threw it to the ravening crows which hung about expectantly in the municipal garden. Either way she never showed any recognition of me subsequently, unlike some of the others – beggars, street vendors, shoe-shine boys, newspaper wallahs and a matted-haired ascetic – who would give me a nod of recognition as I passed them on my fifteen-minute walk between home and the station.

One day I noticed a definite firm rounded bulge protruding from under her sari. As the weeks passed I often saw her contentedly stroke the swell of her pregnancy; she was no longer alone on the crumbling wall. It was a cold January morning when I first spotted the baby. All I saw was a pinky-brown fist clutching up at her blouse, spindly and withered-looking. Beneath the nylon she was suckling her child, looking utterly absorbed, utterly content, and quite untouched and unscathed by the pandemonium around her.

It was hard to imagine how she survived. It is said in India that everyone has someone, some family, but I never saw hers. Was a gallant husband spending his time out labouring to bring in money, sharing the wall with her in the middle of the night, bringing her food and hair oil? If there was I never saw him. Or did she have a discreet lover who fathered her child, then returned to the family home, but continued to keep her in clothes and food? Or did she prostitute herself to the lonely businessmen who arrived on night trains from distant cities? Did someone whisk her off to some seedy hotel behind the railway, without leaving a name, a future, a possibility? She didn't look like the other prostitutes who hung around back-street corners after dark, with painted faces, bright-coloured saris and flowers in their hair, trying to catch the eyes of any loitering men who looked as if they had a bulge in their wallets, to help keep them going another day. And where was the child born? On the wall? In the municipal garden? In a hut? In a municipal hospital? I hadn't noticed she'd been gone. Was the child born yesterday, or last week, or in the very early hours of this January morning?

In the days which followed, the scrawny infant appeared oblivious to all save the constant caring and security of its mother's love. With great precision she lulled her child to sleep, she nurtured and protected it, suckled it and smothered it with kisses. They slotted into the background of humanity like one minute speck from the tip of an artist's brush, behind the triumphantly thundering trucks.

Within a fortnight the baby was gone. A desperate, lonely, childless mother was left behind, crumbling like the very wall on which she sat. Her bereavement had changed her almost beyond recognition. Her eyes, which used to sparkle, were now glazed and lifeless. Her body hung limp, her sari was stained, and her hair matted. She no longer sat still on the wall, but walked up and down it. She crossed back and forth over the road, or stood in the middle shouting out in supplication to an imaginary person, or a deity, holding her arms upwards in utter despair as the traffic roared past and swerved around her, the drivers drowning her wails with shouts of abuse. I never knew if the child had died or had been taken away by a relative, an authority, or some divine power. Not long afterwards, I moved away from that area of town. It was perhaps two years before I noticed the woman on the wall again. At her feet sat a naked toddler tied to railings on the end of a long piece of string, grovelling in dust and garbage. Was it the same child disowned by its 'saviours', abandoned, not wanted, sent back to its mother to fight for survival? Or was it another child, a second one which she would raise against all odds? I shall never know. She no longer shouted or wailed, no longer raised prayers amid choking exhaust fumes. Mother and child played together like a calm duet on a crazy battlefield.

Three years later the wall was pulled down. A high brick wall now stands there instead, obscuring the bougainvillea on the other side. The new wall is too high and too narrow to live on. The anonymous woman and child have gone: perhaps they have found another crumbling wall on another street corner. All that remains of their unseen existence is a frayed piece of string dangling from the nearby railings.

In the Fullness of Youth

In India the precariousness of life seems to add zest and exuberance to the celebration of festivals and other significant occasions. One festival celebrates a moment of particular importance for the original followers of the Buddha. For four months during the rainy season monks went off on their own, or maybe in pairs, to some cave or other basic form of shelter where they would live in retreat. Apart from going on daily almsrounds for food they met nobody, not going into villages or wandering from place to place as was their practice during the other eight months of the year. At the end of their monsoon retreat they gathered together in large numbers to confess to one another anything unskilful they had thought, said, or done while on retreat, and meditate together under the brilliant light of the October–November full moon. This was the coming together of the Buddha's disciples, the coming together of the Sangha.

In Poona, on the day of the full moon of October 1983, the rains were continuing late, so celebrations of Sangha Day had to be held indoors. Obscured by heavy rain clouds, the moon could not be seen. Some four or five hundred people came from all over the city, entering the hall with saris and shirts drenched, sandals sodden, and umbrellas dripping. The hall was the auditorium of the medical college, with a large stage at one end facing tiers of several hundred maroon plush seats. Many of the

Buddhist community came from very poor homes and rarely, if ever, sat on chairs; I couldn't help thinking that some looked rather uncomfortable sinking into the admittedly rather moth-eaten maroon velvet, with their legs folded up beneath them rather as a child in the West might sit in a large armchair. The heavy downpour, and possibly the formidable appearance of the building, meant that fewer people than usual attended this year's celebration.

Siladitya had arrived early. He had been involved in much of the preparation for the evening and was setting up a bookstall on a trestle table. He took each book out of a canvas bag, meticulously dusted it with his handkerchief, and placed it lovingly on the rickety table. Siladitya is a tailor by trade. He makes men's shirts and trousers from his little house in a village just outside Poona. He always looks a little unkempt with his shaggy mop of greying hair, bell-bottomed trousers, and his shirt usually half untucked at the waist – not, perhaps, the best advertisement for a tailor. Having lived a colourful life, he is now a very devout and seriously practising Buddhist. He loves to meditate and I suspect he would happily take himself off to the Himalayas and shut himself in a mountain cave if it were not for his family commitments.

His wife is an unhappy-looking woman, quiet, reserved, and rather drawn. On this occasion, she and her three daughters arrived after the talks had begun. Unnoticed by most, they sidled along the outside gangway towards the back of the room and perched themselves on the edge of some seats. Although Siladitya was standing beside the books at the entrance to the hall, he hardly appeared to acknowledge his family's arrival, as with bent heads they walked past him. This is something I often noticed among Indian families when in public situations. Though I didn't really know the family well, that night for some uncanny reason I was particularly aware of them; the eldest daughter, Vimala, especially drew my attention. She must have been about fourteen years old. The last time I had seen her she looked just like any other little Indian girl, with plaits tied in loops beside her ears and wearing a faded but colourful frock with most of the back buttons missing. Now she looked elegant and mature, and had an air of unassuming confidence. She was wearing a sari, her hair was neatly plaited in one braid intertwined with jasmine flowers, and glass bangles hung from her wrists. I remember thinking how different she and her father looked, as though they could hardly be members of the same family. I learned later that she was wearing a sari for the very first time this evening. I also learned that she had acquired a great talent for dancing, which probably accounted for the poise with which she held herself. She sat behind me with her mother and two sisters but at the end of the evening they quickly faded away into the crowd and I did not see them again. I went home thinking about Vimala: she had struck me as so beautiful, so fresh and blooming, a girl in the prime of her youth. I wondered whether, like so many Indian women, she would lose that bloom within a few years, and begin to look haggard, worn, and burdened as her mother often did.

It was still raining when I returned to my leaking room. I emptied out the pots left to catch drips from the ceiling and replaced them. I strung up my mosquito net, crawled underneath it and tried to sleep. Like the Chinese water torture the dripping prevented me from going to sleep, but even once the rain had stopped I could not sleep. The following day, as usual, I went by train to Dapodi, where Virabhadra and I were running our clinic from a brick hut. Virabhadra was late, so I started the clinic on my own as a crowd of mothers were already queueing up with their babies. It was at least half an hour before he arrived. He sat on the floor next to me as I checked over a child with a bad bout of scabies.

'I have some bad news to tell you,' he said. 'Siladitya's daughter has died.'

I had to ask him to repeat it several times. The cremation would be taking place in a couple of hours. He told me the whole story.

After the previous day's celebrations the family had gone happily back to their one-roomed servants' hut at the bottom of Poona golf course. They had lain down on mats on the stone floor, covered themselves with blankets and gone to sleep. At about 4 a.m. Vimala had woken up feeling something moving on her ear. Putting her hand up to her ear she had felt a sharp sting, and had sat up in time to see the tail of a thin brown snake slithering under the ill-fitting door. Within minutes she had felt dizzy and had woken her father. After hearing the story he got up at once, got out his bicycle, put Vimala on the cross-bar, and raced down over the golf course along deserted roads to the Municipal Hospital. On arrival, Vimala was hardly able to walk; she told him everything was swimming around in her head and that she felt sick. It took precious minutes to find the casualty department. Siladitya carried his daughter in to see scores of people lying around on the floor, but no doctors or nurses. Half an hour elapsed before a nurse gave Vimala the life-saving anti-serum; by then she was already unconscious. Minutes later she died.

I had heard many such heart-rending tales of tragic deaths before, but I was still shocked. The cremation was to take place the same day; the body would hardly be cold. Virabhadra asked if I'd stay and finish the clinic while he went to the funeral. Somehow I managed to continue the morning's work. Early in the afternoon he called at my house: the funeral was over. Some twenty friends and neighbours had attended. Many would not even yet have heard the news, and it might be two or three days before relatives in the family's native village got to hear about it. Virabhadra was obviously quite deeply affected too. We decided to go to Siladitya's house. I sat side-saddle on the pillion of Virabhadra's scooter; we hardly spoke. The reality was only just beginning to sink in. It could have happened to any of us. We crossed over the golf course, its grass lush and green after the rain. Backing on to the golf course which stands in the cantonment area of Poona are the military officers' quarters. Behind and hidden away are the servants' quarters. While Siladitya did his tailoring, his wife did domestic work. Her employers were also Buddhists, also friends of mine, and friends of theirs too, which within the closely-observed hierarchies of India was an unusual and refreshing situation. None the less there was a shocking difference in their lifestyle. The officer's house, which I knew well, with its three or four substantial-sized rooms and plant-filled veranda, was very colonial, very British. Siladitya's residence was a servants' room at the end of a terrace of similar rooms, each occupied by a family of up to ten members. Built of stone, it was very small and dark, and at this time extremely damp; the walls were sweating with humidity, and a smell of mould pervaded the air.

Sitting cross-legged on a tatty oblong strip of rush matting was Siladitya, head bent, reading a book, muttering the words to himself. His wife sat next to him, her sari pulled down over her downcast head, while her youngest child lay beside her, her head in her mother's lap. The other daughter, who must have been about ten years old, sat alone in a corner on the stone floor, slowly and methodically sifting through uncooked rice to remove little stones. The bicycle leaned against one of the walls. All were silent. As we entered through the open doorway Siladitya's wife looked up at us and started crying and this set off the two daughters. Siladitya beckoned us to sit down, which we did. Virabhadra rested his hand on Siladitya's knee, whilst his wife clung to my hand. Siladitya

showed us the book he'd been reading. It was the *Dhammapada*. He began
to read out loud:

Thy life has run its course: thou art come nigh
The king of death. For thine abode
Thou hast no resting place upon the road
And yet hast no provision for the way.
Then make thyself an island of defence:
Strive quick: be wise: blow off the dust
And stains of travel: wipe away the rust.
*So shalt thou see no more birth and decay.**

Only eight hours previously, Vimala, blooming with the vitality of youth,
had been awoken by a small tickle on her ear. Now her ashes were on
their way downstream to meet the mighty ocean.

Alone in the Tushita Heaven

India is not all heat and dust. The most charming of the legacies of the
British Raj are the hill stations, where Europeans, and latterly the Indian
middle classes, retreat during the hottest months. I decided to spend a
month alone in the mountains. I needed a break from an environment
that fascinated but sometimes repelled me, from a place that in a way had
become part of me. But I didn't want simply to escape; I wanted to come
back clearer and more focused. In the foothills of the Himalayas, in the
northern state of Himachal Pradesh, is Dharamsala, the home of the
Tibetans in exile and the Dalai Lama. It was here in a hut in the grounds
of a Tibetan monastery that I spent a solitary month, meditating, reading,
walking, painting, and sometimes just doing nothing. Although it can
easily be misunderstood to be advocating laziness, 'doing nothing' can
be a very effective – if sometimes uncomfortable – practice which provides ideal conditions for developing happier, calmer, and more insight-
ful states of mind.

My journey to reach Dharamsala took me first to Bombay, where the
bloody Hindu–Muslim riots of the previous months had more or less
subsided. From there I was to get a through train to Patankot in the
Punjab, just on the borders of Himachal Pradesh. The Amritsar Golden

* Sangharakshita (trans.), *The Dhammapada* (unpublished).

Temple uprising had occurred only a few weeks before, and the newspapers were still full of Sikh terrorist violence. I was nervous about travelling through the Punjab close to Amritsar, but did not want to cancel my long-awaited solitary retreat. Virabhadra had suggested I fly, but two days before I left the first of a number of planes was hijacked on a run from Delhi to Srinagar and diverted to Lahore in Pakistan, so it seemed that no mode of transport was guaranteed safe. Determined to go, I boarded the train, settled down to read *Sense and Sensibility*, and started the thirty-four hour journey from Bombay to Patankot. The day passed as slowly and uneventfully as the courtship of Jane Austen's heroines in the drawing-rooms and elm-lined carriage-drives of England. Eventually Eleanor and Marianne Dashwood were each blessed with a husband of sufficient breeding and pecuniary competence. At 2 a.m. on the second night the train stopped in Delhi. I turned over on my bunk and went back to sleep, only to be prodded awake and told to get out; the train would be going no further due to fresh outbreaks of violence in Amritsar. As many trains had been cancelled, the platforms were packed with sleeping bodies. A couple of policemen were beating up some youths with their lathis, and in clusters all around there were groups of soldiers and police.

After several hours I managed to get a slow train to Jullandar city, one stop short of Amritsar. It was a train that would have broken the spirit even of the rush-hour veterans of British Rail's Southern Region. We were packed like sardines, black smoke belched in through the windows, the heat was building up, and as I looked around I realized that there was hardly another woman on the train, and indeed only a handful of civilians; nearly all the passengers were fully-armed soldiers. Nervous and tired, but too scared to sleep, I was unable to move because of the crowds pushing against me. I remained cramped in one position for six or seven hours until we reached Jullandar city. From there I managed to get a slow connection to Patankot, where I arrived some eight hours behind schedule.

From Patankot onwards all went smoothly. The bus laboured up winding, mountainous roads, its grinding gear-changes mocked by views of Nature at her most exuberant. Amid rampaging vegetation waterfalls tumbled and rivers seethed, swollen and darkened to a reddish brown from the recent onset of the monsoon. Mountains reared up theatrically towards a cloudless blue sky; and then, as we swung round a corner, a breathtaking prospect of neatly snow-capped pinnacles glistening in the sunlight told me that I really had arrived in the Himalayas. Even by Indian standards my journey had been an ordeal, and I felt tremendously relieved to have arrived safely.

Dharamsala is like many other Indian hill towns, with its bazaar, *chai* shops, Hindu shrines, Hindi film music blaring out of tinny speakers, traffic congestion, ladies dressed in gaudy nylon saris or satin Punjabi dresses, urchins, and beggars. From Dharamsala I hitched a lift in a jeep full of jolly Tibetan monks a mile and a half up the road to Delek Tibetan Hospital, where I was going to spend three or four days with Dharma-dhara, an Order member from New Zealand. He was working there as a doctor but had managed to get some time off to show me round. Another mile and a half beyond the hospital, up a steep and winding road, is Macleod Ganj. Here I seemed to be in a different country. Nearly all the shops are run by Tibetans selling Tibetan food, Tibetan carpets, Tibetan woven cloth, and Tibetan trinkets. In the middle of the village stands a large stupa surrounded by *mani* ('prayer') wheels. Next to it is a small shrine with miniature Buddha figures arranged on shelves from floor to ceiling and a vast prayer wheel in the centre which is constantly revolved by devotees. There appeared to be as many monks and nuns on the streets as lay people, wearing maroon robes and broad smiles. I was immediately struck by the quietness of the place. People spoke in soft voices; there was no shouting and instead of Hindi music blaring out from loudspeakers I could hear only the deep resonant chanting and drum beat coming from a small monastery.

Perhaps the most important treasure salvaged from the Chinese invasion of Tibet is the library of sacred books and books on Tibet and Tibetan culture which was smuggled over the mountains and now housed in the Tibetan Secretariat, a building marvellously decorated with friezes depicting lotus flowers and other Tibetan auspicious symbols. A room above the library contains a collection of *thangkas*, along with ritual instruments found in caves where yogis had lived and practised in Tibet, and several life-sized (and larger) Buddha and Bodhisattva images. They were presented with such reverence and respect for their significance that visitors had stuffed offerings of rupee notes under the wooden frames supporting the glass.

The other great treasure smuggled over the mountains, and for the Tibetan people of more value than any number of books or precious objects, is of course the Dalai Lama; and he is protected by more than auspicious symbols. His palace is surrounded by twenty-foot-high barbed wire, trained dogs, and well-armed soldiers. At the adjoining temple, however, I was able to watch monks, ranging in age from the very young, maybe seven or eight years old, to the quite elderly, engaging in dialectical disputes on the veranda. The master threw questions at his pupils, with a stamp of the foot and forward lunge to which they responded with equal dynamism. They were all beaming and laughing, apparently thoroughly and joyfully engrossed in what they were doing. Many different classes were going on at the same time, sending a loud gabble of voices echoing out across the valley.

Around the far side of the temple were a few women, nuns and layfolk, prostrating themselves in front of an image of the Buddha. One was an old lady who would fall down on her knees with extraordinary grace, place her hands on two woollen pads and, with a movement as light as a gliding bird, slide forward until her forehead touched the ground. Then with equal delicacy her hands would sweep back on the pads until with what seemed like no physical effort she was back on her feet again. All the while she chanted a mantra. She was no more than four feet ten inches tall, and her face was ageless; she could have been sixty or eighty. Her attitude was one of extreme sincerity and devotion; she was never distracted, and her total concentration meant that her movements were all perfectly synchronized. I was very pleased to be able to carry this image of reverence and veneration to my solitary retreat.

The most stark contrast with my experience of life in Dapodi was provided by the Tibetan Children's Village, which Dharmadhara took me to visit, high up on a mountain ledge. The village is funded from overseas, and one of its purposes is to preserve the culture of Tibet. The several thousand children who live here are from exiled Tibetan families dotted all over India. Quite a few are orphans. Others came from Tibet into India on foot with parents who have since returned to Tibet. They are aged from a few days old up to seventeen or eighteen years. Despite the sombre histories of some of them, they looked happy, clean, and sturdy, and a warm and friendly atmosphere prevailed; they were obviously well loved as well as properly fed.

Three days later I climbed up the mountain to my solitary hut with my rucksack full of food supplies, warm clothes, wellington boots, my paints, a few Buddhist books, as well as candles, incense, and a small framed thangka of the Bodhisattva Tara (an archetypal female figure, who represents the actively compassionate aspect of the Enlightened mind). That same day the Dalai Lama was due back from a visit to England. There was a quiet buzz in the air as people gathered in little groups on the roadside. Smouldering fires of pine needles were burning on each bend of the road, on to which people threw sticks of fragrant incense. Some people were collecting wild flowers, some carried candles, and others held lighted incense. As I walked up and up the road, a middle-aged nun was coming down, carrying a spastic child almost as big as herself, tied on her back with a piece of cloth. The nun smiled a big beaming smile, and the child flung her arms about and drooled in excitement. They were going to pay homage to the Dalai Lama as he passed in his vehicle on his way to the palace. I did not see him, as I had already climbed beyond the palace before he arrived.

I soon settled into my solitary hut, which was partly propped up by stilts and set amid pine forests on a steep mountain slope. For much of the month it rained in sheets, and most days I was enveloped in thick cloud. I began to feel claustrophobic, hemmed in and oppressed by the elements. The occasional break in the weather was like a glimpse into some eternal reality: mountains like turrets of crystal, vast and elemental rocks and caverns, blue skies of absolute clarity, and luminous velvet carpets of moss to be felt and stroked. Technicolored fungus clung to tree stumps, and sweet-smelling ferns concealed wild strawberries and lily of the valley. All around me were pine forests, tree after tree standing attentive and covering the whole of the 'Tushita Heaven'. This name, taken from Buddhist literature, had been given to the Buddhist retreat centre. It is the name of the abode of the contented gods, supposedly one of the purest realms of mundane existence. I explored exciting pathways going up the mountains, down the mountains, along the mountains, leading somewhere, nowhere, anywhere.

Apart from the goatherds I occasionally passed on these walks, my only companions were the animals. Large grey monkeys swung through the branches, landed on my roof, and peered cheekily over my little balcony, pulling faces and chattering as if to say 'Come on, don't take things so seriously.' A large mongoose slept under the hut and would make nightly visits to my door where I left scraps for it. A small mouse would sit beside my feet, cleaning its paws, and scampering back under the cupboard door if I moved suddenly. An owl often stared at me from a branch in front of my hut, where he sat motionless; then with a sudden swoop he would fall to the earth to capture an unmindful shrew, which would struggle noisily for several painful minutes before dying. The owl would then bear the tiny corpse smugly back to its branch for consumption.

At night the terrible baying of jackals could be heard over the valley, echoed by the howling of wolves and the barking of dogs. In the daytime it was the 'caw-caw' of black crows, grasping and impatient birds considered evil in Indian mythology. In the cupboard lived a spider as big as my hand, black and hairy with bulging eyes. I never saw it move but each day it had changed its position. A lot of extravagantly coloured butterflies fluttered about, nonchalantly minding their own business. And there were plenty of fleas and mosquitoes whose business was unfortunately with my blood.

Early in the morning I was awoken by an elderly monk from the retreat centre, who came light-footedly down the mountainside with a large kettle full of hot, sweet, steaming tea. He never knocked on the door of my hut, but just stood outside chanting a mantra until I opened the door. In the pre-dawn silence he poured out the tea into my large enamel mug, muttered a few words of Tibetan, grinned, and then made his way back up the mountain to another hut, chanting all the way. In the evening he or another monk would leave food beneath a stone for me to take when I wanted. Occasionally extra pieces of fruit, biscuits, or even a bar of chocolate were left for me at other times of the day. All my needs were catered for; I felt very supported.

What worries I did have were of a deeply personal nature. An internal conflict which had been going on for some time now completely dominated my mind. This was the question of whether or not to have a child. I was thirty-two, I was effectively, if not legally, married to Vajraketu, though we were not living together, and I had a very strong, almost overwhelming, urge to have a child. Vajraketu, however, had mixed feelings about fatherhood and, particularly in India, one can't help reflecting that the world hardly needs more children. There was also the work in Dapodi, which I was loath to interrupt or hinder. And finally, I was conscious of having set a course when I was ordained which had to take precedence over my needs and aspirations as a woman of the world.

It was a very difficult time for me; pulled as I was between reason and emotion I could not resolve my conflict on a purely rational level, and even at the end of a month of inward debate I could not come to a clear conclusion. The Indian government, and its expulsion of foreign aid workers, had its part to play too, for while I was in the Himalayas Vajraketu was having a short break in England, after which he was not allowed to return. We therefore had a nine-month period of separation. Unable to reach a decision, I was glad when the last day came and I went back down the hill to spend a few days with Dharmadhara before returning to the plains.

While I knew that for many of my contemporaries in the Western Buddhist Order having a child had been a very positive and even necessary step in their development, I eventually came to the conclusion a few months after this retreat that in my own case motherhood could be positively relinquished.

Where the Three Valleys Meet

Dharmadhara owned an Enfield motorbike, a great heavy black monster which carried him up and down the mountains to visit patients in distress. Before I began my solitary retreat he had told me about a cave he had visited where Padmasambhava had once lived and meditated. Padmasambhava, or Guru Rimpoche (literally 'Precious Teacher') as he is often called, was a great scholar and saint who took Buddhism from India into the demon-ridden land of Tibet in the middle of the eighth century CE. He was a real person, but his being and his life story have become surrounded with myth and legend. As an individual, he is perhaps the strongest presence in Tibetan Buddhism, perhaps even more so than the Buddha himself, and all monasteries have images and paintings of the great Guru Rimpoche within their intricately decorated temples or *gompas*. Having heard Dharmadhara's tales about the cave I was eager to go there myself, and he was happy to make a second visit. But day after day the clouds burst open and torrential rain made the journey impossible. Fortunately, two days before I was due to depart for the plains, I awoke to a clear, calm, sunny morning. Without too much thought of the consequences should the heavens re-open, we set out on our pilgrimage to trace the footsteps of Guru Rimpoche, through the Kangra valley to a place called Mandi at the foot of the Kulu valley. It took us about seven hours including occasional stops at wayside teahouses.

Sitting on the pillion of the bike I got the better deal, not having to concentrate on the driving. It became slightly hypnotic after a while; the chugging of the engine, the luminous green fields of rice against the stormy black sky, frail-looking bridges crossing gushing rivers, as we travelled up and down from one valley into the next. Sometimes we had to dismount where landslides had partly blocked the road. We chugged past wooden shacks, salt mines, pine forests, sugar cane fields, children shouting and waving, wild flowers, and waterfalls. There was very little traffic, and the only beings on the road were an occasional herdswoman, mountain goats, and a snake slithering across our path. In the late afternoon we arrived in Mandi, having miraculously passed through only one light shower of rain. From now on we were in Padmasambhava territory. In the time of Padmasambhava the area was called Zahor and the historical/mythical context of our pilgrimage is recounted in *The Life and Liberation of Padmasambhava.**

Padmasambhava, 'the Lotus-Born One', can travel through time and space. From his island abode on the Dhanakosha Lake in Uddiyana he sees that it is time to instruct the Princess Mandarava, who is later to become his foremost disciple, along with her retinue. So, 'like the iridescent shimmering of the misty clouds which rise with the sun', he makes his way from his island abode through the heavens to Zahor, where he finds Mandarava with her serving women in their private park. He chooses to appear to her in the guise of a serene eight-year-old youth, sitting cross-legged in the air above the park, surrounded by rainbows, smiling, and exhibiting 'gestures of Dharma'. Mandarava swoons, but Padmasambhava revives her, whereupon she comes to her senses and rejoices. She invites him into the palace, closes the door, and forbids all entry. She makes many offerings, shows great reverence, and thus Padmasambhava 'sets turning the wheel of Dharma'.

The story goes on that 'an oxherd whose karma was impure' sees Padmasambhava enter the palace and starts to gossip, saying that 'a Samanian vagabond, muddling the Dharma with who knows what law, is doing something that is anything but the Dharma.' The king, Mandarava's father, does not believe this at first, but some of his ministers, having made insinuating remarks themselves, want to prove the gossip true. They go down into the place where Mandarava is being taught the Dharma, and there, 'mounted on a lofty throne covered with jewels, the

---

* Yeshe Tsogyal, *The Life and Liberation of Padmasambhava*, Dharma Publishing 1978.

Saint, bright as a mirror reflecting the sun, a radiant splendour dazzling the eyes, was teaching the Dharma, in the resounding voice of Brahma.'

Seeing this, the ministers are too afraid to lay their hands on Padmasambhava. The king, however, is furious when he hears their report, and believing that this foreigner is dishonouring his daughter, he orders that the vagabond Padmasambhava be tied up and burned alive. The punishment for his daughter for consorting with the vagabond is to be thrown into a pit carpeted with thorns, and left there for twenty-five years. The king orders that a dome should be placed over the pit so that the princess may not see the blue sky, and a double screen so that she may not see the sun. Her 500 servants are forbidden to cross the threshold, and if any of them should hear Padmasambhava's voice, they too will be thrown into a dungeon. Mandarava's dungeon is apparently still to be seen in Mandi, although we never actually found it, but we did see the ruined walls of a palace, built on the original site of the palace where the princess lived.

The ministers then go to the palace, and throw themselves on Padmasambhava, some tearing at his clothes, others holding his feet and hands, despite Mandarava's protestations that 'This son of the Conqueror is nothing but my spiritual Master … my heart will break, my body is undergoing intolerable pain, and out of grief my eyes are filled with tears.' Nobody heeds her words. Putting a noose around Padmasambhava's neck they urge him forward with blows, along a track worn by horses and cows, to a deserted place where the three valleys meet. We made the same journey out of Mandi on the motorbike, climbing higher and higher up what is now a tarmac road, and eventually arriving at the very place 'where the three valleys meet'.

The ministers build a pyre with vine shoots and palm leaves which they douse in sesame oil. They put Padmasambhava in the centre, set fire to its four corners so that the smoke goes swirling in clouds throughout the valley, and then go home, leaving the pyre to burn. Soon after, a great earthquake occurs, and various supernatural beings appear, untie the bonds, and pour rainwater on the pyre to extinguish it. Seven days later, smoke is still rising from the valley, so the king returns to the place, and he sees that the pyre has been transformed into a lake of water, surrounded by large ditches filled with fire whose flames are burning upside down. On a lotus flower in the centre of the lake sits an eight-year-old child.

The king can hardly believe his eyes, rubbing them, and looking again and again, each time he looks he can still see the same sight. Realizing what he has done, he is racked with grief, and eventually offers Padmasambhava the throne, which he accepts. Padmasambhava dons the five royal robes and puts on the lotus-petal crown, while the ex-king, his robes removed, puts the cord of the chariot around his neck and pulls it himself. Mandarava is released from her dungeon, and once again with all her heart goes for Refuge to the Three Jewels as embodied in Padmasambhava, who proceeds to convert the people of the entire region to Buddhism.

As Dharmadhara and I approached the place where the three valleys meet we saw, nestling in the centre, a small but beautiful lake – the transformed funeral pyre of Padmasambhava. It was twilight, but before darkness had completely descended we circumambulated the lake. There were two Tibetan monasteries and a Hindu temple close to the water's edge. We were able to stay in the Nyingma monastery (the Nyingma is the oldest school of Buddhism in Tibet, being descended from the teaching introduced by Padmasambhava). At the monastery we were given extraordinary hospitality by Yogi Namgyal, the only resident who spoke any English. He had just completed a solitary retreat of three years, three months, three weeks, and three days, during which time he had completed three hundred thousand prostrations (multiples of three are considered auspicious). He was young, friendly, and relaxed. During the evening an even younger monk from the Kagyu monastery over the lake came to visit. For special festivals the two monasteries have large celebratory pujas together, but otherwise they live and practise separately. The lake is named Tsompema, which means the Lotus Lake, by the Tibetans, and Rewalsar by the Indians. We discovered that it is a place of pilgrimage not only for Buddhists but also for Hindus, who have adopted Padmasambhava as a saint, given him a different name, and proclaimed him a Hindu. Hence I was kept awake much of the night by hymns to Rama and Krishna echoing out from loudspeakers over the otherwise tranquil setting.

At 5.30 the following morning we set out to ascend a steep hill to the climax of our pilgrimage. We climbed on foot through terraces of sunflowers, maize, and marijuana, plants higher than our heads, our footsteps accompanied by the distant deep vibrations of long trumpets from a Tara puja being performed by the Kagyupas. An hour and a half later, amid a fine, misty drizzle, we came to the entrance of the cave where Padmasambhava and Mandarava had lived and meditated. There was complete silence all around. Many prayer-flags were strung across from the top of one large boulder to another, washed white with the rain and fluttering in the breeze. A novice monk, not more than sixteen years old, appeared from a small room carved out of a rock, and took us into the cave. First we entered an antechamber where, until recently, a lama had lived for many years. Ducking down through a narrow opening at the far end, we entered a second chamber, dark, dank, and dripping. There, embedded in one of the walls, was an enormous image of Padma-sambhava, his renowned 'wrathful smile' piercing right through me. A slit in the rock of the opposite wall shed a little light from outside on the image: its vastness alone was quite breathtaking. Apart from a low-wattage bulb dangling from his trident, the cave had not been modern-ized or prepared for tourists in any way. Perhaps because of the steep ascent, very few people visit it. We ducked once again to enter a third chamber, where Mandarava had lived; not a sound penetrated from the outside world. No one knows how long Padmasambhava lived in this cave but it is said that 'For two hundred years he dwelt in the land of Zahor.'

Descending back to Tsopema Lake, with a novice monk as guide we were able to find another cave where Mandarava had lived. It was situated behind a chai-shop in the village, in a great cavernous rock, on which was a bas-relief of Guru Rimpoche said to be carved by Mand-arava. The narrow opening led into a tiny room, brilliantly lit by butter lamps, sweetly smelling of incense which wafted in clouds around thangkas of Buddhas and Bodhisattvas. And there, sitting serenely on a four-foot bed, was an elderly nun, very slowly and mindfully turning a small mani-wheel, chanting softly, completely undisturbed by our intru-sion, just smiling and nodding her head. I could hardly take my eyes off her; for me this was the most powerfully moving part of the pilgrimage. As we left her cave, she came out with us and showed us a niche in the rock: Mandarava's hand print. This nun had lived alone here for count-less years.

Before long we were retracing our steps, back on the motorbike for the seven- or eight-hour ride to Dharamsala. The following day I made the long, and this time uneventful, journey back to Poona.

Through Jaundiced Eyes

Within a few days I was off to Phaltan, a small town some three hours' bus ride from Poona, to do a Marathi language course with an American lady called Maxine. Her bungalow was on the edge of town at the bottom of a private drive hidden from the road by guava trees. Bougainvillea trailed over the fence that marked the boundary of her land, and her garden backed on to the canal. In the bungalow she had designed herself, with its spacious open-plan rooms and immaculately-kept simple stylishness, I could have imagined myself anywhere in the world. It had a fresh water supply, electricity, and even a telephone. Mosquito netting covered doors and windows so that I did not have to cover myself in evil-smelling Odomos, and the noise and clutter of India were kept at bay. It was not that Maxine isolated herself from the kind of India that was most familiar to me. On the contrary, she had already set up an excellent non-formal education class in the centre of town for some of the poorest and most deprived children in the area. But the world inside her home was a refreshing intermission from that, with its books, music, and carefully chosen pictures. She was devoted to her work as a linguist, devoted to her little school, and devoted to her cultured high-caste neighbours.

My baby conflict was forgotten as I plunged into studying, speaking, and trying to understand this difficult language. Two weeks later I was again back in Poona, back to the slums, back to weighing babies and treating scabies. It wasn't long before I started to feel ill. This was not unusual. In the three years I'd lived in India I'd often been plagued with 'Bombay belly', or 'the runs' as it was commonly termed. In fact in retrospect I think I was so often slightly ill that I began to think of my 'fluid' state as the norm, and became accustomed to having to dash to the toilet at inconvenient times. It was interesting to learn that I was not alone; Indians as well as foreigners frequently suffer from diarrhoea and dysentery.

On this occasion, however, I had no appetite for a number of days, felt particularly nauseated, and was overcome by weakness. After about a week of feeling like this, one day I walked halfway to the station to go to work, and just knew I couldn't continue. Dizzy and faint, somehow I managed to stagger home and lie down. Minutes later I started vomiting. My whole body felt poisoned, yet I'd hardly eaten for days. I knew it wasn't just a bout of food poisoning. I had a suspicion of its cause, and when I saw the tell-tale dark brown urine and pallid stools, I knew I was right. A few days later it was apparent to all: the whites of my eyes had turned yellow and my skin was distinctly jaundiced. I had hepatitis. A laboratory test confirmed the diagnosis. Rather than concern, I felt great relief. For at least ten days I had felt so groggy, so run down and nauseated, so unable to do anything that required exertion, that to know and be told I must take complete bed rest came as a welcome gift.

At that time I lived in the servants' quarters of a large, colonial, two-storey 'bungalow' in the centre of Poona, with its name, 'Gladhurst', picked out in stained glass over the front porch – a nice reminder of the modest social background of most of the British in India, for all their airs. And yet in its heyday it must have been very grand behind this suburban doorway, the main wing of the house having large stately rooms with white marble floors, verandas discreetly hidden by trellises entwined in creepers and vines, and wide staircases and wooden columns, all set in a large garden with a sweeping drive, walkways, stone statues, lotus ponds, exotic plants, and flowering trees. Once it had been one of the many homes of the Nizam of Hyderabad: his railway coach could be shunted into a siding whence he could walk up a flight of steps straight into the garden.

With a bit of effort I could imagine how it must once have been, but when I lived there, although the house was functional, it was crumbling away, and the garden was an overgrown mess of broken pillars and columns. The wooden pergola was rotting, bunches of grapes hung from the sides of a couple of cracked and broken stone urns, and weeds grew between the cracks of waterless ponds. Despite its dilapidation the place had a certain romantic charm, although piles of waste – rusty barbed wire, corrugated iron, and broken bottles – heaped in the garden gave a desolate, unloved air to the fading grandeur. When I was there, Gladhurst was owned by Judy Pereira, an Anglo-Indian who went to Mass every Sunday, had a blue and white plaster statue of the Virgin Mary at the bottom of her garden, kept a firm distance from Indians, and thought that Bhagwan Rajneesh was the best thing that ever hit Poona.

In the early days of my illness Virabhadra visited regularly, just to check that I was still alive. As I recuperated, I had the company of Mike the philosopher who lived at Gladhurst, renting a whole wing of the house for his wife, Rosemary, and their two children. He had come to India to write a philosophy book, choosing Poona because of his Buddhist connections. For me he became the ideal nurse and companion. Every morning he walked round from his suite in the main wing to my rooms in the servants' quarters to see how I was. If I needed food he did my shopping and when I developed a craving for Marmite and Rose's lime juice, of all things, he managed to find both in Poona's renowned deli, Dorabji's.

In the second week I looked my worst, shining yellow like the sun, but I actually began to feel somewhat better, and the nausea left me, although I still had little appetite. For several weeks I was so weak that after going downstairs to the toilet I had to lie on my bed for half an hour, shaking as though I'd just climbed a mountain. Several friends in India had suffered from hepatitis and some of them had become depressed when they were ill, but for me the illness brought about high spirits and a state of mental activity, to the extent that my state of consciousness was higher than normal.

I read a lot. Initially it was P.G. Wodehouse, lent to me and earnestly recommended by the great philosopher Mike. Not being in the slightest bit interested in the idiotic capers of the English upper classes, I had given the whole corpus of his writings a wide berth in the past, but now I fell completely under his spell. Then I plunged into feminist literature, biographies and autobiographies mostly of Western women. Apart from reading, I just lay on my bed and let my mind drift. It slowly dawned on me that the warring internal armies of reason and emotion over my baby dilemma had called a truce, and the conflict had, at least for the time being, abated, even dissolved away. I felt remarkably free to move forward again, as though a great burden had been lifted from my shoulders.

The resolution not to have a child had a transforming effect on me. Having being engrossed for so long with my own conflicts, absorbed in subjective musings, my mind now began to flash back over the last three years of living in India, back to people I had known and nursed, places I had visited, situations in which I had been involved. Then something new and rather strange began to happen. I started to build up fictional characters in my mind's eye: a young village girl and her ex-Untouchable family and the place in which they lived began to appear vividly before me. She was someone I had never met or known. For me she was the archetypal Indian woman, and she came alive as keenly as though she were my own sister or even myself. This was Shobha. In my head I worked out her family tree, which consisted of some twenty-five members. I could visualize everyone; I drew the tree and gave many of them names. I knew exactly how Shobha looked, how she thought; I knew her actions and her responses to things. I saw the minute details of her everyday life: her house, her relations, her interaction with others, her dreams and fantasies. I started to write.

Apart from school essays I had never written fiction, but as the days went by I became completely absorbed. I wrote, thought, even dreamed about Shobha and her family; they were larger than life. I could not sleep at night, though it didn't matter for I could doze off in the daytime whenever I wanted. Nights and days merged indistinguishably. I remember no moment when I was either bored or lonely.

Once I was on the mend, my only medicine being sticks of sugar cane and a traditional ayurvedic liver-strengthening potion, Virabhadra stopped his daily visits, and my only regular visitor was Mike, who came for afternoon tea. Overcoming my trepidation at exposing my schoolgirl literary efforts to the philosopher, I let him read 'Shobha'. Disclosing myself in this manner was not easy – I felt as though I was letting out a closely-guarded secret – but I had built up enough trust in Mike by this time not to fear rejection. He did not come to tea the next day and I wondered if perhaps my writing was so excruciatingly awful that he couldn't face seeing me. However, the following day he came round and said he liked what I had written, and that he could suggest some changes which, without distorting the content, could make it much better. He got me to read it out aloud, to listen to the words, to see it as poetry, hear it as music, feel the flow and the rhythm. I learned more in that hour than I had ever learned about writing before, and began to feel very excited. Words began to look and sound quite different. I began to enter into a relationship with them, and soon I felt no fear of showing Mike other bits as I wrote them. Shobha became his friend as well as mine and at one point he said he wished he were writing the same story.

So the days passed. A few Indian friends like Mrs Khandagale visited bringing fruit and flowers. Judy Pereira did not approve of having such people on the premises but they continued to visit, climbing over the back wall. (I eventually left Gladhurst, and spent my last three years in much more cramped and less private rooms in Ambedkar Society, so that my Indian friends could come and go as they pleased.)

Though steeped in a certain aspect of India through my writing, I was quite out of touch with the world at large. I never listened to the radio

Virabhadra had lent me, nor read a newspaper. One morning in October 1985, Judy came rushing round, stood beneath my window and shouted up, 'Hi–la–ree, Hi–la–reeee!' (She was the only person in India who refused to call me by my Buddhist name.) From the moment I had become ill, I had not caught so much as a glimpse of her, though on a couple of occasions she did send up some fruit or a slice of birthday cake, requesting that the servant bring back the plate immediately for fear of contamination. I looked down.

'Indira Gandhi has been shot in Delhi; several bullets have gone into her chest. It's not yet publicly known but friends in Bombay have just phoned to tell me,' she shouted up in her husky voice. 'Don't tell anyone!' Shocked, I tuned into All India Radio, but no news was coming through yet, so I tried the BBC World Service.

'Mrs Indira Gandhi, India's Prime Minister, has been shot several times in the chest at her home in the capital city of Delhi. At the time she was giving an interview in her garden. It is thought the attempted assassination was performed by one of her bodyguards. She has been rushed to hospital and is said to be in a serious condition.'

I tuned back to All India Radio but there was still nothing. The world knew but India didn't.

Then Mike came round. 'Have you heard?' Judy had told him too, with the same injunction to tell nobody else. By the time the news could be heard on All India Radio the BBC was announcing her death. Two hours had elapsed before the assassination was announced on Indian radio. A horrid hush pervaded the streets outside, as though the city had come to a standstill. Mike and I kept our ears glued to the crackle of the BBC while from radios in the surrounding apartment blocks mournful music wafted through the air – the same music that was played after the death of Indira's father, Nehru.

Within hours, communal violence had broken out in Delhi, and soon it spread to other cities, with the death toll rising rapidly by the hour. Curfews were imposed in Delhi and other cities in the north. For the next few nights the streets of Poona were deserted, although it was not under strict curfew, and a few militants did cause trouble in the old part of the city. During the days that followed Mike, Virabhadra, and I sat huddled over the radio in my room. We felt as though we were sitting on a live bomb; anything could happen. A few months previously I had seen the aftermath of Hindu and Muslim violence in Bombay: burned-out huts, buses, and rickshaws, gangs loitering on street corners, fear and hatred hovering thickly in the air. I now felt that violence could erupt on my doorstep any minute.

Several days later I ventured out of the garden for the first time one evening with Mike. We walked down the deserted street to the local restaurant to have supper. It was closed and barred. Everything was shut up. A pall of silence hung over the streets. Quickly we turned back, and cooked rice and dal at home.

Indirectly, Mrs Gandhi's assassination and the subsequent bloodbath put a stop to my writing. Try as I might, I couldn't recapture the all-consuming absorption I had known. The muses had flown. I felt different. With my jaundice gone and the first few grey hairs apparent at my temples, I felt I had been on a long and exciting journey, though I had hardly left my room. I put 'Shobha' on the shelf, where she quickly gathered dust, and returned to work in the slums.

Dr B.R. Ambedkar

My family – I'm the baby

Slums in Dapodi

Rag-picking

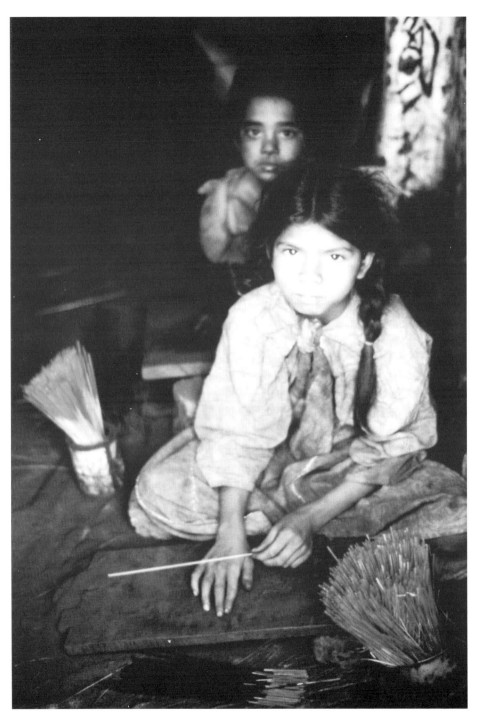

Making incense sticks

Carrying water

A sewing class

Teaching a literacy class

Learning to write

Virabhadra and I off duty

Weighing a baby to detect malnutrition

Vimalasuri after her ordination

Virabhadra outside the Khandagales' house

Meditating

fiction

A Mahayana Sutra is a poetic discourse which contains the Buddha's teachings, advocating the ideal of a life dedicated to the attainment of supreme enlightenment not for one's own sake only, but for the good and benefit of all sentient beings.... The Buddha is the supremely and perfectly enlightened one. When we hear or read a Sutra we may feel we have no choice but to accept whatever the Buddha says whether we like it or not, because, after all, He knows and we don't know, and this may create in our minds a little resistance. But suppose a text is not labelled a Sutra. Suppose you don't have to regard it, as some people do, as 'spiritually authoritative' (although 'spiritually authoritative' is in fact a contradiction in terms). Suppose we can read it quite straightforwardly, just as we read through any other work of imagination – a novel, a poem, a short story? Suppose we can read a Sutra more or less as we read literature, rather than as dogma, read it more as poetry than as a statement of scientific fact or philosophic truth. If we could read it in that way, perhaps then we might be more open to its spiritual influence, might be more receptive to its message, might allow ourselves to be captivated a little by its magic. And this suggests a further thought. It being helpful to read Sutras more as works of imagination, it might be equally helpful to read works of imagination more as Sutras....

SANGHARAKSHITA *in taped lecture 'The Magic of a Mahayana Sutra'*

Shobha – A Story

The Village

Shobha Shinde was born a Mahar, an Untouchable, in 1955. She spent the first fourteen years of her life in a place where generations of Shindes had always dwelt. They lived as an extended family of between nineteen and twenty-five persons in a small, dusty village in central Maharashtra. They were landless labourers save for a small piece of *wattan* land provided for the Scheduled Caste community by the government; but it was rocky ground far from the river, and nothing grew there. Their hut was in the area where Untouchables had always lived, in the Maharwaddha on the outskirts of the village. Their neighbours were six other such families, all Mahars. They lived apart from Caste Hindus who occupied the village centre, and drew their water from separate wells. Caste Hindus and Untouchables did not mix, although Untouchability had been declared illegal in 1951.

The people whose land they worked were of the Maratha or warrior caste. On their land they grew millet and jowari, sugar cane, potatoes, brinjal and onions, chillies, coriander, and garlic. Down near the river which wound its way round the edge of the village was a long narrow strip of flooded rice fields. At the edge of the land grew a field of marigolds, and four straight papaya trees reaching high into the blue sky. On the river bank close to the Shindes' house was a rock-built shrine dedicated to Mariai, the pestilence goddess. Every year they celebrated her *jatra*: having bathed the black image in curds and milk they would dress her in a green sari, cover her head with turmeric and vermilion, and place food and a coconut before her. One of the Shindes' neighbours was her *potraj*, which meant that from time to time she would be possessed by the goddess; on special occasions she carried the image on her head round the village to get rid of pestilence. The Shindes worshipped other gods too, but Mariai was the one they loved most.

The river marked the eastern boundary of the village. Beyond the cultivated land on the further shore the terrain was desolate, a vast region of ochre-coloured earth broken up by black boulders and an occasional spiky cactus. Apart from the four papaya trees there was nothing to break up the vast expanse of sky.

Shobha's father tended a pair of white buffalo which were kept for ploughing and transporting harvested crops to town. Three long-horned water buffalo were kept for their milk. Each day boys from the village would take the buffalo down to the river to be washed, the great black animals slowly lowering their dust-covered bodies into the muddy water. The naked boys would jump on the buffaloes' backs, and holding on to their long curved horns would splash around, scrubbing their black hide with rough stones so that they shone when they emerged from the river into the glaring sun. The Shindes owned no animals of their own, nor any land that could be cultivated; they owned no farm implements, in fact no means of livelihood, save their strong backs and soil-worn hands; but they did keep some chickens for their eggs. Outside their house grew a neem tree; it was very old and gnarled and gave the only bit of shade at midday, and they used its leaves and bark for medicinal potions. Nothing else grew there.

The Shindes' house was long and low like a barn; the walls were of stone and mud, the roof of heavy thatch. It needed repairs every monsoon, but it had been built by Shobha's great-great-grandfather and had stood for eighty years. The inside walls were coated in smoothed mud. Two tiny windows let in barely enough light to see by, keeping out the burning glare and heat of the sun at midday. One end of the room had been partitioned off to serve as a kitchen. On the kitchen walls massive blackened cooking pots hung from wooden pegs. Eight large hand-beaten brass water pots stood piled on top of each other in one corner beside an area of sunken flagstones sloping towards a drain. In another corner was an open fire for cooking, and a hole had been made in the centre of the dung floor to make a place for pounding spices. A rickety wooden shelf held a row of aluminium canisters containing pulses and grains, and beneath that three more long shelves displayed highly polished brass plates, stainless steel plates, *watti*, and *tambia* (cups and little pots). Every item had its place. This was the women's domain, and no man was allowed to enter.

The rest of the hut was an open area where the family members ate and slept, and where the menfolk sat when they were not out working in the fields. Brightly coloured pictures of Hindu gods in worm-eaten frames hung in rows along one wall, and on another wall hung a few faded black and white family photos: grandfather in his turban sitting next to grandmother in her nine-metre sequined wedding sari, uncomfortably perched on studio chairs against a backdrop of a palm-fringed Goan beach at sunset. There were group photos too, each member of the family standing to attention, neatly groomed in their best clothes. The girls' hair was scraped back and pinned away from their faces, with two loops of plait held together with large ribbon bows around the earlobes; the boys' hair was uniformly parted and their arms were held stiffly to their sides in military fashion. Each child, boy or girl, had their eyes outlined with black *kasal*, which accentuated their bemused expressions.

On its own hung a photograph of Shobha's great-grandfather. On the surface of the yellowing glass frame his forehead had been reverently smeared with vermilion powder, and every day a burning stick of incense and a lighted earthen lamp were placed on a shelf beside it by great-grandmother. Before Shobha's birth he had dropped dead close beside Maraiai's shrine when returning home from a day's ploughing in the fields: he was seventy-five years old.

Six metal trunks stacked in one corner contained all the family possessions: some clothes, a mildewed copy of the sacred Vedas, and a meagre dowry of jewellery including nose rings, nose studs, earrings, toe rings, and bangles. Each trunk belonged to one family group, and each had its own padlock. Folded on top of the trunks were stacked a pile of hand-stitched bed covers. No piece of cloth, even when worn into holes, was ever discarded. The smallest scrap was incorporated into a patchwork cover, the cloth being spread out in layers and stitched together to provide a little warmth during winter nights.

Whilst Shobha was still being suckled she slept on the floor next to her mother, Aai, burying her head in folds of soft sari, which gave easy access to a warm cushioning breast. When she was eighteen months old, though she was still unweaned, she was sometimes put to sleep near her grandmother, Agi, whose firm palm continuously patting Shobha's side would lull her to sleep: it was a warm and withered hand, not small and delicate, but strong, feminine, maternal. A few months before her brother was born, the flow of sweet warm milk dried up, but Shobha still enjoyed Aai's comforting nipple to chew on, and seemingly Aai found equal comfort in their closeness and never pushed her away. After the birth of her younger brother Shobha was put to sleep next to her sister Usha, lying beneath a shared cover with their cousins to form a long row against the partition wall. From this time on, she and Usha, who was two years her senior, were rarely willing to be parted. Shobha grew to be strong and healthy, unlike Usha who was frequently sick, had difficulty eating, and often cried with fevers in the night. Usha developed slowly so that before long Shobha had caught up with her in height and they were often referred to as 'the twins'.

The girls had no education. The primary school in the centre of the village was attended by some of the boys, but none went beyond third standard, leaving before they were eight years old. There was work to do on the land, money was needed, and formal education seemed of little use if they were to remain in the village. Furthermore, at school they were humiliated by teachers and fellow students alike. Being 'ex'-Untouchables didn't mean much in practice. Though they were followers of Dr Babasaheb Ambedkar, and though the mass conversions had happened in nearby Nagpur the year after Shobha's birth, they were hardly practising Buddhists yet; they still mostly adhered to Hindu customs. A Brahmin man taught at the school; there were thirty or forty boys in one small hut, too many to fit inside, and it was the Scheduled Caste children who were made to sit outside in the direct sun. They could not see the blackboard or hear the teacher, and they were spat on by fellow pupils and sworn at by teacher and passers-by alike. They had little incentive to learn, rarely did well in exams, and were caned for being ignorant. Before long Untouchable boys tended to play truant rather than be humiliated. Nobody in their families forced them back; instead they started work on the land.

The only member of the Shinde family who had shown any interest in education was Shobha's grandfather, Mukkund. He had learned to read and write, and at the age of thirteen had befriended a neighbour, Ramesh Patil, a boy from the high-caste Maratha. Though Mukkund often went round to his friend's house he would never be allowed to go inside;

instead they'd sit in the Patils' small garden in the shade of a tamarind tree. Ramesh had hopes of becoming a teacher and found Mukkund an eager student. Ramesh's liberal-minded family saw no harm in the friendship – in fact they even encouraged it, and would probably have let Mukkund enter their house had they not known the scandal it would have caused among neighbours. For four years Mukkund continued to see his friend, and his knowledge of a world outside the village broadened into exciting vistas. He learned about towns and cities, about foreign countries and continents, about the deep blue limitless sea, about the cold clear white brilliance of snow. He learned about white man and black man, about wireless and telephone....

It was a sad day for Mukkund when Ramesh told him that he was leaving the village and going to the city to study at a college. Ramesh's family provided a grand farewell supper. Very few boys from the village had ever continued their study towards further education, so there was great celebration among the Caste Hindu community. But Mukkund was not invited because Ramesh's relations and friends would be polluted if he ate with them. However, in the early hours of the morning after the feast, when all the guests had returned to their homes and a stillness lay over the village save for a solitary barking dog, Ramesh stole out from his house and ran down to the Maharwaddha where he found Mukkund outside the house asleep. He woke him up and presented him with two packages. Mukkund fell at Ramesh's feet in deep reverence and respect. But Ramesh pulled him up, embraced him, and, both in tears, they separated. Ramesh stealthily fled back to his home. Before dawn he had departed for the city. One of the packages contained sweetmeats, the other a book, the holy Hindu scriptures of the sacred Vedas. Ramesh never returned to live in the village. His marriage was arranged to a city girl. Mukkund was invited but couldn't afford the fare. Once a year Ramesh returned to the village with his proud, beautifully adorned wife, and later with his children; but though they passed each other in the street Ramesh ignored Mukkund, who painfully swallowed his bitterness and his love.

Mukkund never forgot the stories he had heard, and he would sometimes gather around him a group of his grandchildren and send their imaginations soaring, although he never taught anyone else to read or write. As a young child Shobha used to love his stories. She and Usha would often sit on his lap and gaze up at his furrowed brow, at his pockmarked cheeks and bulbous nose; they'd catch hold of his great coarse hands and tug at the loose end of his magenta turban. He held himself proudly, spoke in a deep slow voice, and emphasized his words with sweeping gestures.

By the age of seven Shobha was almost doing a woman's work in the house. She looked after younger brothers and sisters, nephews and nieces, one of whom was usually hoisted astride her hip. When there was extra work to do in the fields 'the twins' were out there too, squatting down to weed between rows of onion plants in the heat of the day, or to pluck the bright heads of orange and yellow marigolds to be taken into the town and strung into garlands as temple offerings. They picked ripening chillies until their fingers and eyes burnt. At the beginning of the monsoon they would perch on one-legged stools, their feet in the water and their bodies sheltered from the driving rain by a woven shell of bamboo and straw – two among a long line of other workers, similarly clad, sinking the vivid green shoots of paddy into the mud and singing as they worked. It was hard and back-breaking work, and they were paid a pittance, but every rupee was needed.

When Shobha was nine the area fell under a drought. A little rain fell early in the season, then there was nothing. The atmosphere became heavy, but still no rain fell. The earth was scorched and cracked, the crops wilted, the well dried up and the river dwindled to a trickle. The cows and water buffaloes hung their heads low; food was running out. As the weeks went by nothing was left but a small store of the previous year's rice. Tempers flared as the food supply dwindled. The adults lived on boiled rice, the children on rice water. The babies were too listless even to cry, silently enduring cracked lips, mouth sores, and festering scabs. Their skin fell back around their ribs and their bellies puffed out, their eyes sank into their skulls, and folds of flesh hung down like baggy pants from their buttocks. Cattle died, people died, young and old, but the gods were good to the Shinde family; nobody died there but two chickens, which were quickly eaten. Usha suffered from night fevers and Shobha nursed her. By September a little rain fell, but much of the crop had been ruined. The river rose slowly and the well filled up, but nothing could replace the lives that had been lost. Agi declared that fate had ordained it thus.

It was said that to ensure a good yield the river had to touch the bottom step of Mariai's temple three times in a season. 1965 had been a year of little rain: the crops had borne only half their usual yield, and throughout the monsoon the river only once touched the step. The following year, in the first week of July, after days when gales whipped up dust storms across the land and there was nothing left to do but wait, the first heavy black nimbus cloud crept up over the horizon. It was afternoon. All the women and children sat outside and waited. Agi started to sing, pleading with the gods to feed and nourish the earth:

> *We are only poor people,*
> *If we have given you cause for your wrath*
> *Don't take your revenge now.*
> *The children's bellies are empty:*
> *Their ribs are all you see;*
> *They have no food.*
> *My baby is crying;*
> *He wants to live and bring wealth to our village;*
> *Send down your nectar,*
> *Send down your nectar.*

With a baby asleep on her lap she began to rock to the rhythm, her hand beating time on her thigh. At the end of each verse everyone joined in the refrain:

> *Send down your nectar,*
> *Send down your nectar.*

Neighbours came and sat among them. They clapped their hands or slapped their thighs, they swayed to the rhythm of the song as Agi's cracked old voice warbled out her prayer. She sat in the centre of the group as though in a trance, staring up at the gathering black clouds looming closer.

The wind whirled columns of dust into the air. Distant rumbles of thunder vibrated in the heavens and sheets of lightning lit up the darkening earth. The rumbles soon became deafening cracks as though the world would split, and the lightning sheets were interspersed with great forks of light that shot down to earth (Shankar's trident, they said). Agi sang relentlessly on, though she stopped her tapping and raised her hands, joining them together in supplication to the gods, gently bringing them down at the end of each verse to touch her forehead with her fingertips, before returning her maddened stare to the stormy sky. The first few drops of rain that fell were as big as rupees. The children rushed to open spaces. The boys flung off their shirts and threw out their arms and chests while the girls raced around in twos and threes shouting, 'The rain has come, the rain has come!'

The mother of the baby on Agi's lap swaddled the babe in a cloth, picked him up and carried him inside. Agi did not notice. Her verses of entreaty were being answered; the gods were being good. In minutes the heavens tore apart and the rain poured. The children rushed around in circles while neighbours fled to their houses. Agi stood up slowly, the last to go in. Wet streaks of her grey hair hung around her calm face. Her palms still placed together, she fell on her knees, put her fingertips flat on the warm, wet, steaming earth, and bowed her forehead to touch the ground. She made this salutation three times, then slowly got up and walked inside. The children flocked towards her, grabbing her hands or the end of her sodden sari to be near her magic, then followed her into the hut chanting 'Aaiya, Devi …' – Mother, Goddess, Protector.

That night the whole family performed a special puja. They lit sticks of incense, candles, and butter lamps, they cracked open a coconut they'd been saving, and they thanked the gods for sending the rain. When everyone else had gone to sleep, calm and contented, Agi still mouthed her prayers. For three months the rain fell heavily, with occasional breaks in the cloud during the morning when the sun shone and the fields steamed as though on fire. The paddy fields were planted and the rice quickly thrived; the well was full of sweet water to drink; the river flooded its banks but did no harm, and many was the time it touched the bottom step of Maraiai's shrine. It was a yielding, prosperous season.

By the end of September the rains had ceased. The swollen river crept back off the land and followed its natural course. Soon they would be harvesting the rice whose green pregnant ears already swayed drunkenly back and forth with the breeze. The air was fresh again and clear, and the crops flourished under the brilliant blue sky. But it did not last. By Diwali hazy clouds hung low in a dull sky, but no rain fell. A lethargy, an eerie silence, stole upon the air. Damp clothes clung to the body, perspiration gathered in creases of skin, and trickles of sweat ran down temples. Energy seeped away. Even the children stopped playing and lolled around inside the house. Appetites diminished. People hardly spoke, as though there were not enough air to fill their lungs, but the daily routine of work in the home and on the land continued. Relief from the stifling oppression in the atmosphere came from bathing in the river. In the evenings after work, the men went down to the river to wash the day's grime from their spent bodies.

The day of Balu's death was just like any other day. Shobha's papa, her two *kakas* (uncles), and her cousins, had made their way through the fields and down to the river. They were strong swimmers, having bathed daily in the river since childhood, though in the monsoon they never ventured far from its banks. They stripped off down to their underpants, and plunged again and again into the refreshing coolness, ducking their heads, filling their mouths with water and squirting it out in jets. Within minutes they felt revived. But what they did not realize was that although there had been no rain for many weeks, making it seem as though the monsoon was over, 'elephant rain' – a kind of freak storm which sometimes occurs when the monsoon has finished – had lashed down further upstream. Although they couldn't yet see it, the river was rising again, and a strong undercurrent had been unleashed. Unaware of the danger, Balu – one of Shobha's kakas – left the group and swam out alone into midstream.

The others were getting out of the water and wrapping themselves in dhotis, talking and laughing as they shook the water from their hair and rubbed their heels with pumice stones. Not until they had dried themselves did they notice the change in the water level, which was slowly creeping up the banks. Shobha's father shouted out his brother's name, agitated fear in his voice – 'Balu!' The men looked up with sudden terror at the turbulent rapids boiling in mid-stream. But Balu could not be seen. They darted back and forth, peering into the water, screaming out, 'Balu, Bal–oo–oo–oo!'

One of them spotted his body being dragged swiftly downstream, rolling over and over in the water as he tried desperately to swim against the current. The five men rushed down the river bank shouting out to him. Rain was falling in a soft fine drizzle, turning the dried banks to squelching, slippery mud. Balu was dragged under, then reappeared several yards downstream. As fast as they ran they fell, skidded, or sank in the mud, whilst Balu was carried amid surging rapids, whirlpools, and currents that dragged him from one side of the river to the other, further and further from their reach. His screams for help were swallowed up in the noise of the torrent. For three miles they scrambled, covered in mud. The drizzle turned into a driving rain that beat against their sun-worn faces while their hearts pulsed in their throats. Balu had disappeared. Some of the men carried on downstream, whilst others retraced their steps to see if his body had been washed up on either of the banks. As the hours went by they began to realize the futility of their quest. It was well after dark by the time they entered the Shinde house to break the news.

That same night, in the rain and the pitch dark, all the men of the Maharwaddha went out in search parties with flaming torches. But it was in vain. It took two days before the body was recovered, caught in reeds and driftwood ten miles downstream. It was unceremoniously brought back to the village on a bullock cart. Balu was almost unrecognizable, bloated like a pumpkin and stinking with decay. Wood had to be found, and a funeral pyre was built at the water's edge. The wood was bought with borrowed money which it took the Shindes two years to repay. Because of the stench, the body was not taken into the house, but remained under the neem tree where it had been laid. The family women, the neighbourhood women, and women relatives from nearby villages, all sat round the body wailing and groaning, while vultures circled overhead.

Shobha was eleven, and she was witnessing for the first time the death of a loved one. The body was wrapped in a white cloth, only the face exposed to the elements. It didn't look like her Balu-Kaka who had teased her and played with her, who only a few years previously had so proudly brought his new wife into his family home, whose daughter, only five years old, had already learned to knead bakeri dough, and whose wife Meena, after two miscarriages, was expecting another child. Shobha sat close to Aai and looked across the distended body at Meena, whose large brown eyes were glazed with utter despair; she seemed aloof and withdrawn from everyone around her. Pausing for a moment's breath between wails, Agi placed her hand on her daughter-in-law's arm and held it there. In the past Meena had found Agi's constant piety a dampener to her own youthful vitality. Balu used to tease the two of them, helping to dissipate the petty bickering that on occasion broke out between them. One moment he would take sides with his mother, and gently chaff his wife, then he'd turn round and playfully harass and make fun of his mother till she could stand no more and would let rip, exploding, 'What god has sent me this accursed son?' while Meena giggled silently.

The funeral pyre was stacked. The body, tied to a rough stretcher of wooden poles, was lifted from beneath the neem tree and carried on the shoulders of six male relatives. Grandfather laid a few simple marigold garlands across the body. The pall-bearers walked in silence followed by the men of the neighbourhood; the women walked behind with their heads covered and bent, and the children dragged their feet and clung to their mothers. Still draped from the neck down in a white cloth, the body was lifted and reverently placed on the sticks and logs. The men made a semicircle round the pyre, while the women and children squatted on the ground to one side. A sobbing man poured kerosene on the body. There being no son to set the pyre alight, it was Balu's eldest brother who had the task. But the wood was damp, and after an initial flare it only smouldered, billowing forth clouds of smoke. More kerosene was emptied on to the wood and, with a crackling sound and a rush of wind, flames leapt up beneath the body.

A crescent moon had risen in the north and shone down to illuminate the familiar landscape, as sparks from the fire flew upwards to join the stars. The white cloth caught alight, sticks crumbled around the body; somewhere from the darkness came a muffled sob. Flesh, sticks, smoke, and flames merged into one. Shobha lay down and rested her head in Usha's lap. She lay there perfectly still and watched, while her mind drifted back....

It is morning. Agi sits beneath the neem tree stitching scraps of old cloth, the toddlers play with leaves and stones in the shade, the other women are out working in the fields, and great-grandmother sits inside the house beneath great-grandfather's photo, nodding her head. In the kitchen Meena is hunched over the fire cooking bakeri and humming contentedly to herself. Shobha and Usha squat beside the pounding hole. They half fill the hole with dried red chillies then lift the great stone pestle too heavy for one small child, and start to pound. The powder flies up in their faces, making them choke and splutter. Meena lets out a peal of laughter as the children struggle on, then she leaves the cooking and goes over to the girls. She bends down and shows them how to hold the pestle, how to drop it vertically at the last moment into the hole, and then catch it on its upward bounce using a continuous movement and breathing in time. She mimics the twins: their earnest expressions with tip of the tongue on the upper lip, their wrinkled brows and half-closed eyes, their short sharp breath and their inability to drop the pestle straight. They laugh.

Balu returns from the fields for his lunchtime tiffin. Hearing the laughter and smelling the spices, he peers into the kitchen. Looking behind him to see that nobody else is around he sneaks in without Meena noticing, catches her around the waist, swings her over his shoulder and dances around the room. The twins squeal, the bakeri burns. Disarrayed, Meena smothers her laugh in her sari. Just as Balu lets Meena's feet touch the floor, Agi walks in cursing the noise, hits the children and shouts at Meena for burning the bakeri. Balu winks at the twins, grabs his tiffin, slips round the doorway and runs back out to the fields....

The funeral pyre had burned down low. All that remained were blackened bones and a small pile of burning embers. Someone picked up a shovel, gathered the bones and ashes, and threw them into the river. A few marigolds were scattered on the water, and they all went home.

Early the next morning Shobha and Usha went hand in hand down to the water's edge. A charred area of earth, a fluttering piece of singed white cloth, and a garland of marigolds caught in the reeds were all that was left from the cremation. They freed the wilting garland and sadly watched it float downstream out of sight before returning home to collect the brass pots in order to draw water from the well and start the day's chores.

Meena looked tired and worn. Her daughter, Gita, clung insecurely to her side wherever she went but Meena either ignored her or pushed her away. She hardly ate, and performed her daily tasks mechanically. Her eyes were red and puffy and her hair uncombed, her blouse torn, and her sari soiled. She appeared not to notice. Removing her wedding chain she placed it in the trunk, and never again did she apply the vermilion marriage spot to her forehead. Much of the time she complained of aching limbs, and lay unnoticed, unattended, in a corner to rest while the other women continued with the daily chores. Gita cried.

Four days after the cremation Shobha awoke one night to hear agonized moans coming from Meena. Somebody lit a lamp and through bleary eyes Shobha saw silhouetted bodies moving to and fro. She crawled out from underneath the cover and went over to where Meena crouched with her hands clasped around a wooden post. Her dishevelled hair hung about her pained and sweating face, and her sari and petticoat were gathered up around her waist. Her moans became stronger, then louder, then became a deep sigh as she fell back and sat with head resting between her knees. Aai wiped Meena's brow with a cloth; Agi ordered Shobha to go to the kitchen and fetch boiling water and a sharp kitchen knife. As Shobha went she noticed that the men had moved outside and gone back to sleep. The children too slept on.

The kitchen was full of smoke. A blackened water pot stood balanced on the fire, steaming, while one of Shobha's aunts pounded a potion on the floor. At Shobha's request she got down the sharp kitchen knife from a high shelf, and carrying the boiling water and the potion she followed Shobha back to Meena. Meena drank the potion, lay down, and moaned. There was a moment's silence, then again Meena squatted. She pushed down, she heaved, she groaned, she swayed, then flopped back and sighed. The lamp on the floor beside her showed Meena lying with her legs bent and opened. Agi placed a hand on Meena's taut rounded belly while with the other she gently swept her withered fingers around the baby's head, a small crown of straight black hair with a trickle of fluid seeping around the sides. For the last time Aai helped Meena back on to her haunches while Agi folded clean cotton rags. Shobha felt faint; she held the hem of her skirt in her mouth and sat to one side. With an exhausted moan, a final push, a final heave, a groan, and a shriek, the baby's head was out. Meena lay back and panted. Then the baby's head rotated, a shoulder appeared, arm, trunk, legs, and the snake-like cord all slithered out into Agi's grasp. A rush of blood-stained fluid gushed to the floor.

Agi's hands were in perfect control. She held the baby's head and wiped its face. She clasped its feet and hung it upside down. She hit its feet, then gently laid it down and blew on its face. It opened its eyes and jerked its legs. Agi slapped its buttocks and it let out a little whimper. Meena lifted her head and looked over her deflated belly; it was a son. Agi wiped his body, wrapped him in rags and laid him on Meena's belly. Meena cried softly. Agi continued with her work: she held the umbilical cord and gave a slight pull on it. The cord lengthened so she tested it again until the placenta swam out, a large, red, jellified mass. Agi took the knife and cut the cord, then tied cotton thread around the umbilical stump which she proceeded to smear with cow-dung. When that was done she carefully placed the child in Meena's arms. With a dampened rag Aai washed the drying blood from Meena's soft fleshy thighs, and sprinkled the pool of blood on the floor with ash, while Agi lit candles and incense before pictures of the gods in gratitude that a son had been born. The placenta was buried outside as the first cock crowed. Meena fell into a deep sleep.

The baby had come early and became more frail by the hour. He didn't cry or even whimper; he only slept in the crook of his mother's arms, his breaths quick and shallow. The morning passed and he had not the strength to suck on the breast.

The day grew hot.

Then the afternoon sun beat down.

Long evening shadows stretched across the land.

Night fell.

Before the sun had risen again the baby had died. He was buried in the wattan land; there was no ceremony, no wailing, few tears. Meena hardly spoke. Gita grizzled and clung to her mother's side but was ignored, or cursed and hit till she cried.

The days passed by, the work went on; the rice was harvested, the fields were ploughed, and the nights turned cold. Meena looked thin, haggard, and lifeless. A measles epidemic spread around the village and some children died. Gita contracted the disease. Her fever rose and her little body sweated and shook as she went into convulsions. Meena became anxious for her life and rocked her in her arms or patted her side. She sang to her and prayed for her, fed her spoonful by minute spoonful of rice-water, hugged and stroked her, kissed her and wept for her. Gradually the convulsions stopped and the fever went down. Gita asked for food and drink which her mother prepared and gave. Meena felt something returning in herself, vitality seeping back into her veins. One day as she combed and plaited her long black hair, she peered into the tiny cracked mirror, and a faint glimmer of a smile looked back at her. She sighed deeply.

When the festival of Holi came, mother and daughter returned to Meena's native village, thinking to move back to her family home. But widows are bad omens, and her own father refused to let her stay under the same roof, even for a night. Her mother wept and embraced her, but Meena had to return to her dead husband's house that very evening.

Usha remained short while Shobha grew tall and slender. Tiny breast buds swelled under her blouse, and her firm hips swung from her nimble waist as she walked through fields or balanced a water pot on her head. When she worked she gathered her bright-coloured ankle-length skirt in the middle and tucked it in at the waist. Her strong muscular calves tapered to fine delicate ankles, around which hung loose silver chains, faintly tinkling as she walked. The balls of her feet were steady and buoyant, the heels cracked and dry; her long flexible toes spread to grip the ground as she glided over the burning dusty earth. When she was thirteen her bleeding started. As Shobha was getting up one day from sifting through rice for stones, her mother noticed a small stain of blood on Shobha's skirt. Shobha felt bewildered and frightened; for a moment she was confused as she remembered the birth of Meena's son, the blood, and the pain. Her mother tweaked her cheek proudly and gave her a reassuring hug. Usha showed Shobha how to wear the rags, and they giggled together down by the river bank. She bathed in a separate place where the women washed out their rags, laid them in the sun to dry, and replaced them with dry ones before returning to the house. When the bleeding stopped she bathed where she had always done. All the women in the neighbourhood knew, and it made her feel adult, mature, womanly.

Throughout her childhood Shobha's father had been a shadowy figure, a vague presence in her woman-dominated life. All day he worked in the fields, and at night he sat with the other men or went to the houses of neighbours, returning late at night when Shobha was already asleep. He never played with his children, and rarely spoke to his wife except to give orders which she patiently obeyed.

One hot afternoon the women sat beneath the neem tree sewing cloths and sifting millet, chatting and laughing. Even great-grandmother had moved from her dark corner beneath her deceased husband's photograph to sit outside. She leaned hunched against the gnarled tree trunk, eyes closed, her untamed wiry white hair bushing around her sleepy nodding head. The young children lay naked on cloths, arms and legs flung out, flies buzzing around in circles and landing on their hot brown sleeping bodies; noses twitched and tiny grubby hands rubbed their faces, but they didn't wake up. Papa returned home early from the fields. He staggered alarmingly towards them, red eyes rolling. He was drunk. For the first time there was violence in Shobha's house, and for the first time Shobha saw her mother cry. With her sari torn and half-unravelled, and bleeding scratches down her face and body, she wept bitter angry tears into her mother-in-law's shoulder. Great-grandmother awoke from her sleep and mechanically let her head nod up and down. Usha and Shobha ran down to the river for solitude.

They had seen drunken men before. A neighbour used to beat his wife and abuse his brothers and children, and they had seen men from the village lying in the gutter looking half dead, clutching bottles to their chests, and men stumbling down the road swearing and slurring their words. They had laughed then. Now, frightened, confused, and ashamed, they sat on the river bank aimlessly plaiting reeds until the sun went down. At dusk they gathered their skirts and walked slowly back to the house.

As the weeks went by things got worse, though Aai became stronger and fought back when her husband attacked her. More silent than ever, great-grandmother was a ghostlike figure hunched in the corner. She still burned incense and lit the earthen lamp every day, but she never spoke except to mutter inaudibly to herself. She had passed her eightieth year. The worm of insecurity crept in at Shobha's heart. Papa began to shout and swear at her, at her brothers and sisters, her cousins, her aunts and uncles, at her mother, and at his mother.

During this period Shobha's eldest brother's marriage was arranged, to a girl from the neighbouring village. Papa and Aai argued over the dowry. When the new wife arrived they cavilled at her meagre jewellery. Papa shouted at the bride while Aai took her under her care and ignored him. She was a scraggy-looking scared young girl of fourteen. She was not pretty; but she cooked well and knew how to embroider.

The following year Usha's and Shobha's marriages were arranged. The twins were to have a joint marriage ceremony to cut down on the expense. They were to be married into the same family, to the two sons of their father's aunt, who lived twenty miles up the river. As a small child Shobha had met these cousins but their next meeting was not until the wedding day. Shobha's future parents-in-law came to the Shindes' house one day in March to make the contract. Shobha changed out of her faded multicoloured skirt and blouse, and for the first time wore a sari, borrowing one of Meena's. When Aai had helped her to dress, she walked up and down inside the house feeling self-conscious, adjusting the yards of material as Meena did. She oiled and neatly plaited her hair; then she made a design of *rangoli* (a coloured powder sprinkled in intricate designs on the ground) on the trodden-down earth in the doorway of the house as a sign of welcome.

The two sets of parents discussed dowry details while Shobha and Usha served special tea with milk and ginger, and laid out in front of their guests the sweet *ladu* and *karangi* which they had prepared. When papa wasn't drunk he could be cordially hospitable to outsiders, and on this occasion he laid on the charm with a will in order to sweeten his relations. The local astrologer was called in, the two couples' horoscopes were matched and, according to what was favourable in the stars, the date and time of the wedding were fixed for three weeks thence. Nervous and excited, the twins were also happy to be entering into the same household. Shobha had just turned fifteen.

They journeyed by bullock cart into the nearest town to buy their wedding garments. For years grandfather had saved money for his grandchildren's dowry, keeping it in a metal box that his friend Ramesh had once given to him, buried under the cow-dung floor of the house. His dying wish the previous year had been that his grandchildren should be married properly. Every now and then Agi dug up the box and counted the coins. Now was the time to spend them. In the sari shop the twins sat on mattresses while yards of luscious, tempting material were thrown out in billows before their gaping eyes: silks and satins, organdie, cotton, and American georgette; saris with gold borders, silver borders, and silk-stitched borders; hand-embroidered saris, sequined saris, plain colours and prints; white, cream, yellow, red and orange, sky blue and violet, all the colours of a monsoon rainbow. They chose two dark red cotton ones with narrow gold-threaded borders and blouse pieces to match. They bought the first sandals they had ever worn, making their elegant gait a little clumsy. They bought gold earrings and large beaded nose rings as part of their dowry, along with shining plastic hair clips and green glass bangles. Coconut oil was bought for their long black hair. A neighbour fitted and stitched their tight sari blouses. There was not a rupee left to spend.

The wedding day arrived. Outside beside the neem tree a *pandal* had been set up: a raised platform with patched white awning from which hung frills of kingfisher blue with a dark blue backdrop. Blaring out of a gramophone speaker rigged to a generator on a bullock cart was music from Hindi movies, interspersed with songs dedicated to Dr Babasaheb Ambedkar and Gautama Buddha. Placed in the centre of the stage was a table covered in a worn woven cloth on top of which stood a plaster Buddha image painted luminous orange and gold. Next to the image, propped against a stone, rested a picture of Dr Ambedkar set in a gold plastic frame. Both picture and statue were garlanded with marigolds and petals were strewn across the table.

The bridegroom's party had arrived and sat in the shade of the neem tree while Shobha's cousins offered them water to wash their faces, hands, and feet, and water to drink. The grooms wore white open-necked shirts and white bell-bottomed trousers. The shirts were too loose and the trousers too long. The girls peeped round the door, and it was pointed out which husband was for whom, but they could not make out their faces. The two grooms, like the brides, wore a halo of flowers round the crown of their heads from which strands of flowers hung down the sides of their faces, half-obscuring their eyes. They sat cross-legged nibbling at *chewdar*, nervously jerking their knees up and down. The twins, equally nervous, played with their bangles, counting them, twisting them, clinking them.

Friends and relatives arrived and sat on the ground in front of the pandal, the women in the direct sunlight covering their heads with their saris, the men to one side in the shade of the tree, the younger ones wearing white Nehru caps and the older ones turbans. Children rushed up and down, and danced to the music. The air buzzed with excitement. The *purohit* who was to direct the ceremony arrived and gave orders on the procedure to be followed. The brides sat on one side of the stage on a mattress, the grooms on the other. In call and response, Buddhist Refuges and Precepts were recited, followed by an inaudible string of verses chanted by the *purohit* alone. Life-long vows were made, garlands exchanged, mangala suttas placed around the necks of the brides and silver rings on their toes.

The day seemed hotter than usual, Shobha's hands sweated and her head swam. A sea of faces looked up at her through the stifling sweet fragrance of jasmine garlands and incense smoke that wafted up towards her in the breeze. Once the ceremony was over everyone threw flower petals over the newly-weds and the music started up again. Then came gifts of cooking pots, plates, and glasses which were placed solemnly on the platform, while the donor of each had their name announced to all. Finally there was a feast, all the men sitting down in long rows, to be served rice, dal, and a potato curry on banana leaf. Once the men had finished eating the women ate what was left.

Night fell. Shobha had not yet exchanged a word with her husband, Vilas Gaikwad, had not even looked into his face. For three days the bridegrooms stayed with neighbours but ate at the Shindes' house. On the fourth day, Shobha and Usha, laden with their gifts and a small metal trunk, left their childhood home. Aai wept hysterically not only at the loss of her daughters, but remembering also the day she had been married and moved into the Shinde household. She had been ten years old. Everyone else cried too, and even papa wiped away a tear with the end of his dhoti. No longer the property of their parents, they were now owned by their husbands.

By bullock cart they made the day-long journey to their new home with their husbands and relatives. Shobha and Usha sat next to each other without speaking a word, covering their heads in their saris, as the great wooden wheels bumped over the sand and rocks, following the course of the river. By late afternoon they had crossed the river on a rickety raft and arrived at the Gaikwads' house. It was larger than the Shindes' house and occupied by only two families: eighteen people, three generations. As well as labouring for the big and corrupt landowners, they farmed their own wattan land, a one-and-a-half hectare strip down by the river where the main crops were rice and jowari, just enough for the family requirements. They also grew brinjal, onions, chillies, and potatoes, and coriander which they sold in the small market town, saving enough money to buy a buffalo in order to have milk to sell.

Shobha had been warned by Meena what to expect on her wedding night. She had also observed the coupling of dogs and buffalo in the village. She submitted with fearful fascination to what was expected of her, even though she had still not looked Vilas in the eyes. Meena had reassured her that she'd get used to it after a while, and this was true. Only occasionally at night, when each couple took it in turns to sleep behind a thin partition wall away from the rest of the family, did husband and wife ever spend time with each other. The girls rarely had a sight of their husbands, who were out all day working on the land, and they were never allowed to be alone in the house together. Apart from the infrequent hours together in the middle of the night, there was no physical contact, and little exchange of words except to discuss the day's work. Only when husband and wife caught each other's eyes outside in the fields did they ever look one another in the face.

The Gaikwad family were generous and kind. Sassubai, their mother-in-law, loved her new daughters-in-law like the daughters she had never had. She had produced five sons, and suffered seven miscarriages. Her only daughter had been stillborn after three days in labour. At that time she nearly died too, but her husband had managed to bundle her into the bullock cart in agonizing pain to see the doctor. After that she had been sterilized.

Within a year Shobha had been delivered of a daughter. For the birth she returned with Vilas to her native village where Agi aided the new baby into the world. They named her Amrita, which means 'nectar of the gods'. Shortly after the birth Vilas returned home, but Shobha remained in the Shinde household for three months, where Aai and Agi looked after her until her strength returned, and her body had resumed its former shape. Vilas was immensely proud of his wife. When she and the baby returned to his home, he went into town and bought her a pink nylon sari printed with a design of yellow and pink flowers around the border. At rare moments alone in the house Shobha took the sari out of the metal trunk to look at it, feel it, admire it.

Usha remained frail and did not conceive, which made Sassubai agitated. She brought in magic healers to perform conception rites and Usha was given potions and tree roots on which to chew and special prayers to recite. They did not work.

Soon after Amrita's birth Vilas announced his intention to go to the city. Sharp and ambitious, he had been educated up to eighth standard and was the pride of his parents. A stable job in a factory would earn good money to feed and clothe his family and send his children to school, on top of which he would be able to send money back to his parents and brothers. A schoolfriend named Rahul wrote a letter, the only letter the Gaikwad family had ever received, from the city where he had moved the previous year, saying there was a plot of land next to his where Vilas and Shobha could build their own hut. He talked of good prospects, high pay, and little caste discrimination. Shobha was not so eager. She had been into a large town only three times, and could not imagine what it would be like to live in a city. But she did not voice her opinions; the choice was up to the rest of the family.

Within a month the day of departure arrived. Everyone in the Gaikwad house was up before sunrise. Shobha's husband's family stood outside the mud-built house. Usha stood apart from the gathering, burying her tear-stained face in the end of her sari, unable to look Shobha in the eyes. Vilas, carrying Amrita in his arms, climbed into the bullock cart followed by Shobha, and they sat together squashed between a few items of clothing tied in a bundle and a small metal trunk. Vilas suddenly stood up, pushed Amrita into Shobha's arms, leapt down from the cart and fell down at his father's feet weeping. The women turned their faces away, hiding their tears in their saris. His father laid his hand on Vilas's shoulder, saying nothing, until Vilas, keeping his gaze turned to the ground, got up and climbed back into the cart. He looked ahead.

They skirted the village keeping the house in sight. Shobha looked back. Her eyes followed the tracks of the cartwheels until they rested on the family group still standing there. She could see all the houses, the village, the whole district, and the river threading its way through the earth like a silvery snake. The landscape beyond the village grew broader with shimmering horizons. From the east a massive red ball of fire rose into the sky; dawn had broken. The cartwheels bumped over the rocky terrain stirring up clouds of dust in their wake. They reached the brow of the gentle slope, and Shobha looked back for a final glance.

The City

Samsar

Ah the married life, the married life,
Just a pan on the stove;
First you get burns on your hands,
Then you get the bread.

Oh the married life, the married life,
Never call it worthless;
The very crown of the temple
Should never be called a brass pot.

Oh the married life, the married life,
Do not cry or whimper;
You fool, the garland around your neck,
Don't you call it a noose.

Oh the married life, the married life,
Break off the cucumber from the vine;
One end may be bitter,
All the rest tastes sweet.

Shobha hummed the tune of this song which Agi sometimes used to sing while kneading dough in the kitchen at home. She and Vilas spoke little. For two hours they travelled by bullock cart, Shobha's brother-in-law steering. The sun was well up in the sky when they arrived in the town. Without speaking the three of them waited, squatting on the ground by a chai stall for over an hour until they heard the roar of a bus turning a corner. As the bus came to a screeching halt, they stood up, and Vilas bade farewell to his brother, clasping his hands.

They journeyed for sixteen hours through the day and the night to reach the city. As they passed wayside shrines passengers threw out coins, and on crossing rivers they touched their foreheads and mumbled a prayer. A white man and woman slept on a seat near the front: the man was young and unkempt, his shoulder-length hair matted in clumps about his face, his arm loosely flopped around the woman, whose curly blonde locks rested on his shoulder. Vilas slept. As night fell the bus stopped in a crowded bazaar. Shobha and Vilas got out and stretched their legs, combed their hair, and bought a glass of tea to share, and four bananas. Awoken by the break in the droning, lulling motion of the bus, Amrita started to cry, so Shobha returned to the bus and discreetly suckled her beneath her sari.

The conductor, chewing betel leaf which had stained his teeth red, shouted for people to return to their seats as the bus belched black exhaust fumes from under the chassis. Vilas jumped back into the bus for the final overnight stage. By dawn they were approaching the city and all the passengers were expectantly sitting up in their seats, talking with their neighbours or looking out of the windows. On the streets the noise of engines and menacing hooters was loud and continuous, and the stench of factories and stagnant water made Shobha feel sick. People lined the streets and bullock carts ambled along amid the crowds. Urchin children ran up and down behind fat wealthy men, holding out their hands, tilting and scratching their heads. They were ignored.

The bus passed through bazaars and shanty towns, and rumbled past factories and hovels. They passed carpenters' workshops, metal workers' foundries, and areas where dyed cloth hung in the sun to dry. They swerved round corners, round people, round animals, dodged around cars, rickshaws, and cyclists. They crossed over bridges, screeched round roundabouts, drove under a railway line, through a dark tunnel.

Stopping at broken-down traffic lights they waited till a policeman signalled them on.

As they entered the cantonment area the crowds became fewer and the noise less pervasive; there were open spaces of fresh green grass on either side, large bungalows set in overgrown gardens with shaded verandas encased in white wooden lattice, and bougainvillea of magenta, orange, mauve, and white such as Shobha had never seen cascading over crumbling walls. They passed down avenues lined with trees: the tall erect ashoka tree with its long drooping glossy leaves, the spreading branches of the majestic flamboyant, the feathery-leafed tamarisk with its vivid mass of scarlet blooms; the small graceful upright laburnum with its rough dark brown bark and streaming clusters of bright yellow blossoms hanging from its branches in a golden shower; and the massive banyan trees, whose dark green foliage was covered in dust, whose lower branches touched the ground to take root, and whose upper branches joined overhead to form a shady arcade.

Beyond the cantonment the hustle and bustle of life on the streets began again. Now they were in the heart of the city. Small open-fronted wooden huts sold sandals, books, savouries, and sweets. Colourful saris and lungis hung in a tempting array outside shops, blowing in the polluted breeze. There were bakeries and restaurants, an imposing hotel, a towering block of flats, and dingy offices inside which could be glimpsed spectacled men hunched over enormous wooden desks stacked high with papers, fans whirring beside them. The bus passed a school where boys crouched on the ground playing marbles and girls ran around the compound in pink tunics with bows in their hair. Shobha wondered if her Amrita would attend a school like that one day.

There were stalls where sugar cane was put through a press and served in cracked glasses with ice. There were fruit barrows piled high with bananas and mangoes, chikku fruit and papaya. Street vendors sat on the pavement selling hair slides and combs, rubber bands and mothballs, safety pins, earrings, and ribbons. Displays of luminous painted plaster parrots, plaster tigers, plaster gods and goddesses, all for sale, filled the gaps between one vegetable vendor and the next. Printed handkerchiefs hung against the walls with pictures of blue palm trees, orange birds, lapis lazuli film stars, scarlet animals, and golden bejewelled ladies. There were fortune tellers and snake charmers, shoe-shine boys, and bicycle repair boys. There were *pan* stands and *bidi* stands. Gaudy pictures on glossy paper, some faded in the sun, were displayed, offering likenesses of Lakshmi and Krishna, Shiva, Ganpatti, the Buddha, Mahavira and Muhammad, Mahatma Gandhiji wearing a white dhoti and holding a stick, Prime Minister Nehru wearing a small white cap, Indira Gandhi with her sari pulled over her head, Babasaheb Ambedkar with dark-rimmed spectacles holding a book, Shivaji in a turban raising a sharp curved sword, Sai Baba in the orange attire of an ascetic seated with one leg crossed over his knee. Everywhere people were bawling their wares.

Rickshaws honked and bicycles frantically rang their bells as the bus roared round a corner and into the bus station. The conductor got up and continuously rang the bell by its cord in a double staccato rhythm while the bus backed its way into its allotted niche and jerked to a halt. The back door flung open, people pushed, people pulled, people shoved, a child vomited. Baggage was hoisted overhead or dragged between legs, voices were raised, and greetings were exchanged, as one by one they tumbled out of the bus. Vilas got down first and collected the trunk which was up on the roof, then waited for his wife. Shobha flipped the end of her sari over her head and clasped it in her teeth. In one arm she carried Amrita, in the other a bundle of cloths and pots.

Bemused and dazed they squeezed on to the end of a wooden bench and looked around. Hundreds of people squatted on the ground or sat on benches, or rested on bundles and packages. The white man and woman, barefoot, hand in hand, carrying big orange packs on their backs, made their way to the tea stand. An indistinct shouting crackled over the loudspeaker and a large group of people got up, jostling each other as their bus arrived to take them away. Amrita cried. Different smells filled the air: bidis, petrol, urine, masala, and perfume. A mangy, half-bald dog with festering sores on its body and legs sniffed at their feet then sloped away. A beggar limped up to Vilas. He had one arm and one leg; stopping and leaning on his crutch, he touched his head and held out a hand, then muttered some words and passed on.

The cloth in which Amrita was wrapped was sodden, so Shobha changed it for a dry one before handing the baby to her father. Then she went over to the public latrine, which was indicated by a picture on the wall of a woman's profile painted in black with shapely curved eyebrows, long modest eyes, and a curl of hair in front of her ear; her lips had been painted scarlet and a matching splash of *kumkum* dabbed on her forehead;

a black plait hung over her shoulder. An arrow pointed the way in. The place stank: there were two holes on the ground over which to squat while water hissed out from a break in the pipe and splashed to the floor. Dried human excrement lay like offerings on the cracked concrete. Shobha smothered her nose in her sari.

As she came out a long browned mirror faced her; removing the cloth from her nose she looked up and was surprised. A tall, shapely, elegant woman looked back at her, although her skin was darker than she had imagined. She moved a little closer. Her upturned nose had flared nostrils, accentuated by a small gold ring which hung from the left one, her thick lips sloped gently at the corners, and as she opened her mouth a little her teeth shone white. Her *kumkum* had smudged so she wiped it away with the back of her hand and replaced it with a dab of vermilion powder kept in a tiny box caught in the waist of her sari.

Her skin was clear, though little wrinkles ran out from the corners of her large brown eyes. Stepping back two paces she continued to look at herself. Her hair was straggly, parted at the centre with strands bleached brown in the sun. Shobha covered it quickly with the end of her turquoise sari. She smiled at herself, held her head high, twisted her body to left and to right and, realizing she looked like her mother, felt pleasure, followed by pangs of nostalgia. Two women came in. Smartly dressed, with their shiny smooth hair gathered into buns, they wore large gold earrings and gold bangles, and had gold chains around their necks. Shobha meekly lowered her eyes, covered her head, slipped round the doorway and walked back to her husband and child. Rahul had arrived and now sat on the bench next to Vilas deep in conversation. Demurely Shobha went up to them and was introduced to Rahul who, holding his hands together and slightly nodding his head in recognition, said 'Namaskar'.

'Namaskar,' Shobha replied shyly, quickly looking to her child who whimpered and squirmed in Vilas's grasp. He passed Amrita back to Shobha. Ignoring mother and child they carried on their conversation while Shobha sat cross-legged on the ground at their feet, pulled the end of her sari around her shoulder to hang down loosely over her breast, discreetly lifted up her tight-fitting blouse and suckled her child. Amrita had fallen asleep by the time Rahul stood up, tapped Shobha on the shoulder and said 'Come, let's go.'

Shobha adjusted her sari and stood up, by which time Rahul was already striding ahead, snaking his way through the pressing crowd. Vilas half-ran to keep up with him, carrying the small metal trunk on one shoulder. He turned round to Shobha who lagged behind with a bundle on her head and Amrita in her arms. 'Keep up with us otherwise you'll get lost and we'll never find you again in this crowd,' he snapped. Amrita felt heavy in Shobha's arms, but she quickened her pace through a vegetable market where the vendors clamoured, bargaining, arguing, laughing, shouting, and into the station precinct with its high vaulted ceilings and mosaic floor. She skirted laden families, coolies in red, sweeper women in blue, and people speaking different tongues, exotically dressed, huddled in groups on the station platform.

They rushed up some steps and over a railway bridge towards their platform. Steam from the engine was puffing up into their faces through the wrought iron steps, hissing and belching; then they heard the whistle blow. 'Quick, quick, hurry, hurry!' cried Rahul from the platform back to Shobha, who was only just beginning to descend the steps. The men leapt into an open carriage of the waiting train. Vilas put down the trunk, ran back to lift the bundle off Shobha's head and throw it through the open door, and caught her by the arm, jumping into the train as it jerked to a start.

Shobha squatted by the open door while the men stood and swayed inside the carriage, holding on to leather straps that hung from the ceiling above their heads. The train rocked as it gathered speed. From the doorway Shobha could see men working on the tracks, dressed in lungis hoisted to the thighs and white vests, and swinging pickaxes. Some had small towels wrapped around their heads like turbans. Women went to and fro carrying rubble in large metal pans on their heads from one site to another, a continuous chain of fetching and carrying.

Tents made from sackcloth had been erected alongside the tracks where tribal folk lived and worked. Shobha stared at the tribal women who were tall, strong, upright, and muscular. Instead of saris they wore yards of bright-coloured patterned cloth gathered into skirts which swung from left to right as they walked, and rather than the standard gold jewellery of Maharashtran women they wore heavy silver bangles, anklets, nose rings, and weighty silver hair-clips and ear-clips. Shobha gaped at them incredulously.

The train stopped at several stations.

'The next stop is ours,' said Rahul. 'Get up and push yourself to the doorway, and keep tight hold of your bags.' As the train jerked to a halt they were pushed out of the door. They had arrived on a narrow platform where groups of men sat around playing cards in the shade of a dilapidated station building.

'Jai Bhim!' said one of the card players, an elderly white-haired man, as Rahul passed by. 'Are these your new neighbours?' he continued, touching his forehead. 'Yes,' replied Rahul. The old man nodded, smiled, then carried on with his game.

They crossed the railway tracks, ducked through a hole in the wall and emerged in a shanty town. Children milled around their feet, women cleaned their pots in the mud and shouted at each other or hummed to the melodies wafting from their radios while a large fat black sow and her seven piglets lay snorting and squealing in the acrid-smelling, overflowing gutter.

Strips of corrugated iron merged into beaten-out tin cans to form dwellings barely high enough to stand up in. For several minutes they wound their way through tiny alleys where if they had stretched out their arms they could have reached the houses on both sides, between mud huts with corrugated roofs, corrugated huts with tiled roofs, brick huts with asbestos roofs, and wooden huts with scrap metal roofs, the roofs held down with stones and old tyres, each hut propping up its neighbours. Rahul's house stood at the end of a line of other huts; beyond lay a small open space which had become a rubbish tip, and running at a right angle from that had been erected another row of huts running to the left and the right.

'This,' Rahul proudly announced, 'is my house, and that plot,' he pointed to the open space splattered with litter and excrement, 'is where you can build yours. It's dirty now, but we can easily clean it up. My plot looked the same before I started building.'

Shobha felt a lump in her throat and tears welling up in her eyes, but she kept her emotions to herself. During the following week Shobha, Vilas, and Amrita lived with Rahul, his wife Nirmala, and their two young sons while they built their own house next door. First they erected a wooden frame, eight feet square and seven feet high, on to which were affixed pieces of scrap metal. The roof they made from corrugated iron bought with money which Rahul lent them. Shobha covered the floor with cow-dung, just as she had done on so many occasions in the village.

Vilas built shelves on which they stacked their few pots and pans. Within a week they had moved into their new home, the finishing touch being a picture of Dr Babasaheb Ambedkar, bought and framed in the bazaar, which they hung over the door and garlanded with marigolds. The day they moved in Shobha prepared special sweets and invited Rahul and his family in to bring good fortune.

For the first five months in the city Vilas worked as a labourer on building sites for eight rupees (60p) a day. He'd come to the city on the assumption that he would get a job in the chemical factory – factory jobs being highly prized – but by the time he arrived the factory was cutting down on unskilled staff and many men had been made redundant. This was a big blow to Vilas but he didn't despair. He applied to other factories, and by the time the rains came he had secured work in a cotton textile mill. This meant a regular wage, a pension scheme, medical insurance, and even possibilities of promotion.

Now his wife and family would be safe; now he would have money to send back to his village. Shobha was pregnant again, but with a proper job he'd be able to educate his son – this time it would definitely be a son – and buy his wife a new sari and bangles. Maybe later they'd be able to move out of the slum and into a housing colony; one day they might even be able to buy their own apartment. Within a year Vilas would be able to buy a bicycle, later a scooter … the possibilities stretched out temptingly before him.

By 6 a.m. Vilas had got up and washed in the water that Shobha had collected an hour earlier from the communal taps, heated on the shegadi stove and put ready in a bucket. After washing he sat cross-legged in the open doorway and, perching a small mirror on an upturned pot, methodically shaved off the stubble from his pointed chin. He combed his moustache and oiled his hair. Then he sprinkled baby powder into the palm of his hands and smoothed it on his face to try and conceal the darkness of his skin. By 8 a.m. he was ready to leave the house and walk to the main road where the company bus would take him to the factory.

In the evenings, although he was often tired, Vilas returned home happy and cheerful. Before eating his supper he and Rahul would sit on a metal bed frame balanced over a gutter which carried thick black sludge-like waste outside in the lane while their wives prepared the evening meal. Because he worked hard at his job the foreman was pleased and soon put his name forward for promotion. Before long he had not only repaid Rahul the money for their roof but had also saved fifty rupees which he sent to his family in the village.

Once a month on a Thursday night he and Shobha would go to see a Hindi movie at the local Amitabh Talkies. In the back row Vilas would drape his arm around Shobha's shoulder so that his hand fell down limp on to her breast, but when the interval came and the lights went on he'd discreetly remove it. Though she could not follow much of the dialogue Shobha already knew many of the songs from hearing them on radios down the lane, so she'd hum along to the tune; and as the film stars ran and sang, she too imagined herself running through Himalayan pine forests, swinging around trees, rolling in the snow – something she had never seen in reality – standing in a sequined sari beneath a waterfall, being chased and provocatively teased by Vilas till they'd fall on the ground and roll over and over together down a hillside.

At first she hated their slum locality and longed for the vast open spaces, the fields of marigolds, the crops and cattle, and most of all her sister Usha. But as time passed she made new friends and wore better clothes and sandals on her feet, and whenever she wanted she could gaze at the colourful materials in the bazaar and admire the shining pots and pans which stood in piles for sale. They had a wide choice of vegetables, and on special occasions they even ate fruit. There was the monthly outing to the cinema, and she dreamed of her yet unborn son going to school, studying hard so as to gain a place in college, and of the beautiful wife that she and Vilas would choose for him, and then all of them living together in a pristine apartment, with white walls, a bed, and running water from their own tap.

It was the Wednesday just before the festival of Diwali. Thursday was a factory holiday. Shobha had been busy preparing sweets and tying them in cloth bundles strung from an overhead beam to keep out the ants and rats. All her neighbours were doing likewise. That evening Vilas arrived home earlier than usual. Shobha was chatting and gossiping with the neighbours. They giggled at the mad woman who lived down the lane, they complained at how Sundabai always smelt, didn't change her sari every day like all the other women, however poor, and only did her washing every second day. They whispered in indignation at how Mr Kamble always flirted with the ladies, and they scorned the way proud Pushpa held herself aloof from her own community and was always trying to mix with people from higher castes. When Tarabai got up and left the group of women Shobha told the others how Tarabai's husband had been seen, in broad daylight, walking down the street with another woman – everyone knew, even Tarabai knew – but Tarabai never spoke about it. As her brother-in-law had taken a second wife, infidelity obviously ran in the family, the gossiping group concluded. Sitting outside Nirmala's house some of the women worked while others just passed the time of day. Shobha helped another woman sift stones from her uncooked rice while Amrita crawled in the dust, naked save a patchwork bonnet tied in a bow under her chin.

The shadows were still short when Vilas walked slowly down the alley towards them. Amrita, seeing him first, crawled off to meet him, but he walked right past her. Surprised to see him home so early, Shobha stopped her gossip, passed the rice back to her friend, and followed her husband into the house. The other women fell silent too, and pretending not to notice carried on with their work.

Shobha thought he must be ill. He sat on the floor resting his back against a wall with his gangly legs outstretched across the room and his chin buried in his chest. Shobha made him a cup of tea but she didn't ask questions. In silence he drank the hot sweet tea and in silence removed his trousers and wrapped a lungi around himself. He spread a cloth out on the floor, lay down on his back and placed his forearm over his eyes. A neighbour peered through the narrow doorway to enquire what was the matter, if there was anything they needed. Shobha shrugged her shoulders, but Vilas remained silent and motionless so the neighbour left. Shobha bit her lip and frowned at him, too frightened to ask questions or even to speak.

Not moving, Vilas lay there for more than an hour without saying a word, just grunting and sighing occasionally. Shobha lit the shegadi stove. The fumes made him cough and he turned over on one side and buried his head under his arm. She cooked the rice and dal, and plucked the green leaves of methi from their stalks. When the sun had gone down and the evening meal was ready she fed Amrita and patted her to sleep on her lap. Then she forced herself to speak.

'Eat your food, you must be hungry!'

He did not stir.

'Eat your food,' she repeated.

He turned over on to his other side and groaned.

'Eat yours, I won't be eating tonight,' he replied sulkily.

'Are you ill?' she asked in genuine sympathy.

'No!' he grimaced.

'Then what's the matter?' she snapped back.

'Nothing, you stupid woman. Just eat your food and don't ask questions.'

'I've never eaten before you so why should I change today?' she replied, wiping beads of perspiration from her brow. 'Just tell me what's the matter and I'm sure we can get some medicine.'

Vilas sat bolt upright and turned to face her. She felt frightened at the way his eyes glared, his nostrils twitched and his bottom lip quivered.

'I've lost my job, that's what is the matter. Now do as I say, eat your supper and stop pestering me.'

With jerking movements he stood up, pulled on his trousers, grabbed his shirt, and went storming out of the hut, buttoning his shirt as he went.

Two hours passed before Vilas returned home again. As he ducked through the open door he was talking and muttering but his words were slurred and inaudible, and he sprawled across the floor. His breath stank sourly, making Shobha shudder at the bitter memory of her father. She clutched her sari to her neck and cowered. Within a few moments he heaved, wrenched himself back out through the open doorway, and vomited into the gutter. He stumbled inside, lay down, and within seconds was snoring loudly. Picking up Amrita, Shobha took her outside into the alley and there they lay down together in front of the door.

Several days later Vilas admitted that he had been caught stealing. He worked in the packing rooms, every day stacking newly-woven saris on shelves piled high up to the ceiling. The checker had left the room just for a few minutes. It was so easy to take down one of the bundles of cloth, to slip it into his tiffin bag where nobody would see. But after just a few moments the checker had returned to collect a forgotten paper, caught Vilas cramming his bag, and despite the offer of a bribe to keep quiet had alerted the foreman.

He was told he'd get beaten up if he ever entered the doors of the factory again. Vilas had intended to keep the sari a secret and give it to Shobha after the birth of their son; he knew the colours would suit her and he'd never be able to afford such a costly one. He had once overheard Shobha complaining to Nirmala that she hadn't had a new sari for over a year and he wanted to please her, to make her happy. Now he made out it was her fault, but Shobha refused to take the blame. It was an unhappy Diwali.

Every day now Vilas hung around the house; apathy set in. They told their friends and neighbours he'd been made redundant. Only Shobha felt the shame; she alone swallowed the humiliation. Vilas hardly spoke to her now and he ignored Amrita. It was around this time that Shobha developed what started as a niggling cough but soon developed so that she was wheezing, hacking, and coughing up thick yellow mucus streaked with blood. She became weak and lost appetite and weight. A magic healer who came to her door one day gave her medicine, chanted mantras, and tied a special stone round her neck, but the coughing continued.

Her illness coincided with her time for delivery, which was fast approaching. Having prepared herself to return to her mother's house, not having been back there since Amrita's birth, she hoped that Vilas would come too. But the money they had saved had run out, and they could not afford the fares, so she had the baby at home; another daughter was born. Vilas sulked and complained of the expense; girls only brought trouble. How would they ever find dowry to give the new baby's husband? Why hadn't Shobha given him a son? Now they only ate rice and potatoes cooked with chillies.

After Vilas had loitered around the house for several weeks he eventually got another labouring job on the roads, but he consumed much of his meagre earnings in illicit liquor before returning home and forcing himself upon her. Shobha didn't cry any more, nor did she smile or laugh. Her youthful bloom faded to a sickly pallor, large dark rings hung under her downcast eyes, her laugh wrinkles became heavy furrows, while her hair lost its sheen and fell out in handfuls as she combed it. She became thin and wasted and her baby was always hungry, chewing on a hardened nipple.

She decided to take work herself and earned two rupees a day doing other people's washing in the river. She walked around the alleys carrying a large pan on her head, the baby tied in a sling around her hips and Amrita running along behind, shouting out her services. The women piled her pan full of their dirty washing; then she walked through the alleys and down to the river where she beat the clothes on the bottom step of the burning-ghats. If a cremation was taking place she would move further downstream and beat the clothes on rocks before returning them to their owners to be dried. Being constantly tired she did not enjoy the work, but she desperately needed the money for food.

The weeks passed, and the months. Shobha lived for her children. She became pregnant again; she told Nirmala, but not Vilas. Mixing with the other women was hard; they asked intimate questions which she tried to avoid answering. She barely spoke with Vilas. It wasn't till he noticed her bulging belly that he guessed she was pregnant. He slapped her and beat her. She winced and flinched but she carried on with her daily chores.

It is just before dawn. Shobha slips stealthily out from under her patchwork coverlet made of old cloth. She always enjoys the first hour or two alone. She reties the waist tape of her petticoat, which she had loosened before she went to sleep, readjusts the front pleats of her cotton sari, and with a slight bend of the knees places her heels on the bottom edge to iron out the wrinkles. She picks up three large brass water pots, placing one on each hip, their lips caught in the crook of her arms, while she balances the third on her head. She walks feebly through the alleys to an open piece of land where she joins a queue of about twenty other women waiting to fill their pots from the trickle of water that dribbles out of three water pipes. Shobha puts her pots on the ground beside her and waits. She doesn't talk to the other women; she watches the early morning sun rise up above the corrugated iron roofs, over the sackcloth and plastic sheeting, the red tiles, and the factory chimneys, and she gazes at the smoke that belches and puffs up into the cloudless pink sky, while her mind drifts back to her childhood.

She recalls her earliest memory: gazing up at the clouds of smoke that rose out of the dung fire and were drawn to the ceiling, as though the smoke was being sucked up the shaft of sunlight from a gap between the wall and the thatch. Her mother, rocking her back and forth, was grinding steeped lentils on a rough stone. She must only have been three years old at the time, but as she rocked between her mother's rib and thigh she was safe and utterly content. As she grew older she was sent out to play with Usha, but given the opportunity she would steal back into the house to watch the patterns of smoke. Even now she could imagine the special smell of spices her mother used and the particular odour of her body.

Now Shobha looks up at the black smoke from the factory chimneys, and smells the rotting waste and open gutters. The queue hardly seems to be moving. She squats down on her haunches, rests her forehead on her knees and starts coughing. Her chest hurts, her ribs ache; weak and faint, she gasps for breath. Two women leave the taps with their full pots balanced on their heads. Shobha shuffles a couple of paces forward. The woman in front of her holds the end of her purple sari between her teeth, stoops down, picks up a stone and throws it at a balding dog who has come sniffing around the pots. The dog yelps and limps away. A strip of sunlight falls on Shobha and begins to warm her body; she rests her head in her hands and feels their roughness against the softness of her cheeks.

Her whole body aches: she yearns to lie down on the ground and fall into a long deep sleep. Two women are now arguing, almost breaking into a fight. Some try to calm them while others join in, taking opposing sides. Shobha tries to ignore them all. Two more women have now filled their pots and walk away together. Though probably the same age as herself, she thinks they look younger, happier, more contented. One has a small child running along by her side, reminding Shobha of Meena and her daughter. Shobha stands up and moves a pace forward, then looks down at her sari. It is soiled. For weeks now she has been feeling so weak and lethargic, so ill, that she rarely has the strength to do her daily washing. When she recalls how proud she used to be of the way she looked and dressed, she feels sad. 'Poor Meena lost everything,' she thinks.

The queue in front is getting shorter though many others have joined behind. Shobha moves forward again and squats on her haunches in an ever-increasing patch of sunlight, folds her arms around her knees and very gently rocks back and forth as she watches a small child playing in the dust. She coughs. Picking up a twig she starts drawing pictures in the dust. The heat of the sun begins to penetrate her pores and she starts to relax. She breaks the twig in two and throws the pieces into the air with a strange little giggle.

'Eh, Shobhatai! What are you dreaming about?' shouts the girl behind her. 'There's no time for fantasies in our hard life. Move your pots forward or someone will jump the queue.'

Shobha shuffles forward without speaking, looks down at her feet, twists the silver rings on her toes, coughs, and spits. Children are crying, voices raised, pots and pans clanking. The fumes from recently lit shegadi stoves catch her throat and make her cough more. Dogs, mangy and bald, fight and bark. Lorries rumble along the distant highway and trains rattle down the line. Nowhere is there peace and quiet; even down by the dirty polluted river the city noises float across. There is nowhere to be alone just with a friend, nowhere to spend time idly plaiting reeds as she and Usha had done. As a state transport bus roars past she puts her hands over her ears, and remembers the day she and Vilas left the village, filled with such hopes and prospects.

Arriving at the taps at last, she places her pots under the trickle of water and watches them slowly fill up. As she does so she is overcome with sadness: regret for what she has left behind, and fear of what might lie ahead. Knowing that her cough is likely to be a symptom of tuberculosis, she has not told anyone, not even Nirmala, for she knows that a lot of stigma is attached to TB, but she often wonders if her neighbours have already guessed. Vilas has never shown even the slightest concern. Utterly weary, she experiences her youthful life wasting away. Her lips quiver, a heavy pressure pushes behind her eyes, she can hold back her sadness no longer and large, warm, salty tears trickle down her cheeks.

At last the water pots are filled, and balancing them on her head she slowly straightens her knees and mechanically walks back to the hut. Vilas has been out the night before and has not yet returned but Shobha is neither worried nor surprised, for it is not the first time. She ducks through the open door, places the pots around the washing space and starts to cough, clutching her ribs as she does so. Holding the edge of her sari to her mouth she sees streaks of blood in her phlegm. As she coughs she feels as though her chest will rip apart.

She stumbles out into the alley, still coughing, and starts to run. The huts swirl around her, and ugly distorted faces stare at her from the open doorways and shout out to her, but she does not stop. She passes the water taps, crosses some open land, and stops at Mariai's shrine strewn with dead flowers. There, holding on to the concrete, she catches her breath. Seeing the river beyond the public latrine, she clambers through a barbed wire fence, crosses a field littered with human excrement and reaches the river. Her breathing is rapid, her head spins, she coughs and spits, the blood-filled phlegm glistening on the dusty earth. There is a sudden silence. She can no longer hear the distant clanking and banging from the slum, no longer hear the dogs or the street vendors, the playful children and angry mothers. She can hear no trains or buses, bells or hooters. All is utterly silent.

Sitting on a rock near the burning-ghats she gazes into the water, into a deep pool cleared of water hyacinth where the women wash their clothes. Puffy silver-edged clouds are reflected in the water, their edges blurred by tiny ripples. Like the melting wax of a candle the clouds melt into the water, and the concrete and factories on the further shore fall into the depths of the river bed. As a sunlit ripple runs its natural course, it merges concrete blocks, corrugated metal, wooden planks, and plastic sheeting into insubstantial fluidity.

Pulling her sari around her shoulders and clutching it to her breast, Shobha lies down on the rock. Her gaze lifts to the sun now surrounded by clouds; they swirl and mass but the sun is not obscured. The clouds darken until large drops of rain begin to fall on her face, but she remains serene, even refreshed. She is no longer coughing. Her body is limp; she cannot move her head. She tries to touch her face with her hand but her hand will not move. She has no fear. The wind grows stronger and she watches it blowing through the folds of her sari. Looking down on her body she sees her face; her eyes look up to the clouds, yet it is her body she sees. People are coming towards her, gathering around her. She sees their mouths opening and closing but she hears nothing. The heavens open and the rain falls; it pours and pours. She laughs and laughs shouting, 'I can fly, I can fly,' but nobody hears. Vilas is there among the crowd. He lifts her up while Nirmala and Rahul stand to one side holding her children.

A blank darkness descends.

Opening her eyes, Shobha sees the wick of the oil lamp and hears the soothing bubbling of water on the clinkers. Squatting over the stove, Agi is rolling out chapattis. Vilas sits against the wall reading a book, and the children lie near her, asleep. She wipes her hand over her face and tries to sit up, but her body is aching and weak. She coughs. On seeing her stirring he puts down his book, comes over to her, and sits beside her, saying nothing. She wonders how long she has been asleep: hours, days, weeks? She can remember nothing. Agi comes over and saying 'Drink this' hands Shobha a cup of warm, sweetened milk.

Shobha slowly sips the milk but she still does not speak. She feels a tiny flutter inside her and puts her hand on her barely pregnant belly.

'Usha had a son last week, you know,' says Agi. 'I would have stayed to look after her, but Vilas's telegram made me drop everything and come here first. You haven't been looking after yourself properly, have you, child?'

Shobha can feel the milk soothing her empty stomach.

'Take some more,' says Agi, 'and eat this chapatti with it; you haven't eaten for days.'

Shobha dips a chapatti into the milk and lets it melt in her mouth.

'We want this son of yours to be healthy,' continues Agi.

For the first time Shobha speaks. 'How do you know it will be a son?

Agi looks Shobha in the eyes: 'I know these things, Shobhatai, you know I do.' Shobha smiles weakly; Agi is always right. She watches her grandmother return to the stove and listens to her singing.

Oh, the married life, the married life,
Break off the cucumber from the vine;
One end may be bitter,
All the rest tastes sweet.

communication

A great rain cloud rises above the world
Covering all things everywhere,
A gracious cloud full of moisture;
Lightning-flames flash and dazzle,
Voice of thunder vibrates afar,
Bringing joy and ease to all.
From the one water which issues from that cloud,
Plants, trees, thickets, forests,
According to need receive moisture.
Each, according to size, grows and develops
Roots, stalks, branches, leaves,
Blossoms and fruits in their brilliant colours.
The great holy world-honoured one
Proclaims abroad this word:
I appear in the world
Like unto this great cloud,
To pour enrichment on all parched living beings,
On honoured and humble, high and low,
Law-keepers and law-breakers,
Those of perfect character
And those of imperfect,
Orthodox and heterodox,
Quick-witted and dull-witted,
Equally I rain the rain of the Dharma,
Unwearyingly.

PARABLE OF THE RAIN CLOUD, *from the White Lotus Sutra*

The Madhouse at Phaltan

I came back to India from a visit to the UK in October 1985 to find that visa restrictions had been enforced. I would be allowed to spend six months a year in India, but not to do medical aid work. So for the next four years I was to spend six months of each year in the West, doing mainly fund-raising work, and six months in India, teaching Buddhism.

Left without the support of Virabhadra and Vajraketu I felt a bit shaky, though Lokamitra was still around, the restrictions not applying to him because he had an Indian wife. Before my return I was anxious about the flight, and my plane was delayed for four hours at Heathrow due to a bomb scare. Police and sniffer dogs searched all the luggage and the inside of the plane which some people had already boarded.

There was also growing unrest in many parts of India. Once I was over the jet lag, I plunged straight into my new work. I was about to depart on a four-day tour of villages and small towns to give talks on basic Buddhism to some of the ex-Untouchable Buddhist community of Maharashtra, when I read in the local newspaper that violent clashes had broken out between a militant Hindu group and some Buddhists, in the very town where I was to give my first lecture. A curfew had been imposed, and though there was a strong possibility that it would be lifted by the time I got there it seemed wiser not to risk provoking bad feelings, and to steer clear of the town. I continued with the rest of the tour, however, as venues had been prepared and people were expecting me. I travelled with Malati, a woman in her twenties who was to act as interpreter, and various other people, mostly men, accompanied us for different parts of the tour.

When I first met Malati she seemed shy, and was always accompanied by members of her family, especially her father, so I didn't immediately have an opportunity to get to know her. It took me a while, therefore, to realize that, having been to an English-medium school (where all the teaching is in English), she spoke some of the best English I'd heard within the Buddhist community. One cannot assume that an Indian person who has passed both school and college exams in English and attained good marks necessarily speaks the language very fluently, or even grammatically. Those whose parents don't speak English and have not had the advantage of any formal education, of whom there are millions, are at a great disadvantage, and often fall behind during their first years at school because they get no help with their studies at home. On the other hand, some children who are English-medium educated, and speak the language well, do not really master their mother-tongue, Marathi, which makes it difficult for them to communicate with their parents. The worst case of all is that of a child who ends up learning neither language thoroughly, and is consequently ill-equipped to communicate in any language.

As well as speaking excellent English, Malati could express herself equally freely in Marathi, and had no problems changing quickly from one language to the other. When I first knew her she was twenty-three, and held a Bachelor of Commerce degree, a qualification which is highly regarded by members of the ex-Untouchable Buddhist community into which she was born, all the more so when it is attained by a woman. She has four older brothers who have all married and done well. Malati, though, is by far the most sociable, and perhaps even the most confident, of them all.

Malati's family lives in a flat in the centre of Poona. When I first visited it, with its three rooms and large hall, I thought it was quite spacious. As I gradually realized the full size of the extended family, however, I saw it differently. Between eighteen and twenty people lived there, from Malati's ageing grandfather down to her baby nephews and nieces, and a constant flow of guests also passed through. When I first got to know Malati, she was giving tuition classes in her home to small schoolchildren, helping them to cram for their end-of-term exams. These exams were very important, even for infants. If they failed, they would not move up a class, and would often be made to feel even more of a failure by ambitious parents with high, sometimes unrealistic, expectations. If a child fails more than once it seems an easy option to drop out of school altogether, and this frequently happens with slum children, who rarely have access to extra tuition, even though they probably need it most. Around examination time there is a frighteningly high suicide rate among pupils at matriculation and college levels.

Though Malati had done well, and no doubt could have found a good job or career, her rather protective father thought it more appropriate that she stay at home – though there were plenty of aunts and sisters-in-law, as well as her mother, to do the cooking and other household chores. Her BCom would qualify her to look for a husband at least similarly qualified, and her 'home-loving nature' would no doubt impress future parents-in-law more than the image of a modern working girl who might be no good in the home.

None the less, her father seemed happy for her to spend time with me, as companion and interpreter. Whether this was out of generosity or because he thought that being seen with a foreign woman would add to her assets and finally clinch a marriage deal, I never dared to ask. Malati herself was always keen to help, and happy to be away from the steady trickle of eligible suitors that her father brought from all over Maharashtra to see her. This seemed to be the main occupation of his retirement. The subject of marriage was becoming a bit of a headache for her as she was by now nearing thirty and in Indian terms almost on the shelf. Although she had turned down the suitors her father had found so far because she really couldn't imagine living with them or their families, there would soon come a time when her father would put his foot down, and in effect force her to marry. Though independent-minded, and well aware of the freedom of people in other cultures, Malati would not disgrace the family by fighting an arranged marriage beyond a certain point.

Malati travelled with me on and off for three years, to villages and cities all over Maharashtra, interpreting my talks on basic Buddhism and helping to lead and interpret for me on women's retreats. She was a skilful bridge-builder when it came to putting people at their ease with the tall English Dharma teacher and her strange ways and customs, particularly the people in whose houses we stayed. She had an infectious laugh and an ability to bring a smile to the most unhappy face. It always astounded me to see how she would fit into a stranger's home as though they were lifelong friends, helping roll out chapattis, playing with the children, and fetching water; and she was never shy or coy in front of men, under no circumstances allowing herself to be seen as inferior to them, but always responding in the most natural and happy manner.

Lack of self-confidence is the greatest hurdle ex-Untouchables face. Unfortunately, as soon as they achieve a sense of self-esteem, perhaps through getting an education, their first instinct is sometimes to distance themselves from those still on the wrong side of the hurdle. Malati, however, still maintained a heartfelt though unsentimental empathy with those dwelling both physically and psychologically in the most dire conditions, and thus became a friend to all who crossed her path. I noticed that as she meditated and studied the Dharma more, her natural desire to help people grew stronger and she became more able to find the most appropriate means of doing so. Her ability to express herself with confidence had the effect of giving confidence to others.

It was mid-afternoon when Malati, Vaijanath, who was one of our escorts, and I, arrived in Phaltan, the same small town that I had been to the previous year to do my Marathi course with Maxine. I thought rather wistfully of her bungalow as, after a tedious three-hour bus journey, we were taken to a rather seedy hotel, perhaps the only one, in the centre of town.

In England I think I would find it nerve-racking to give a public lecture to 500 people, perched, arms folded, on their upright seats, coolly waiting for me to entertain and inform them. In India, though at first I was certainly very wobbly at the knees, I never found it quite so daunting. It could even be fun, mainly because it all took place in a relatively relaxed atmosphere. Usually talks were given in the open air, on large pieces of wasteland between slum huts or in gaps between tenement blocks in the cities, and on any piece of open land in the villages. Large numbers of local Buddhists would attend. It was possible simply to arrive somewhere, and with the co-operation of local Buddhist leaders muster an audience on the spot by going from door to door telling people about the event, but the more successful events were those to which someone had given some thought beforehand, arranging for handbills to be given out around the Buddhist neighbourhood, fly-posters to be stuck on walls and lamp-posts, and a chalked board advertising the event to be placed on the land where the event was to take place.

On the morning before an evening talk the land would be cleared of debris and swept, and a stage would be erected with backdrops and roof flaps made from brightly coloured cloth and decorated with Buddhist flags. However far away the source of electricity, a PA system would be rigged up, and fairy lights dangled across the awnings and backdrop, in many cases with extravagant loops over the huts and tenements in the surrounding area as well. Cotton rugs would be laid on the stage, with mattresses and bolsters as seats for the speakers. Centre stage would be a shrine made out of tables, boxes, or chairs, usually covered in orange and blue cloths. On the shrine would be a Buddha image and a picture of Dr Ambedkar, surrounded by flowers, candles, and incense.

On this tour I was to be the principal speaker on the topic of basic Buddhist practices and principles. Various groups of people came and visited us in our hotel room, bringing us garlands and bowing at my feet. I had by this time become reasonably accustomed to this sort of formality, though I still felt rather uncomfortable about it, especially when frail elderly people bowed before me with a reverence and sincerity which would have befitted some kind of goddess. As one who practised and taught Buddhism, I was treated not as a dignitary, but as a guide, an inspirer, someone to look up to. It seemed that it was not necessary for me to earn their reverence in any way, but I was careful not to abuse such heartfelt respect.

At around 9 p.m. Malati and I were escorted to the venue, where three to four hundred people had gathered. As we arrived, people started arguing about who was supposed to make the introductory speeches, and who was supposed, or allowed, to garland whom. There was a strong whiff of politics in the air. Sadly, many followers of Dr Ambedkar, despite considering themselves Buddhist, and despite Ambedkar's own call for harmony, have split into various factions, and they were unwilling on an occasion like this to give way to one another in matters of precedence and prestige. Malati and I sat patiently on the stage feeling increasingly uncomfortable as the discussions went on around us, while the audience looked on. It took some fifteen minutes before decisions were reached and the event could start.

At a later date I had a similar experience in a large village in central Maharashtra where I had been asked to inaugurate a new shrine. Hundreds of people had turned up for the occasion and it was a very beautiful shrine. I hadn't yet spoken, but already people whose names were read out were advancing one by one to collect a garland from a great pile of flowers beside one of the organizers. Mounting the platform, they each placed a garland around my neck. I then removed each garland and placed it on a table to one side, before the next one was hung around me. The whole process took nearly ten minutes.

I was relieved to see that there was only one garland left, until I realized that a fight had broken out between two youths. One started shouting angrily, and the other hit him. Onlookers tried to pull them apart, while the audience got restless and began to complain, some getting to their feet. My interpreter stood up and, speaking into the microphone, told people to sit down and keep calm. As if aware that the audience would appreciate a better view, the two men leapt up on the platform, still fighting.

I was quickly ushered to a seat inside the shrine as the men were dragged off the platform to continue their fight behind the shrine, where they were joined by a number of others, to a chorus of barking dogs. I later learned that the two troublemakers were leaders of different Buddhist factions and that as they were one garland short they were fighting over who should present the last one to me. I had never had men fighting over me before and I was not at all flattered.

At Phaltan the disputes did not escalate into violence but by the time the event got going it was well past 10 o'clock, and halfway through members of the audience, particularly the mothers with sleeping children on their laps, started to get up and walk away. Most of them, I discovered, worked in the fields, which meant they would have to be up before dawn; so sleep was more important than my talk. We returned to our hotel to be kept awake all night by a lot of noisy men wandering up and down the corridors, some of them decidedly drunk, and by bed-bugs and mosquitoes. I lay thinking of Maxine's netted windows and doors and wishing I'd asked to stay there. Malati and I were, I think, the only women in the hotel.

The following morning we were taken on a sightseeing tour of the town, to places I'd not seen when staying with Maxine. First we called at a very ancient Hindu temple which had once been Buddhist. There were still a couple of Buddhist sculptures over the doorway but inside it was full of lingams and images of Hindu gods, on which had been scattered offerings of ghee, sugar, sweets, and coconut milk. A pulp of flower heads and vermilion powder squelched underfoot. The air was suffocating; candles burned, dripping and smoking at the feet of the deities, but no light of day was allowed to enter the inner sanctum. I sensed a psychic darkness and was glad to leave.

Our guide then took us for a short walk out of the town to visit the local 'madhouse'. In India many psychologically disturbed or mentally ill people are not locked away as they so often are in Western countries, not hidden from society as though they don't exist. Every village, and every locality in any town or city, will have one or two such people who just become part of the community life, as in the past English neighbourhoods always had and accepted their 'village idiot'. They may get teased by children or laughed at, but at least they are acknowledged and catered for. None the less, there are those, even in India, who cannot be absorbed into the community, perhaps because of violent or other anti-social tendencies, and for them there are institutions such as Poona's massive mental hospital, which I once visited with a friend who worked there as a music therapist. Though by English standards it was archaic, and seemed more like a prison than a psychiatric hospital, it was infinitely better than what I was about to see.

Phaltan's 'madhouse' (the brutally straightforward terminology made me suspicious) was a place where the mentally disturbed were 'looked after by the gods'. I felt as though I had been whisked out of the twentieth century and plunged into the Middle Ages. As we walked through the gates I saw men stumbling around with their legs chained together: great sores opened in their ankles where the metal links ripped into their skin with every shuffle and clank they made around the courtyard of the temple. Their eyes were blank and their expressions distorted. Women, their skin transparent over their skulls, were carried in the arms of friends, relatives, or wardens, emitting strange eerie shrieks and moans. Unlike the Poona hospital, which catered for hundreds of patients, this house of the gods had only about thirty 'patients', and they all lived in nooks and crannies of the temple complex, in the shade of a stone wall, or beneath an archway, perhaps moving inside the temple itself when the rains came.

The place had the fascination of a macabre fantasy by Hieronymus Bosch. It would have been easy to imagine monsters and devils appearing from the cracks in the walls, or leaping out of the mouths of the distorted faces that looked up expressionlessly at me. My mind refused to connect what I was seeing with what I knew of as human suffering. I realized I was gaping like a child watching apes at the zoo. I was asked if I would like to see more, but I had had enough.

Returning to the temple gateway, I looked through an open door, and there, in the cool interior of a marble-floored chamber, sat the temple priest, an immaculately dressed young man with delicate features and deep piercing eyes. He was dressed in shades of salmon pink and his lungi, long shirt, and turban were starched and neatly pressed. He reclined on a high bed bolstered by satin cushions, reading a newspaper, while two visitors, on their knees in front of him, presented gifts of fresh fruit. Putting down the paper he accepted the fruit, and then he looked towards the door and saw us. He looked me in the eyes, nodded his head, and smiled sweetly. I met his gaze and nodded in reply. We left the temple complex. What real care or treatment was given to the inmates it was hard to determine, or even imagine. The idea seemed to be that being in the presence of the priest and gods was enough.

'Who Let Down the Great Golden Bucket?'

Our next port of call was Walchanagar, a punishing bus ride through barren country, relieved only by cacti and other desert shrubs. We passed only bullock carts and an occasional bicycle. It wasn't really possible to appreciate the stillness, the serenity, and the bare beauty of the landscape through the clouds of dust that rose around us as we bounced along dirt tracks, or above the roaring and grinding of the ancient engine, and the constant chatter of people when the bus paused, which it frequently did to negotiate a boulder or a ditch.

The bus was crammed with people carrying enormous loads, the men in cerise or magenta turbans, the women mostly in emerald green saris, faded and torn but still retaining a glitter of gold or silver thread at the border. Some of these women did not wear the traditional tight-fitting sari-blouse of city women, but pulled the end of their sari over their shoulder to cover an otherwise exposed breast; and many spread their toes wide to grip the floor. Their skin was worn, wrinkled, and weatherbeaten, and lay in folds over cheeks, ribs, and arms. One or two of the passengers stared at me throughout the journey; very possibly I was the first white person they had ever encountered. Every fifteen minutes or so the bus stopped to pick up a passenger or two. It was hard to imagine where they had come from, for as far as the eye could see all was barren:

no settlements, no huts, no water, no sign of life from the roadside to the shimmering horizons. Yet they had come from somewhere to catch the daily bus, and they boarded with their bundles or their woven reed baskets full of chickens. There were children, babies, pregnant women, old men in turbans, young men in white Nehru caps. Perhaps they had walked for an hour, a morning, even a day, to reach the road that would take them to Walchanagar. We of course had our luggage too, consisting largely of Dharma books, magazines, and leaflets. For this part of the journey, from Phaltan to Walchanagar, we had two escorts, Vaijanath and the elderly organizer of the tour, Mr Langade, to help us heave this burden of knowledge on and off the buses.

After a change of bus, and a long wait in the middle of nowhere, we eventually arrived at Walchanagar. We were led from the bus station down an avenue of blossoming sweet-smelling trees to the government guest house, set amid well-tended flower gardens. In a great cool hallway we found sofas and armchairs surrounding a large low table on which we were instantly served tea. Fans whirred softly overhead. In England I had never been a great tea drinker, but in India tea is another substance altogether. The tea leaves are boiled up with water, sugar, and buffalo milk to make a thick syrupy drink that gives an almost instant buzz, probably because it contains so much sugar. It is not drunk by the mugful, but sipped from dainty coffee-sized cups after a couple of glasses of water to quench the thirst. It is often poured into the saucer to cool it, and sipped from there. 'What else is the point of a saucer?' I was asked when I raised my eyebrows in surprise during my first days in India.

In our en suite bedroom, Malati and I showered, ate lunch, and slept. By 8 p.m. I had prepared my talk, and we were escorted from the guest house to the open ground where the talk was to take place. Along the tree-lined roads I saw printed fly-posters advertising the event, with pictures of the Buddha and Dr Ambedkar alongside the heading. I was never quite sure what to expect at such an event. Even if someone told me how many people would be there, I was never sure what to believe. In India numbers are often wildly inaccurate. A promised audience of 200 may turn out to be 50, while 100 may actually mean 500. People would often tell me what they thought I would like to hear rather than what they knew to be the case.

When I had been in India only a few months I was asked to give a talk to a Mahila Mandala. When I asked how many women belonged to the

Mandala, and therefore how many would be likely to attend my talk, I was told 'about fifteen': a nice, manageable number for my first talk. It was late evening when I stumbled through the alleys between shanties to a tin hut where, sure enough, about fifteen women were waiting, seated on the floor of the tiny stuffy room, looking expectant. I sat down on the bed, ready to speak. I was offered water, then tea, then, a bit later, snacks. I kept saying to my interpreter, 'Shouldn't I be starting now?' but he kept replying, 'There's time, there's time; eat your snacks first.' People kept coming and going from the hut, until eventually a man came in and said everything was ready now and I could start. As the women were getting up and pushing out of the low doorway, and as nobody told me otherwise, I assumed that we were moving to another hut. Several minutes later, however, I arrived in a brilliantly lit open space to find some three or four hundred people awaiting my talk. My heart missed a few beats. Angrily, I turned to my interpreter: 'Why didn't you tell me it was going to be a big event?' 'Well,' he said, 'I could see you'd be nervous, so I thought it better to keep it a secret.'

People had seen me arrive so I could hardly turn back. I wasn't sure how, or even whether, I was going to be able to improvise; talking intimately to a group of fifteen women in a small tin hut is very different from addressing a mass gathering.

'If you get stuck for words,' said my interpreter, 'I'll just fill in for you; nobody will know.'

He jumped up on the stage, and directed me to where I should sit while the introductory speeches went on. I rapidly scribbled a few notes on the back of a bus ticket, and the show went on. Though my début was hardly distinguished, neither was it a disaster.

Arriving at the meeting space at Walchanagar, I realized that this was going to be a very big event indeed, and estimates afterwards put the number at between 1,000 and 2,000. Malati began to panic.

'I can't do this. I can't speak in front of so many people,' she quavered.

Though somewhat overawed myself, I knew that beyond a certain size it didn't seem to make much difference whether there were 500 or 2,000 people in an audience. However, even right up to the end of my stay in India, when I'd had a lot of experience, this knowledge didn't stop me getting stage fright. I knew, however, that it would be no help to Malati if I showed my nerves as well, and after all I had the benefit of a well-developed stiff upper lip.

'Please make the talk easy,' she pleaded; 'don't use too many difficult words.'

I had briefly gone over the talk with her back at the hotel. She had heard some of the stories I would be telling on other occasions and I was confident that she would do well. Before the event began I was asked to garland a larger than life-sized statue of Dr Ambedkar in the park. As I walked from the platform to the statue I hesitated. I had three things to handle: a ladder, a large and weighty flower garland, and my flowing sari. If I held my sari decorously in one hand and the garland in the other, I would have no way of holding on to the ladder. If I held the garland and the ladder my feet were likely to get caught in the hem of my sari, releasing five billowing metres of sky-blue chiffon, an embarrassment I often dreaded. But if I held the ladder and my sari, there was no way I could hold the garland except by slinging it around my own neck, which would have been considered very irreverent.

I doubt whether anyone else was aware of the rapid survey of all the various possibilities that raced through my mind in the thirty seconds it took to walk from stage to statue, watched by some two thousand pairs of brown eyes. But perhaps the man who stood at the bottom of the ladder holding the garland noticed. When I reached him he said, 'You go up first, then once you're steady I'll hand the garland to you.' So, holding my sari with one hand, and the ladder with the other, I climbed up. Even that was complicated by the fact that one of the rungs was missing, forcing me to expose a forbidden length of calf. Once I was at the top, the man climbed up the ladder behind me and passed the garland to me, and, stretching perilously, I managed to get it over Ambedkar's head to cheers and applause from the audience. I descended the ladder relieved and rather pleased with the success of this delicate operation. Then Malati was asked to do likewise, but she just stood at the bottom of the ladder and asked the man to present the garland on her behalf, which seemed to be perfectly acceptable. I learned something here.

Before leaving the guest house for the event, we had met in the dining-room a policeman, like us from Poona, who evidently found me intriguing and began asking a lot of questions. I refrained from telling him why I was there, partly because I was often chatted up by men whose motives were dubious, and towards whom I always tried to be pleasantly discouraging, but also because I was not sure of my visa position, and wanted to keep as low a profile as possible so far as the police were concerned. For a big event like this, however, the local police would be informed as a matter of routine, and one or two would be on duty during the talk. Now, to my slight dismay, I saw that this policeman had followed us from the guest house and was sitting to the side of the stage with the other local police. I had by now discovered that he held quite a high position in the force, that he was neither a Buddhist nor a local, and that he was in Walchanagar on 'official business'. It was just possible he could cause me trouble.

Once I started speaking I forgot all about him. It was a brilliant evening. I spoke on the importance of the three most precious things for a Buddhist, the Three Jewels: the Buddha, the ideal human being that we too can strive to become; the Dharma, the teachings of the Buddha that we can try to put into practice; and the Sangha, the spiritual community of all those who are attempting to tread the Buddha's path. I explained why Ambedkar had chosen Buddhism, and I wove into the talk examples, similes, and stories. One of my favourite stories, and one which I used on this occasion, is about a family of frogs who live at the bottom of a deep dark well:

'Generation upon generation of these frogs have lived there. All they can see from the bottom of the well is a little pinhead of blue sky. Every day buckets are let down into the well, sink into the water, fill up with water and then are quickly drawn up into the open air again. Try as they may, the frogs can never get into the bucket. They are never given the chance, and often the bucket just hits them on the head, making them see stars. By the time they come round the bucket has gone.

'One day a very different sort of bucket is let down into the well. It is large, round, and made of gold, and once it has reached the water it waits there until all the frogs have jumped in. When the last one has got into the bucket, it is slowly pulled up into the open air and placed on the wall of the well. The frogs jump out of the bucket and on to the wall, and are amazed at the things they see around them, things they have never seen before. They see beautiful green fields of rice, a meandering river, high mountains, deep forests, wild flowers the colours of the rainbow, and overhead an eternal blue sky. Some of the frogs just sit on the wall, but others are more adventurous and go exploring: they play in the fields, they jump up the mountains, they swim in the river, they keep cool in the shade of the forest.'

Then I ask the audience what all this means. By this time young and old are usually gripped by the story. Its simplicity, even naïvety, is enjoyed as much by educated as by illiterate Buddhists. Some may already be guessing the ending, but will still roar with laughter and cheer when it is spelt out, even on a second or third hearing. So I continue:

'The deep dark well represents the conditions under which you existed as Untouchables, living in the dark, trying to get out but unable to, nobody giving you a helping hand, and many trying to push you right under the water. This is not just you, but generation upon generation of Untouchables.'

I look up and see nods of recognition. Then I ask, 'Who let down the great golden bucket?' Usually at least a couple of people shout out the name of Dr Ambedkar. 'Yes, it was Babasaheb Ambedkar.'

A round of applause breaks out as a sea of smiling faces looks up at me.

'He lifted you out of the dark and showed you the light. He freed you from your old intolerable way of life and showed you things you'd never seen before. So what are the fields, the mountains, forests, and rivers? These are the different teachings of the Buddha. They are beautiful and refreshing; as we explore them, we start to tread the path to Enlightenment, the path to freedom.' Again I hear applause and see affirming nods of the head.

'Some of the frogs go and explore their surroundings; in other words they try to understand and practise the Dharma. But others just stay sitting on the wall saying, "Isn't it beautiful, isn't it beautiful!" These frogs are like the thousands of people who call themselves Buddhist, but don't do anything about trying to change themselves. Dr Ambedkar said he wanted his followers not just to admire but to try to understand and practise the Dharma.'

Malati excelled herself, interpreting with a vigour and clarity that I had not heard from her before. Working with a good interpreter is a matter of harmony and synchronization, like dancing, each sentence being kept short and pithy so that the audience doesn't get bored waiting for the part they understand. The only mishap on this occasion occurred about halfway through, when a three-foot long poisonous centipede got in among the audience, causing a large number of people to stand up and start shouting. Not knowing what was going on, I assumed that a fight had started, as we were not far from Baramati where an outbreak of civil violence had recently forced us to cancel a talk. Quickly I moved out of the glare of the floodlights, but within a couple of minutes I was informed of the nature of the problem. The centipede, no doubt terrified, had sprinted away as fast as its little legs could carry it, and the talk continued.

The audience was receptive, nobody walked away, the speeches of thanks were exuberant, and I could tell people had been very moved. Many bought books while others invited me to their localities or villages to give a talk to the Buddhist people in their area. Late at night after the last Buddhist verses had been chanted, we returned in high spirits to the guest house, to be greeted by the policeman. Absorbed in my lecture, I had forgotten all about him. He had been inspired by the talk and wanted to buy us tea, snacks, even a meal. He kept saying it was 'beautiful, beautiful'. 'Your stories are perfect for these ignorant people,' he went on. Our Buddhists here in Maharashtra don't know anything. Ambedkar, Ambedkar, is all they say – they are just like the frogs on your wall,' he chuckled smugly. 'They don't understand anything; they are very foolish, these people.'

I could feel myself becoming irritable, and if it had been anyone else I would have contradicted him. Though during my talk I had made several digs at the Hindu caste system which didn't appear to bother him, and though he obviously had no intention of reporting me to any authority over the question of my holding a tourist visa, still I didn't want to try my luck. For the sake of politeness we accepted a cup of tea with him, but at the first possible opportunity we hurried back to our room, pursued by a peremptory, 'We will take breakfast together tomorrow!'

As it happened, we took two breakfasts, but not with the policeman. We were invited to two Buddhist households in the neighbouring locality. There were other invitations too, but time was short and all too soon we were back on another bus for the last leg of our journey. We arrived mid-afternoon at Daund, the home town of our organizer, Mr Langade, but nobody appeared to be expecting us, except a Mr Gaikwad, who had received a message only an hour before our arrival. The two men relieved their embarrassment with a short argument, and we were taken to Mr Gaikwad's house, where Mrs Gaikwad insisted on cooking a meal for us. This took her, her daughters, and various neighbours, all working steadily, three hours to prepare. Although we said that we would be perfectly happy to eat in a restaurant, it was made clear that the option was not available to us on this occasion.

The evening event was equally disorganized, this time held in a hall where some people walked out because they had expected a political meeting and others drifted in late, angry because they hadn't been informed earlier. By the end I felt slightly irritable; a stark contrast to Walchanagar. But that was so often my experience of India, a land of complete contrasts where I swung from elation to weariness, from buoyancy to dullness, from brightness to gloom, but rarely felt neutral.

We slept at the Gaikwads', rose at 5 a.m., and returned to Poona by train, arriving in time for breakfast.

Born Untouchables

By the time my role had shifted from medical work in Dapodi to Dharma work all over Maharashtra, I had also moved out of my quiet and exclusive residence at Gladhurst. One reason was that my Anglo-Indian landlady continued to make a fuss about my Indian friends visiting me there. Also, now that I was concentrating on more directly Buddhist activities, I wanted to live in the Ambedkar Housing Society where some of my closest Indian Buddhist friends lived. Built in the sixties by some of Ambedkar's followers, it provides decent and reasonably-priced homes for Buddhist people. Each single-storey house has two or three rooms and a veranda. Each is painted an ochre colour and surrounded by a small plot of land. There are some 200 houses in total, with rough tarmac tree-lined lanes running between them.

Even during the eight years I lived in India life in the Society changed rapidly as its inhabitants placed more and more emphasis on material values. Where once a radio was enough, now nearly every house displays a TV antenna on its flat roof. Fences or even high stone or brick walls now separate houses which previously had nothing to separate them from gossiping neighbours, playing children, and rummaging pigs and chickens. Some houses have acquired pretentious gateways, open verandas have been turned into closed-off rooms, extensions have been added, and some have even acquired a second storey. Concrete slabs have replaced cow-dunged areas in front of the houses, where the women sit and the children play. Gardens with flowers and shrubs are springing up behind the high walls. Parked outside many of the houses a moped or scooter can be seen where once there was only a bicycle. All the houses have electricity and running water, though the water is turned on only for a few hours morning and evening and stored in tanks, drums, and brass pots.

In other words, the majority of people who live in Ambedkar Society are middle-class Buddhists. Most of the men have skilled, white-collar jobs. Their children all go to school, and many are sent to the highly-prized English-medium schools. Some houses are occupied by extended families, others by nuclear families, the latter usually hiring what they are proud to call a 'maidservant' to do the domestic chores such as cleaning the house and washing the dishes and clothes, while the woman of the house goes out to work.

The first TBMSG centre was established in Ambedkar Society. When I arrived in 1982, we were renting a house there which served as centre, office, and Lokamitra's home. By the time I came to live in Ambedkar Society the centre had moved to purpose-built offices in Dapodi, with at least twenty office workers, telephones, filing cabinets, overhead fans, and even an air-conditioned room housing a computer. We now have at least a dozen huts in Poona where regular Dharma classes are held, and other similar premises in many other cities throughout Maharashtra. Early in 1990 a very large purpose-built Dharma centre had its public opening in Dapodi. When I moved to Ambedkar Society I rented the back room of Block No.14. Three women lived in the house: Kadlacbai, a frail, white-haired widow of about sixty-five, her daughter, who had once been married but had run away from a cruel husband without having produced any offspring, and her grand-daughter Surekka (the daughter of her son), who had been orphaned as a young child.

Surekka was about fifteen when I moved in, and attended an English-medium school. There was a striking gap between Surekka's sophistication and her aunt's and grandmother's simplicity. Even so, they all slept together in the kitchen. The veranda was used for tuition classes, and Surekka ruled her young charges, all cramming for exams, with a rod of iron. As the months progressed, Surekka's tuition classes became larger and noisier. At exam times the six- and seven-year-olds would come to the house at about 6 a.m. for a couple of hours when I was trying to meditate, and return in the evenings at around 5 p.m. At the tender age of fifteen, Surekka had clearly already come to the conclusion that to spare the rod is to spoil the child. Unable to avoid hearing everything that was going on through the thin doors, I had to listen to the frequent sound of a ruler thwacking knuckles. A general infantile hubbub I can live with, but childish cries of pain were too much and many was the time I had to go in and tell Surekka to stop. She would, but not for long.

I spent six months there. When I wasn't out of Poona leading a retreat, on tour giving Dharma lectures, visiting centres in other cities such as Bombay, or out leading Dharma classes, I would spend my time in and around Ambedkar Society, where I had many friends. Everyone in the Society knew me, by face if not by name, and I knew most of them, but those I got to know best were the women who attended the Dharma classes and retreats I led.

Right from the early days I was helped enormously by a woman called Manorama. Without her support and kindness, I doubt if I would have made any progress with women's Dharma activities in Maharashtra. I first met her when she was living with her husband and two young sons in an old bungalow in the cantonment area of town, near the up-market Mahatma Gandhi Road, and I lived with them for a few weeks after I got to India. At that time her husband was professor of physics at the Military Academy. Becoming deeply inspired by Buddhism, he went on to be ordained, and left his secure and prestigious job, which also meant giving up the house and much of his income, to work full time as secretary for Aid For India and the Karuna Trust.

Meanwhile Manorama and I became friends. We are the same age. At our first meeting she was very shy of me, and I thought she understood hardly any English. Later I learned that, although she was Marathi-medium educated, she had a very good grasp of the English language. Having had to drop out of college in her first year to take on household responsibilities, only now in her mid-thirties was she able to further her studies, doing an MA course in English literature. The first woman ever to interpret for me, she had a remarkable ability to learn English words quickly, and her growing enthusiasm for the Dharma was reflected in the spirit and inspiration of her interpretation. At first she was not altogether happy, and in fact felt rather threatened, at the idea of her husband resigning from his secure, potentially influential, and upwardly mobile job. For one thing, it meant that her status would be lowered in the eyes of her friends and colleagues. But she soon saw the importance of what he was doing, and was sometimes even proud of him.

From her I learned a lot about Indian customs, and about the fallacy of the romanticized Western image of the contented, passive, home-loving, happy-to-be-subservient Indian woman. She talked about how she often felt hemmed in and frustrated by the constraints of patriarchy, and showed me how hard even well-educated women like herself have to work. When I stayed in their bungalow she would be up at around 5 in the morning preparing lunch-boxes for her husband, elder son, and herself, as well as making breakfast. She would wash the clothes and take a bath before leaving home for her work in a laboratory, which involved looking down a microscope all day at blood slides to screen for malaria. Her youngest son stayed at home with his grandfather, and a girl came in twice a day to wash the dishes. Returning home late in the afternoon, Manorama would start preparing the evening meal. This might entail sifting through wheat to pick out little stones, then taking it to the mill to be ground into flour before she could start to make the chapatti dough. At that time her life seemed an endless round of serving her husband and her sons, and often there were visitors too. I soon came to realize that this was nothing exceptional, and that nearly all women had to do the same, some much more. It was her choice to take up a job, against her husband's wishes. Though the work was boring, she liked to get out of the house. When she started meditating, she'd get up half an hour earlier to fit it into her daily routine.

When her husband resigned from his teaching job, the family moved to Ambedkar Society. She talked freely with me about herself and some of her family difficulties. She always wanted to know about how we live in England, the way men treat women, the way husbands treat wives, the expectations of in-laws, the freedom of women, and much more. On occasion the gulf between her conditioning and mine seemed enormous, and I had to tread carefully. What in the West would be regarded as a mild feminist attitude might in India seem like a threat to the foundations on which Indian society is built. It was not always appropriate to express my views openly, though I often felt as though I was sitting on a seething volcano. Sometimes I felt weak for not saying what I really believed, yet when I did it wasn't always helpful. I was constantly treading a delicate line between expressing what I really thought and felt and thereby being true to myself, and trying to be as helpful as possible within the situation, which often meant not saying what I thought. For many years Manorama was the one Indian woman who knew about the relationship between Vajraketu and me. Having plucked up courage to tell her, half-imagining that she would be outraged, I was pleasantly surprised to find that she was not the least bit shocked, although she did think we should get engaged.

Mrs Diwal was another resident of Ambedkar Society, a small, plump, white-haired woman who always had a gentle kindly smile on her lined face. She sometimes giggled like a shy adolescent. The rooms inside her Ambedkar Society house were painted pink and mauve, which somehow suited her character. She lived with her frail, amiable husband, one of her three sons, his wife, and their two young children. Towards the end of my time in Poona, this son ran off with another woman, and the daughter-in-law returned to her family home in Bombay with the two children, to sue for divorce – a difficult and painful situation for the benevolent older couple. Mrs Diwal was like a mother to me, often dropping in to give me pieces of fruit, making sure that I took enough rest between the events of my sometimes hectic lifestyle, and often inviting me round for meals. Despite being older than me by thirty years, she would often call me 'Mother'.

We were attending a small retreat in the countryside once when she told me her life story. Eight or ten of us sat in a circle outside. The balmy night air caressed us, a half-moon gave almost enough light to read by, and the stars winked in the velvet sky. A small paraffin lamp in the centre of the circle glowed on dark faces, and cast long shadows out beyond the circle. She began her story.

She was born in a village in central Maharashtra in 1922. Both sides of the family worked on the railways. There was some education on her mother's side, but little on her father's. They were Mahars, the predominant Untouchable community of Maharashtra. Despite being an Untouchable, her mother's side of the family insisted that she be educated, so she was brought up with her maternal grandparents so that she could go to a nearby mission school. She said, 'My grandmother always made sure I was clean and so the teachers liked me.' She was seven when she started school, one of only two girls from the same caste. She passed her exams well, and when she was eighteen, both she and the other girl got jobs as teachers: 'Dr Ambedkar's revolution was starting, I very much felt part of it. We were not only the first Untouchable women teachers in Kandesh, but the first women teachers at all in the area. My family was very proud of me.'

But despite her education the area was full of caste prejudice: 'Even the dhobis wouldn't wash our clothes for fear of pollution. We did have one

146 BUT LITTLE DUST

dhobi who befriended the family, but he had to wash my father's white railway uniform at night, so as not to be seen, otherwise he might have been beaten, even by members of his own caste.

'When I was still at school, I once wanted to buy some cloth. I was told by the neighbour that if I were to step over the threshold of the shop and the shopkeeper were to find out I was an Untouchable he'd beat me, so I had to buy my cloth standing outside the shop.

'When the Untouchable well dried up early in the hot season, which it often did, we were not allowed to draw water from the Caste Hindu well. I would have to stand by their well with my pots, hoping that someone would feel sympathy and fill them for me. If I had drawn the water I would have polluted their well and they would have had to perform ritual ablutions to purify it. If they did not fill my pots I had to go without, or walk a mile to the nearest river.'

I had read a lot about caste prejudice in books, including stories of Dr Ambedkar himself. He had to sit outside the classroom to hear his school lessons as a little boy, and once when he was asked to write on the blackboard he was accused of polluting the lunchboxes of the other children which hung behind the blackboard. I was appalled to learn that, according to the *Manu Smriti* – the sacred law book of the Hindus which still gives scriptural authority for the inhuman treatment of the Untouchables – if Untouchables so much as hear the holy scriptures they should have molten lead poured into their ears. The same book also states that if an Untouchable should touch a Caste Hindu even by accident, the Caste Hindu would have to go away and perform ritual ablutions to cleanse himself from that touch. At one time Untouchables were not allowed to walk in the streets at sunrise or sunset, in case their shadow should fall upon a Caste Hindu, thereby polluting them. Caste Hindu children, even toddlers, having developed a rudimentary grasp of their 'superiority', would tease and torture Untouchable children of their own age; their conditioning started from the moment of birth.

In 1936 Mrs Diwal heard Dr Ambedkar speak. At that time he already felt that the only way out of the caste system was for people to change their religion, and he was looking at the possibility of Islam. 'He was a great inspiration to us all; he was a father, a teacher, a saviour; he was like a god to us. He spoke out in a way that nobody else dared to speak, he criticized Hinduism, he said what he felt. He was our only hope.'

I looked round the circle of attentive faces. There was not a dry eye.

Mrs Diwal's uncle encouraged her to perform in plays which brought out the injustice of the caste system. 'We all had to do our bit. I was sometimes scared but I knew I had to do it.

'Friends of mine wanted to arrange my marriage to a teacher. I met him but he wore a funny kind of uniform, a red dhoti and open shirt, which I didn't like; I couldn't imagine being married to someone who looked like that. Also, he only got paid every two or three months. I got a job in the school where I had been a student. But despite my misgivings, my marriage was eventually arranged, and as it turned out he has been a very good husband.'

Inspired by Dr Ambedkar, her family threw all the pictures of Hindu gods from their house into the river, only her mother clinging to the old gods. At her wedding her uncle changed the vows of the wedding ceremony in accordance with Dr Ambedkar's teaching. 'We lived by what Dr Ambedkar taught us.'

After her marriage she moved to Poona, got a teaching job, and started a Mahila Mandala. During the Pakistan–India war she made food and took it to the wounded of the Mahar Battalion. Her family was very poor indeed, her husband having to sell ghee (clarified butter) from door to door in the mornings and teach in the evenings, while she looked after her first son. Later she went on to get a BEd and tried to get a job with the corporation, but at that time they did not want to employ an Untouchable woman. Her husband was earning fifty rupees (£2) a month, and they were supporting his parents as well as the child. Later she did get a job with the corporation, but was still so poor she only possessed two saris: 'I'd wash one in the morning when I got up, wear the other one all day and night, and then wash that, and wear the clean one.'

She stayed in the corporation job for fifteen years, and very soon after the mass conversions to Buddhism under Ambedkar's leadership, she too became a Buddhist. She remembered Sangharakshita coming to Poona soon after the conversions; he was the first white man she had ever seen. She recalled him explaining the meaning of a Buddhist shrine. Although she was nominally a Buddhist, and gathered with other Buddhists to chant the Refuges and Precepts, it wasn't until she met Lokamitra that she began to understand that Buddhism was a path of self-development. It meant cultivating and maintaining positive qualities, not just reciting precepts but putting them into practice. 'Like rice absorbing the water in which it is cooked, I was absorbing the Dharma.'

A vibrating stillness hovered over the circle.

'As a child I was given presents when I passed my exams but once I was married I was given nothing but work. When I went on my first Dharma retreat I could hardly express my joy at having been given something so precious after so many years.'

The silvery moon shone high above, silhouetting the ancient Buddhist caves of Bhaja in whose shadow we sat, caves where 2,000 years ago monks, or maybe even nuns, had once lived and practised, caves where the Dharma had once flourished. Here we and the Dharma flourished once again. I thought of my teacher, Sangharakshita. In silence we lifted the lamp and climbed the steps to our shrine-room. In silence we meditated. In silence we rolled out our beds, turned down the wick, and went to sleep.

I was a familiar sight in Ambedkar Society, riding the bike I'd bought with generous donations from friends in England before my departure. In London I was used to riding a five-speed racing bike with drop handlebars. Here, by contrast, it was rather pleasant sedately to mount my shining black, old-fashioned, heavy, upright ladies' cycle with no gears. I even learned to ride it wearing a sari, by hitching up the folds of skirt into the waist to prevent the material from getting caught in chain or wheel, allowing the thick petticoat alone to cover my knees and calves. During my first few years in Poona I cycled all over the city, happily dodging in and out of the chaotic traffic. Towards the end of my time there, the traffic had become so congested and the air so polluted (and I'd seen so many fatal accidents), that I used my bike only to ride in a mile or two's radius of my base, preferring to use other modes of transport into the city.

The Gadankushes lived at the other end of the Society from me. I quite often called in on them, usually going on my bike as there was little danger of being knocked off it in the Society. Virabhadra lived in an extension room in the Gadankush house, and had quickly been made to feel one of the family, as I was when I visited him there. When he left for England, although I didn't actually live there in his place, my visits became a substitute for his much-felt absence.

Before his sudden and unexpected death, Mr Gadankush ran a shop from the veranda of the house, selling biscuits, matches, tea powder, cigarettes, eggs, and sweets. It was more of a retirement hobby than a profit-making business. He died shortly after I arrived in India. Mrs

Gadankush lived with her four grown-up sons. The oldest two were married, one having a son, the other a daughter, and both their wives worked from home. While I was there the third son was married to a local girl, and moved out with his new wife to live elsewhere. Aniruddh, the youngest, unmarried son, lived at home and went to college.

I used to leave my bike at the garden gate and walk in and out of the house as though it were my own. The doors were always open and the family always seemed pleased to see me. They were the first people I got to know in India who really accepted me just as a friend, rather than a special guest. For example, I could go into their house and not always have a cup of tea thrust into my hands (which is the usual, almost compulsory, greeting for a guest in an Indian household). Later I was treated similarly in many other households. Usually, I would sit in the Gadankushes' front room on one of the two beds which formed an L-shaped space in the small room. In one corner of the room stood a metal cupboard with a full-length mirror set into it, in another was a TV, and a large poster of a blonde-haired little girl with big blue eyes hung on the wall. On a wooden shelf over one of the beds was a plaster image of the Buddha with a pot of plastic flowers beside it. Over the doorway into the kitchen hung a picture of Dr Ambedkar, and over the head of Mrs Gadankush's bed hung a photo of her dead husband.

Aniruddh, her youngest son, was one of the few Indian men I got to know well. In the eight years I lived in India I saw him grow from an adolescent into a good-looking, intelligent, warm and sensitive young man. Through his English-medium education and his contact with Virabhadra he had perfected his English to the degree that his Indian friends told him he spoke more like an Englishman than an Indian (there is quite a difference between Indian English and English English). As time went on he became less shy of me, and he would often come round to my house to have a chat. When he and his best friend fell out over an unfortunate misunderstanding he came round to my house in tears to tell me. He liked to ask about England, about Buddhism and the FWBO in England, about English society. One day I was at their house helping Sunanda, one of the daughters-in-law who did tailoring work, to sew some buttons on a blouse. Aniruddh was sitting on a bed supposedly trying to study. He'd been reading an article in a magazine which mentioned hippies. He had heard about them before, and as a young boy had seen people passing through Poona who he suspected were hippies. But what was their philosophy? Why did they grow their hair long? Why, when they could afford to buy shoes, did they go barefoot? Why, when there was plenty of water, did their clothes often look dirty? Why did they take drugs? I tried to explain that their behaviour, dress, and the use of drugs implied a rejection of conventional values. I spoke of their 'Make love not war' philosophy. He was fascinated, though somewhat bemused. I went on to say that hippies were a cult of the past, and talked of punks, describing pink and green hair sticking up in spikes, safety-pins and razor blades used for decorating the body, and punk music, characterized by obscene lyrics and aggressive actions. This he could not understand, not of 'educated' people. 'Pink hair? Men dying their hair different colours and making it stick up, and hanging razor blades from their ears?' he asked incredulously, sitting cross-legged on the bed with his shirt neatly ironed, his trousers pressed, and his hair well combed.

He could make more sense of what I said about yuppies. He thought that Indians were more likely to become yuppies than hippies or punks – and he was probably right. All the while Mrs Gadankush was sitting on the other bed beside me. She couldn't understand a word we were saying, but laughed and laughed at Aniruddh's expressions. I couldn't find the Marathi even to try and explain it to her. Aniruddh left for college, I finished sewing on the buttons, and Sunanda went into the kitchen to prepare lunch. I could hardly explain these Western 'cults' to Aniruddh, a relatively Westernized, broad-minded young man. They would have made no sense at all to his mother, despite her very early connections with the British.

She was born in 1928. Her father was a cook for an English family, and his family lived in the servants' quarters of his military lodgings. When she was ten, their much-loved English sahib died, and his wife and family returned to the UK. Mrs Gadankush's engagement was arranged when she was eleven, and she was married at the age of twelve to a man thirteen years her senior. At fifteen, she had a son, who died before he was three weeks old. It was five years before she conceived again, but she went on to produce four sons. As we sat there on the bed together, my mind still idling on the subject of hippies and punks, I forced myself to steer the conversation towards something more appropriate. I looked up at the picture of Ambedkar. I asked her if she had ever met the great doctor. Yes, she had walked several miles to hear him speak in Poona, but her strongest personal memory of him was of the time of his death.

'As soon as we heard of his death and that the body was going to be taken to Bombay for cremation, my husband rushed out of the house and got the first train to Bombay. I was distraught; I didn't want to stay at home, I too wanted to be in Bombay. I had no money for a ticket, but was determined to go. I took my two baby sons with me. The train was packed. People hung out of the doors, they held on to the window bars from the outside, they sat on the luggage racks, they sat on the roof, they hung on to the chains connecting one carriage to another. Nearly all the Mahar community of Poona was heading for Bombay.

'Once in Bombay, like a great heaving, writhing snake the crowds wound their way towards the cremation ground. When they got there, hundreds of thousands of people sat on the ground and waited. Some had lost their sandals in the crush, others had been separated from friends and relatives; children were lost. I clung to my sons. Then a voice came over a loudspeaker, "His body has not yet come, but it will be coming."

'We waited and waited. Nobody shouted, nobody fought; only sobbing could be heard. Eventually his body did come, and we all stood up. It was covered in a white cloth, but the face could be seen. Mounds of flower garlands were placed on top of the cloth. Everyone was crying and weeping, "Oh Baba, oh Baba!"

'The police announced that people should make a queue and only close relatives could come near the body. But we all wanted to see him, to touch him. The body was carried around the city and hundreds of thousands of people followed in its wake, but I stayed in the cremation ground sitting on the ground. As I sat there, I remembered a time when I was about six years old and my grandfather was dying. I knew that one day I too would have to die. Now our "Baba" was dead; even the greatest of men have to die.

'We were distraught, lost; it was as though our own father had died. Eventually the body was brought back to the cremation ground, laid on the pyre, and burned in sandalwood. There was no room for all the people; many were standing in the sea. As the body burned, cannon shots were fired into the air.

'Babasaheb had only converted to Buddhism six weeks previously. He was due to conduct a conversion ceremony in Bombay, so instead U Chandramani, the seniormost Buddhist monk in India at the time, from whom Ambedkar himself had taken the Refuges and Precepts, conducted the ceremony for us. Nearly a million people converted to Buddhism at that time.

'I returned home terribly distressed. All over Maharashtra condolence meetings were held. Choked with grief, people could hardly speak. He died on Thursday, 6 December. From then on people started fasting every Thursday for a while, and then on the sixth of every month.'

Mrs Gadankush wiped her eyes and nose with the end of her sari. Sunanda had come in quietly and sat on the floor looking up at her mother-in-law. Her niece sat on her lap and pulled at her gold earrings; her other daughter-in-law stood in the doorway listening silently. They both wiped their eyes.

'Come, let's eat,' said Sunanda. We went into the kitchen and sat on the floor, and Sunanda served us lunch.

t r a n s f o r m a t i o n

The Buddha went to the Eastern Bamboo Park where three of his disciples, Anuruddha, Nandiya, and Kimbila, were living in the open air. After they greeted each other the Buddha said, 'I hope you are all living in peace and harmony, as friendly and undisputing as milk with water, regarding each other with kindly eyes.' 'Surely we do, Lord,' replied Anuruddha. 'And how do you live like this?' asked the Buddha. 'It is fortunate for me that I am living with such companions in the Holy Life,' replied Anuruddha. 'I act, speak, and think with loving kindness towards these friends both in public and private. I think "Why should I not set aside what I want to do and instead do what they want to do?" and I act accordingly. We are three in body, Lord, but one in mind, and in this way we live diligent, ardent, and self-controlled.'

ADAPTED FROM A STORY IN THE PALI CANON

The Maharashtra Express

Just once during the cold season of 1988, the Maharashtra Express left Poona on time. I arrived ten minutes before the scheduled departure time in no particular hurry, confidently holding fast to the usual assumption that the train would be late. I had been having supper with friends, and we all agreed that there was no point rushing, not for the Maharashtra Express. It was renowned for its tardiness. Every time any of us had been on that train it had always been late, and hanging around on stations late at night is not a very enjoyable occupation; so, we concluded, one might as well go late and not rush.

But we were all wrong. That night the Maharashtra Express made history. It came in on time, and – as I could see as I hurried down the platform – it was going to depart on time. By the time I got there it had already been waiting in the station for fifteen minutes, and was due to depart in five.

At least I had missed the crush that ensues when everyone tries to board the train at the same time. It is no fun being jammed between silk-sari'd women and red-clothed coolies, men armed with briefcases and families carrying all manner of things: tiffins, water bottles, scrolls of chapattis wrapped in newspaper, suitcases, bundles of bedding and clothing, and children. Everyone trying to get on the train is encumbered with quantities of luggage while other passengers similarly encumbered are trying to get off it, and frequently both groups get locked in a stalemate in the doorway, those behind crying 'Forward', and those in front crying 'Back'....

I had missed this initial rush, which was popularly believed to be a necessity in the non-reserved compartments, though I could never fathom why it should also occur in the reserved compartments, where the battle to board the train as soon as it arrived was just as fiercely fought out. As I expected, Malati had been waiting there for nearly an hour. She was standing by an open doorway with her father, who saw me first and waved. He grabbed my bag, plonked it under the seat, said a quick goodbye, and left the compartment. When we had squeezed ourselves on to a bench and I had got my breath back, Malati told me off in no uncertain terms for being so late, and then immediately forgave me. Malati shared with other Indians a wonderful ability not to bear grudges for more than a few minutes if they can express their grievances. Relieved, we both collapsed in laughter.

There were eleven men, women, and children in our compartment, which was meant for six ladies, but there was no point in worrying about it now; things would gradually sort themselves out as the train got going. There was a time when I would march into a compartment flashing my seat reservation and demanding that 'my' seat be vacated immediately. This would cause a terrible musical-chairs commotion, after which, having got my much sought-after seat, I had simply increased the crush on the seats. Feeling claustrophobic, I dared not move, as much because I'd lose face as for fear that someone else would take my seat.

After a few train journeys I realized that in any case at least half the people inside a train before it goes are not passengers but well-wishers, unwilling to jump off the train until the whistle blows, or even until the train is actually moving out of the station. As a retired railwayman Malati's father knew the ropes, so he hadn't waited this long but now stood outside, giving last words of warning not to eat unwrapped food from the stations, to try to get top bunks, and so on, concluding his spiel by giving us the exact time of our expected arrival in Wardha, a twenty-hour journey from Poona Junction.

Each carriage contains one closed compartment for ladies only, for the few women who travel alone without male escort. We could now take notice of each other. A tired and drawn-looking middle-aged woman was travelling with a girl of no more than twenty, presumably her daughter-in-law, who had on her lap a little girl eating *bel puri* (a spicy snack) and dropping bits of it on the floor. The two women hardly spoke during the whole journey and any conversation was directed through the little girl, who couldn't have been more than three years old and was soon asleep. There was also a friendly student, carrying just one small bag. She was studying at Poona University, but a relative had died in her native village, so she was going home to be with the family for a few days. She seemed happy to have someone to talk to as it was the first time she had travelled alone on a train overnight.

The sixth occupant, who was fat and bossy, commanded a lot of space in the compartment. Enthroned in her seat by the window, she leaned her fleshy arm on the window ledge and scowled at the rest of us. She demanded that the light or the fan should be turned on or off, and ordered the student first to close the window and then to open it again, quelling any stirrings of democracy amongst the lower orders with an imperious sweep of the hand and a forceful note in her voice that was not to be challenged. It seemed easier to do as we were told. She asked Malati and I where we were going, and my reply that we were going on a Dharma *shibeer* near Wardha seemed to satisfy her, as no further questions were asked. There is a Gandhi ashram near Wardha to which both Indians and foreigners make pilgrimages, either just to visit or to stay and imbibe the Mahatma's non-violent judiciousness. He spent several years at this ashram, and on display there are various mementoes of his simple and non-violent lifestyle, such as his sandals and loom. I suspect the fat lady thought we were going there, for little else would attract a foreigner to Wardha.

Half an hour after we pulled out of Poona station the bunks were let down. Heeding Malati's father's advice, we claimed the top two bunks and our claim went uncontested. I laid out my rubber yoga mat, covered myself with a cashmere shawl, and was very soon rocked to sleep. At one station I woke up when the train jerked to a halt, sleepily opened my eyes to see whether it was still dark and drifted off only to be woken again by a great commotion going on further down the corridor. The first rays of dawn were starting to shine through the slatted canopy over the station platform. The fat woman sat up, turned on the light, opened the compartment door, and peered down the corridor. People were walking to and fro, a child could be heard crying, and someone was shouting. I asked what was happening. The fat woman said she wasn't sure but that someone had shouted 'Thief, Thief!'

Eventually a pleasant elderly man who appeared to know the fat woman told us that a man on the platform had tried to snatch the golden mangala sutta from around the neck of a woman who was sleeping with her head next to the open window. She had awoken, seen the arm and screamed. Her husband had leapt down from the top bunk in an attempt to catch the thief and twisted his ankle. The arm had disappeared and the gold chain was still where it belonged.

All was well, the whistle blew, and the train was off again. The fat woman now not only locked the compartment door but closed and locked the window too, before rolling back on to the bunk again. Within minutes she was snoring, but her vibrations were soon drowned by the noise of the train as it gathered speed. By 10.30 it was beginning to get very hot and by midday we were in the centre of India. The landscape was arid and the dust gathered thick on our seats, our faces, and our clothes. I lay down and read *Silas Marner*, with the fan whirring a few inches from my head. The damp pastoral scenes of George Eliot's England, with their fog, mists, and rain, seemed far distant from the relentless parched ochre landscape outside my window. The fan did no more than create a little movement of hot air and my skin felt dehydrated and cracked. The water in my bottle was warm, even when taken fresh from a station tap, plastic-tasting yet delicious. A heavy lethargy hung over the carriage as the train trundled along the now single track stretching far into the shimmering noonday horizon.

Garlands of Marigolds
At 3.20 in the afternoon the train drew into a substantial-looking station and people began pushing their way down the corridor. This was Wardha; after twenty hours we had arrived fifteen minutes early! We clambered from our bunks down some tricky little rungs just big enough for the ball of your foot, stuffed bedding and books into our bags, and joined the other passengers in the corridor trying to force a passage through a picket of cold drink wallahs, chai wallahs, and samosa wallahs who were shouting out their wares and not the least bit disconcerted by the onslaught of bodies and baggage.

We had been told someone would be meeting us, and before we had even stepped down on to the platform the reception party, a group of about twenty people, had spotted us and were standing by the open doorway, placing garlands round our necks and pressing flowers into our hands, showering us with petals, shouting 'Jai Bhagwan Gautam

Buddha, Jai Doctor Babasaheb Ambedkar, Jai Dharmacharini Padmasuri, Jai Malatitai!' followed by a clamorous refrain of, 'Vijai-so!' Looking back at the train, out of the corner of my eye I saw faces pressed against the bars of the windows. The fat lady from whom even Malati had failed to draw a smile throughout the journey, was looking out of the window and smiling. The little girl waved, stretching out her arm through the bars. I waved back and handed her one of my flowers, which she snatched from me greedily. Malati and I, unable to move forward, stood on the platform trapped between the train and our 'disciples', as one after another they presented garlands of flowers and bright-eyed smiles. People we already knew hugged us too, squashing the sweet-smelling flower petals.

People were stopping and asking questions with the natural human curiosity which in England is suppressed by the notion that you should mind your own business.

'Who are they? Where are they going? What nationality is she?'

The answers were equally direct: 'She's a Buddhist.... She's our teacher.... She comes from England and has come to lead a Dharma shibeer.... The girl with her is her interpreter.... Yes, she's a Buddhist too.... Yes, she speaks excellent English.... Yes, she's got a BCom.... No, she's not married....'

I let the others do all the talking; on such occasions it was useful to let people think I spoke less Marathi than I actually did.

The sudden exit from the train, together with the heat, the crowds, and the sickly smell of jasmine, all combined to set my head reeling, so that I found myself clinging to Malati and asking for a drink. Immediately a young boy rushed off and came back with a cool bottle of Limca which he thrust into my hand. Gratefully I tipped my head back and drank it down in one gulp, ignoring protestations that I should have been given a straw. I was now deemed sufficiently fortified to answer questions myself:

'Yes, we've had a good journey, though we're tired.... Yes, we'd like to go to someone's house and wash.... No, we'd rather not take a cycle rickshaw or an auto-rickshaw, as they invariably break down in Wardha anyway. Do you remember the last time?... It's only fifteen minutes' walk, and it would be good to stretch our legs....'

Our arms were full of flowers, our bags and bottles having been whisked from us and taken ahead by others, as we crossed over the railway bridge in a wave of chattering excitement. We were ushered past the ticket collector as though we were international dignitaries, and he was far too interested in us to be bothered about whether or not we held tickets. I looked back to see our train drawing away on its last lap up to Nagpur. After twenty hours of rattle and lurch, the solidity of the ground seemed most strange; and after the seclusion of the carriage, suddenly emerging into the street was quite a shock. Brightly turbaned drivers of rickshaws and tongas were shouting out 'Where are you going?' throwing their arms up in despair and shrugging their shoulders when we told them we wanted to walk.

Although we were leading our procession, Malati and I hardly knew where we were going, but we were sure someone would tell us if we were wrong. It was still very hot and the sun glared down into our faces. Many of the little stalls and cloth shops in the bazaar were still closed, their owners having their afternoon siestas just inside, or curled up on a rickety step at the entrance. This part of town was run-down and dirty, even by Indian standards. A busy bus station froze into a common expression of intent interest as we passed. Particularly in Malati's company I stuck out like a sore thumb. It was not only that I stood nearly head and shoulders above her, nor that I was a foreigner with short brown hair. We presented a contrast in another way too, I looking dishevelled in my crumpled cotton sari, with a large bundle of garlands clutched to my chest, while she somehow managed to look neat and well-pressed in her purple silky synthetic Punjabi dress. I wished I could carry a little sign saying 'Actually she's just as mucky as I am.'

As we walked along, little children ran along beside us appealing for *baksheesh* with well-practised importunity. They also asked lots of questions to which I replied in Marathi, much to their surprise and delight. Very few foreigners speak Marathi; those who do learn an Indian language almost invariably take up Hindi.

Crossing the road, we entered the grounds of the hospital, where we found the two-roomed house of Shendebai, a nursing sister. On the threshold we were asked to wait while one at a time the eight or so women who had accompanied us from the station poured cool refreshing water over our hot dusty feet, a custom still strongly adhered to in this region when welcoming an important guest or relative to one's home. A few children joined in too, slightly embarrassed, moving fast and jerkily like an early movie. Inside, we sat on the only bed in the cool dark room and placed the mound of marigold garlands beside us. We were offered water which was wonderfully cool and sweet. Saucers of Bombay mix and a small cup of hot sweet milky tea were also served to us. Within minutes I felt remarkably revived. Many of those who had followed us from the station or joined the procession on its way now sat on the floor in front of us, watching as we ate and drank as though they were following some action-packed drama.

This was my third visit to Wardha, and the second time that I was going to lead a Dharma shibeer for women in the vicinity. Like the previous year it was to be held in a marquee some six miles out of town. I had sent a message ahead to say that I would like a day's rest in Wardha before the retreat started, both to get over the journey and to prepare myself physically, mentally, and emotionally for the coming days, but when we arrived I was informed that the retreat was to start that night. Yes, they had got my message, but they wanted as much time as possible on retreat with me; and really I didn't have to do much tonight as all the organization was taken care of; and it was too late now to inform people otherwise. They were coming from many of the surrounding villages, and in fact many would already be on their way and some would already have arrived and be waiting for me. I frequently found myself thus presented with a *fait accompli* during my time in India.

I suppose I could have refused to go until the following day, but that might have caused ill will and anxiety, particularly for those organizing the retreat, so I decided, after some hesitation, to submit to their plans. I also made it clear that should this happen again I might not comply so willingly. I asked if they understood that I might be tired; of course they understood, they said, but somehow I still felt that either they didn't really understand, or else their emotional response to me was so over-whelming that they couldn't connect with how I might feel. When I had given the go-ahead, the unspoken tension that had built up in the room immediately dissolved, and the whole issue disappeared as though it had never been raised. The retreat would start tonight with me, and they would do everything to look after my needs and comfort – that I was sure of.

Before it got dark, Malati and I went into the 'bathroom', an unlit cubbyhole furnished with tap and bucket, and bathed and changed, after which I lay down on the bed to rest while Shendebai prepared food and her twelve-year-old daughter massaged my swollen feet and ankles. Malati, true to form, went to help in the kitchen. Soon we were sitting on the floor with Shendebai's husband and their small son, eating chapattis and potatoes, rice, and a very garlicky dal. Shendebai refused to eat with us, but insisted on serving all of us first, though had her husband not been there I am sure we could have persuaded her otherwise. Only after we had all finished and they had cleared away the plates did she and her daughter eat in the kitchen. Mr Shende called an auto-rickshaw, and Malati, Shendebai, and I climbed in with our luggage squashed in at our feet and on a small shelf behind our heads. Mr Shende and the two children stood to wave us off. Their daughter was tearful, as she wanted to come on the retreat too; but exams were nearing, and she needed to study.

Beneath the New Moon

The motor rickshaw swung out of the hospital compound and into the bazaar, which was now alive and bustling. Beyond the bazaar we drove through some shanty towns and eventually out to a long straight road which stretched ahead into the darkness. The new moon was just appearing, and gave very little light. Once well clear of the town, our driver set aside the precision dodgem tactics which he had deployed so skilfully in the crowded streets, and his desire for speed took over. He twisted his accelerator handlebar towards him, jerked into gear, and was off, oblivious until almost too late of the occasional wobbly cyclist and the oncoming overloaded trucks with their blinding headlights. Like most Indian roads, this one was only wide enough for one truck, so when they passed each other one would force the other to swing off the road, churning up a cloud of dust. Often there is no space even for a truck and a rickshaw to pass one another without one of the two, usually the rickshaw, having to dive on to the verge. Despite the obvious handicap of size, our driver still wasn't going to give in without a fight. I sometimes wondered whether oncoming trucks could even see us with our single miserable headlight flickering on and off. When the two glaring, unblinking lamps and the roar of the juggernaut's engine were almost on top of us, I would close my eyes, cling tight to Malati, and start chanting a mantra. The rickshaw would lurch on to the verge, throwing us and the baggage in a heap against the bars at the side, then swerve back on the road again, leaving a muddle of bodies and baggage to be sorted out before the next heave. The driver, Malati, and Shendebai all hooted with laughter every time I told the driver to slow down. Naturally he went even faster.

About six miles down the road, by which time my eyes were firmly closed and my heart was thumping in my throat, we swivelled to the left on to a bumpy dirt track. As we continued nearly as fast as on the open road, I was relieved that we passed no other vehicle. There was still the distinct possibility of overturning, but I thought at least we would survive. Though my head was banged repeatedly on an overhead metal bar as we rode the bumps, I found myself still able to reflect how remarkable it was that these extraordinary little three-wheelers seemed never to get punctures. With great relief I saw the one light of Shelu Kate (pronounced 'kartay') village ahead, hanging outside the first house we reached. A crowd of people stood in front of the light awaiting our arrival. Joyful shouts greeted us, and I too felt like shouting for joy just to step out of the rickshaw. Again I was honoured with marigold garlands, and children thrust petals into my hands.

The retreat was to be held in a field outside Shelu Kate. I suspected that the crowd of forty or so who had given me this wonderful welcome were the entire Buddhist population of this small settlement. They lived as Untouchables had always lived, on the outskirts of the village. One farmer among them, for reasons I never quite grasped, had done exceedingly well and now owned a considerable amount of land which he was only too happy for us to use for our retreat. He also encouraged every Buddhist woman in the village to attend. Having met him the previous year I soon spotted him standing at the back of the crowd, a tall, white-haired and weather-beaten gentleman, leaning on a big black stick, just watching.

We were led forward in a procession through the silent, dusty, unlit lanes, past mud huts lit by oil lamps, where faces peered out at us in the dark. We walked until we came to an opening between huts, a kind of village square, where a small village shrine had been erected. Everyone took off their sandals and bowed to the shrine. I was directed to sit next to it, in the light of candles brightly burning; also on the shrine was a plaster image of the Buddha and lighted sticks of incense. I said a few words to thank the people of the village for their welcome; then we chanted verses together and recited the Refuges and Precepts, and I offered flowers before the image of the Buddha.

The previous year it had been light when I'd entered the village, and I distinctly recall the beautiful walk from the village to the retreat site across what looked like sand dunes over which magenta-turbaned farmers drove bullock carts, bringing in their evening loads from the fields and throwing up clouds of dust. Palm trees were silhouetted on the horizon against an enormous red sun. Tonight, though, visibility was down to a few yards. Between the twenty or so of us we carried three feeble torches. The thong of my sandal had broken so I walked barefoot, tentatively feeling my way over sand and boulders. An unknown woman came and linked arms with me and another took me by the hand. We had gone only a couple of hundred yards beyond the village when I was informed that it had been arranged that I should go the rest of the way by bullock cart. Sure enough, as I looked up from my concentrated downward gaze, I saw two large white bullocks staring back at me.

I had just been getting used to the dark and enjoying the feeling of the warm earth on my feet, overcoming the fear that I might step on a snake or a scorpion, and I wasn't at all sure that a bullock cart ride would be any great treat; it would certainly be less comfortable than walking. But it was another *fait accompli* and I could hardly refuse the kind offer; my only fervent hope was that the charioteer would not be another speed merchant. Luggage, along with sacks of vegetables and grain, was loaded on the cart, followed by Malati and me. I clung to the worn-smooth wooden cart rails as we bumped along, little faster than walking pace, the rest of the women following behind us. Nobody talked. The only sound was the creaking of the wheels, the heavy breathing of the bullocks, an occasional whip-crack and 'ksh-ksh' from the driver, and the solitary cry of a night bird. In an indigo sky, rich with stars, hung the crescent moon. I felt overcome by a sense of the strangeness of the role in which I found myself.

By the time we arrived there was quite a chill in the air. Jowari was now growing in the field where we had held the previous year's retreat, but a few hundred yards further on we rounded a corner up a steep embankment and rolled along what in the dark appeared to be a dyke. There in front of us, lit by some incredible feat with electric tube lights, was the colourful marquee, and fifty yards or so to one side was a small awning of khaki canvas. The marquee was not exactly like the white ones used in England for wedding receptions and May Balls, neatly rigged together over metal frames with doorways and windows. Nor was it like the princely tents that were apparently used in the days of the Raj, with Kashmir carpets on the floor and tiger skins lining the walls. Our marquee was roughly tied around wooden poles at irregular intervals, and its walls were striped yellow, blue, red, green, and orange. The flat roof was made from orange cloth which rippled in the breeze and the doorway was one strip of cloth rolled back and tied with fraying sisal. Faded and worn cotton rugs served as a floor over the black earth.

Our driver pulled the reins hard and the bullocks came to a halt. Malati and I slid neatly off the cart and were immediately ushered into the marquee where we were greeted by everyone individually and yet more garlands of sweet-smelling pink petals were offered. Old wizened faces, wrinkled and furrowed, wrapped in shawls and scarves, and lit by piercing brown eyes, looked up into my face, thin shrivelled weather-beaten arms came out to touch me, then the hands were brought together, and withered but firm bodies bowed before me. Some women touched my feet. Some faces were radiant and smiling, others bewildered and questioning. There were young faces and beautiful faces, tired faces, intelligent faces, and faces that looked blank and ignorant.

Each woman in turn presented me with something: a garland, a flower, a single petal. Some made their offerings with great zest, some with caution, but most with a deep reverence. When the last woman had presented me with her gift I walked slowly down the aisle in the centre of the marquee and placed all the flowers on the saffron-decked candlelit shrine. I bowed before the Buddha image. It was late, and people were tired, having been waiting several hours for my arrival, so I just said a few words by way of introduction before we recited and chanted a puja, and went to bed.

The khaki tent had been rigged up for me, and there was even a forty-watt light bulb dangling from one of its support poles. The tent was made from scraps of material bound together and was just high enough for me to stand in the middle. Inside, I was touched to find a narrow metal bed and mattress. Probably nobody there would have believed me if I had told them that during my many years of camping holidays in Europe I had not only never slept in a bed, but had never even used an air-bed. Certain things were accorded to 'important' guests, and the town folk had informed the village folk that a bed was a necessity for a foreigner. Malati, Shendebai, and one of the other organizers slept on the ground beside me.

I took off my sari – something an Indian rarely does at night, but these three had become accustomed to my strange ways – and put on a T-shirt and sweater over my ankle-length petticoat, plus socks and a woolly hat, and climbed into my sleeping bag. I'd remembered from last year how cold it got at night, and how I'd lain awake shivering. At my request Shendebai unscrewed the light bulb and the three of them huddled close together for warmth, sharing out their meagre blankets. The other hundred women slept in long lines in the marquee beneath the white glow of the strip light, using their spare saris and other bits of clothing as blankets. Soon the last excited voices stopped, and in the deep stillness all I could hear was the high-pitched drone of cicadas and the distant barking of dogs in the village. Within minutes I was fast asleep.

'Open is the Going Forth'

The first three days of the retreat were open to any Buddhist women, but the second part, lasting four days, was only for those who meditated regularly at home, attended weekly Buddhist classes, and had been on previous retreats. The first part of the retreat would be a taste of a different life, an experience which would have far-reaching effects on the women's lives; the second, a deepening reflection on the Buddhist life. Each morning we woke to a bell at 5 o'clock. It was still dark and very cold. That first morning many had not slept very well, because of excitement and anticipation, or the strangeness of the place or, in some cases, the cold. I had the benefit not only of being well accustomed to sleeping in strange places in my wandering existence, but also of my feather-filled sleeping bag and the cotton-filled mattress beneath me. Many of the others did not possess shawls, blankets, or even cardigans; they had only the closeness of each other's bodies to keep themselves warm. Despite the cold, some had already been up since three-thirty, drawn water from the icy well, taken a cold bath outside, changed their clothes and washed yesterday's sari; these women were used to working in the fields.

We started with a meditation which I introduced and led through, Malati translating everything I said into Marathi, keeping it simple and direct. By the time the meditation finished, dawn had broken and the first shafts of sunlight were bringing the colours of the marquee to life. I stepped outside on to rich black crusted earth, a field doubtless just harvested and awaiting another crop. We were surrounded by emerald fields of wheat, fields of cotton, of cabbages and chillies, aubergines, and peanuts. The flat landscape was edged in the far distance by palm trees. Between the fields of wheat and cotton stood a deep dark well. A motorized pump was turned on daily to irrigate the ripening crops. There was a miraculous limpid beauty to this little oasis in the midst of an arid desert.

To defecate I would take my little tin can of water (the custom being to wash oneself rather than use toilet paper) into a distant field of thistly stubble and squat carefully on my haunches, watching the sun coming up or going down. I love this outdoor life, away from the noise and dirt, the hustle and bustle of the city. The Buddha himself probably lived more or less like this. The cooking was done outside by a hired man and his two women helpers over ditches of burning wood, in great blackened cauldrons in which they simmered a variety of beans, flavoured with hot chillies to make a potent brew. Two-foot wide chapattis were rolled out by the women, cooked on large metal trays, and cut into pieces to eat with the half-cooked beans and a porridge of dal.

We meditated at regular intervals throughout the day, we discussed Buddhism, and I gave talks about what the Buddha taught, using stories and parables to illustrate points and principles. Probably sixty per cent of the retreatants were illiterate, never having had the opportunity of education. We practised being clear, honest, and friendly in our communication with one another. There were times for walks, for bathing, and washing clothes near the well; there were times for helping to cook and times for eating. There were also times for singing songs, often dedicated to their great leader, Dr Babasaheb Ambedkar, without whom they would not have been on this retreat.

For many of them, it was the first time in their lives that they'd left their homes and come out on their own or with other women. They had come from villages and towns within a twenty-mile radius, some travelling much of the way on foot to attend the retreat. Locked as they were within a strongly patriarchal society, a retreat like this might be the first time that they experienced a glimpse, or at least a glimpse of a glimpse, of their own individuality. Although this first retreat was only three days long, by the end of it women said they felt freer, as though they had been lifted out of the dark and shown the light. These were no polite, meaningless comments to flatter or please; they meant it from the bottom of their hearts. I wasn't asking them to have blind faith or believe in dogma. I simply showed them the possibility of change, telling them that we can change ourselves and become happier and more aware just by recognizing our own potential and by making an effort as the Buddha had done. As was often necessary, I clarified a common misconception, pointing out that the Buddha was a human being who gained a state of perfection called Enlightenment or Buddhahood, rather than being, or even becoming, a god.

Though Buddhist devotion may look very similar to the worship of God or gods in other religions, there is in it no sense of placating some powerful deity. The Buddha image represents on the one hand our own potential to transcend our condition as human beings, and on the other a focus for the expression of natural feelings of reverence and gratitude towards those who have opened the Way before us, and of our resolve to follow. It is not a sacrament but a practice. I encouraged the women on the retreat to test out the Dharma for themselves and not just merely go along with it unquestioningly. The freeing effect of meditation was something they had to experience, as well as the company of other women who lived as they did, and who, having become to some degree happier and more aware, were continuing to change through their own efforts. They had come together not just for an outing or picnic, but in order to discover why Ambedkar had chosen Buddhism, and to help fulfil his vision of a world that lived for the highest ideals not only for the individual, but for society at large. My role was to be a guide, a shower of the way, showing them that they could choose to set out on a path that promises salvation not after death, but here in this lifetime, offering hope and encouragement not only to themselves but to their children and their children's children.

As I explained that Buddhism is based on ethical precepts of love, generosity, abstention from sexual misconduct, truthful speech, and clarity of mind, I was interrupted by many 'buts': 'But my husband/ mother-in-law/neighbour drinks … beats … swears … steals … is unfaithful … is jealous … manipulates … tells lies …, so why should I be ethical myself?'

I was often horrified, particularly in my early days in India, at the way some of these women were treated, and indeed by the way they sometimes mistreated one another. But besides sympathy, we need clarity, strength, and conviction to stand by what is true and honest even if others around us are not willing to change. A very basic principle of Buddhism is that actions have consequences; we plant seeds whenever we act, and we reap the fruit of what we have sown. This teaching, along with the five ethical training principles, was the main theme of study during this first retreat.

The difference in temperature between day and night was severe. By 10 a.m. it was quickly soaring towards 100° Fahrenheit, making the marquee an intolerable airless furnace. There were very few trees around to give natural shade, but we used the shade there was. Only early in the morning and at night did we move into the marquee; the rest of the retreat was held outside beneath the trees. At night and in the early morning I could see my breath, and as I meditated I would curl up my toes to see if they were still there. My lips and heels became cracked and sore.

On a large retreat like this (more women arrived in the early morning of the first full day so that we were 128 in all), where it is impossible to have contact with everybody, it is hard to assess how the retreat is going and how much is being understood, though a good deal can be read on people's faces. So on the last evening I held a question-and-answer session, asking the retreatants to formulate and write down their questions (those who could write helping those who could not). As well as helping them to think clearly, this allowed me to see how much they had understood. On this occasion the questions were very practical, relating to meditation. I emphasized that meditation is not just a flight into escapist fantasies, nor a means of cutting off from real experience, but, on the contrary, a way of becoming more aware of oneself and others which leads to the development of clear understanding and compassion. I described it as a tool for the systematic cultivation of positive mental states.

Many had had experiences of their minds 'wandering off' when they tried to concentrate during meditation; others had 'visions', or were plagued by bodily discomfort. I talked about these as distractions from the practice, and offered ways of trying to overcome them; even the visions, though they might be very pleasurable, could become a distraction. I pointed out that meditation can take one deeper than this; that it is fine to enjoy the visual or other sense experiences which arise, but it is best not to cling to them. It was interesting to discover how many of the women very readily conjured up images of the Buddha, or flowers, or light, in their meditation.

They also asked questions about the differences between Hindu and Buddhist practices. It is written in the *Manu Smriti*, the sacred law book of the Hindus, that women, even high-caste women, are not allowed to recite the sacred Vedas. This venerable authority explains:

'Women have no right to know religion because they have no right to know the Vedas. The uttering of Vedic mantras is useful for removing sin. As woman cannot utter the Vedic mantras they are as untruth is.'

This attitude is deeply ingrained in Indian society, even if people are not aware of its source. One belief of many women, even quite highly educated women, is that during the time of menstruation they are 'dirty' and polluted, so one of their questions was 'Is it all right to meditate when you have a period?' When I had emphatically answered in the affirmative, they went on to ask, 'But is it all right to bow before an image of the Buddha, or light a stick of incense or a candle before the Buddha, when you have your period?'

These were very real questions, questions I'd never been asked when teaching Buddhism in the West, and which I knew these women would never have asked in front of men. These questions showed that they were realizing that Buddhism was something to be practised, not just talked about, something they could take home with them into what, in many cases, we in the West would consider to be dire and difficult living conditions. They could make changes in their attitudes and their lives, and many left the retreat resolving to do so.

In three days a lot of changes had taken place. If nothing else, the women looked refreshed and more youthful, but for some, Buddhism had touched a deeper level of their being, and would not simply be forgotten before the week was out. On the morning that the majority of the women left they brought me flowers with the dew still on them. They bowed to my feet, and wept, clutched me by the arm or shoulder and said, 'You've shown us the light of the Dharma. You must return here soon; being here is like being in mother's house.' This is one of the greatest compliments they could have given me. Many of the older ones would have left the love and security of 'mother's house' by the age of ten or twelve, when they were married and moved into the unknown territory of their husbands' families, some to be treated little better than servants or even slaves. Many had experienced a kind of suffering that I had never glimpsed. They would remember this retreat for years to come, through a life of severe drudgery and hopelessness, a life lived only for basic survival, where old age has descended before youth has been lived.

Twenty-three of us were left. We sat beneath the only tree which provided enough shade for all us, to study a text called the *Pabbajja Sutta*. In this discourse Ananda, the Buddha's cousin and close disciple, has gathered together some friends and is telling them about a time before the Buddha became a Buddha. He describes how the young Siddhartha, the Buddha-to-be, 'he who sees', 'he who understands', recognizes that home is not a very desirable place to be when compared to a life of non-attachment: 'Cramped is this life at home, dusty indeed its sphere. Open is the Going Forth. He saw this and went forth.'

The women glanced at each other and laughed, nodding their heads, appreciating this understanding of their situation. We discussed how, though we might not literally be able to leave home, dusty though it might be, we can still try to acquire the mental attitude of moving away from our tendency to cling on to things, people, and situations, moving away from the harmful actions, speech, and thought that continue to bind us to this cramped and dusty life.

Later King Bimbisara sees the young Siddhartha wandering from place to place on his begging round. He looks so different from other wandering ascetics, of which there were many 2,500 years ago, that the king sends out a messenger to discover the whereabouts and lineage of this man of great beauty and nobility. The messenger tracks down Siddhartha, returns to the king, and says, 'This monk sits at the east of Pandava Hill, great king. A very tiger, a bull, a lion in his lair.'

When I looked around me, a bull or a lion seemed a not inappropriate image for some of these women. Born into desperate circumstances, often maltreated and malnourished, they were, in many cases, still treated as outcasts of society, and in all cases they endured the humiliation of being women. Yet time and time again I saw, in those who had not been crushed by their circumstances, a leonine vigour, firmness, and strength to conquer. A wry sense of humour is a good indication of such stamina, and this quality was evident in every word, gesture, and song of the great majority of these women.

All too soon the retreat came to an end. They said how much they had learned from the retreat, how their lives were a mixture of pleasure and pain but how here they had experienced only great happiness. One took a vow never to slip back but only to move forwards, while another said that from now on skilful action would be her path. They praised the Buddha and they praised Babasaheb Ambedkar. They didn't want to leave. They hugged me, they hugged Malati, they hugged each other. People from the village joined us for the final puja and said we had brought great joy to their village. The farmer whose field we had been using was silently sitting there among the crowd with his dog. Each night he had come and slept at the edge of the field beneath the haystacks, not only to protect his crops from thieves but also to protect us. A group of young boys came to dismantle the tents, to fold up the rugs, and let down the Buddhist flag which for a week had fluttered in the middle of the field. They had come with bullock carts to take back the surplus grain, which only at this point did I realize had been donated by our benefactor, the owner of the field.

As I was about to set out on the dusty road home I felt a tap on my shoulder; it was Shantabai. She had arrived in the midday heat of the previous day. Though no more than thirty she was thin and frail. I remembered her from the retreat the previous year, particularly for her incredibly sweet singing voice. She had dreamt that I had returned to the area and was leading a retreat. Nobody had told her whether or not this was the case, but she had made some chapattis and some peanut chutney, packed a spare sari, and walked four miles out of her village, telling no one for fear they might prevent her coming. From there she took a bus and then walked the last two miles. In Shelu Kate village she was told that the retreat was indeed taking place. When she arrived she had looked into my eyes as though seeing a vision. We had given her food and drink and she had sat down with us and meditated. Now she came to thank me. She had to face the wrath of relatives back home, but she didn't mind; her short time on retreat had been worth it, and she would come again next year.

We stopped in Shelu Kate on our way back to the main road. The farmer had invited all the remaining retreatants to his home, mainly in order to meet his wife who had sent her daughter-in-law to the retreat while she stayed at home to look after the children and grandchildren. A crowd of people stood in the courtyard of the wattle-and-daub farmhouse. Malati and I were shown to a charpoy on which we sat at the feet of a larger than life statue of Dr Ambedkar, bespectacled and holding the Indian Constitution in his hand. They asked if I would like to garland the statue, which

I did, extremely glad of the opportunity of thanking this family for all they had given so that we could hold the retreat.

Two women were residents of the village itself, so the rest of us bade them farewell and made our way through cotton fields to the road. I refused to take a rickshaw, saying I was perfectly happy to wait two hours for a bus if need be. As we stood there I wondered when I would be back; I had made no promises. Timeless days had merged together and the rickshaw drive seemed months ago. Maybe it would be several years before I would visit Shelu Kate again, if I ever did. I looked at the women who remained and marvelled at how different they looked from when I had met them just one week ago. Now they appeared strong, determined, and confident, and a soft but bright alertness shone from their faces. Within ten minutes a bus arrived and we pushed our way in. Others going in different directions watched us go. With two rings on the bell the bus crunched into gear and we were off, hanging out of the open door to wave our goodbyes.

We spent that night back in Wardha at Shendebai's house, where a constant trickle of visitors came to see us. For two hours the following day we were taken from one house to another visiting women who had been on retreat and wanted Malati and me to see their homes, as well as women who hadn't managed to go on retreat but still wanted to meet us, and women who had been on last year's retreat but for a number of reasons hadn't come this year. We were given tea or lemon water and offered an assortment of snacks at each house and at noon we sat down to an enormous and delicious meal. At twelve-thirty, with no time to digest the food, we set out in the midday sun towards the railway station, for the last five minutes walking along the railway tracks. Some thirty or forty people, men, women, and children, came to see us off. They plied us with fruit, biscuits, sweetmeats, and flowers. One little girl even gave me a pen. The train was late and as we sat on our bags in the shade a huge crowd of onlookers gathered around us with the same questions as when we had arrived.

After half an hour, the distant huffing of the steam engine brought everyone to their feet, and the sleepy platform was suddenly buzzing with activity. Our carriage was filled with passengers, most without reservations, and we had to persuade some of them to move from our reserved seats. We held the hands of our friends, thrust between the window bars; everybody was laughing and crying, smiling and waving.

The whistle blew, the train slowly pulled out of the station, leaving our friends running along the platform, and Malati and I settled ourselves for the long haul back to Poona.

The Way to Bhaja

India is the birthplace of Buddhism. The Buddha was born and lived there 2,500 years ago, and it was from there that Buddhism spread abroad. But for a very long time, from about the year 1000CE until the mass conversions in 1956, Buddhism virtually died out in India. There were a number of reasons for this, not the least being the Muslim invasion which led to the massacre of thousands of monks at the great Buddhist university of Nalanda. Those who escaped the massacre fled India altogether to China, Tibet, and Japan. Apart from a few Sri Lankan monks, and of course the Tibetans in exile, there are few Buddhists alive today in India who are not connected to the mass conversions under the leadership of Dr Ambedkar, little more than thirty years ago.

Nevertheless, there do remain from those glorious days when Buddhism flourished in India historical monuments and ruins dating back to the time of King Ashoka, and even earlier. Some of the finest Buddhist remains are to be seen in Maharashtra, which is where most of the new Buddhists live, and perhaps the most famous are the rock-cut temples and monasteries of Ajanta. Set within a spectacular horseshoe cliff, they contain reliefs and paintings of outstanding quality. The site first became important in the late second or first century BCE, when two temples and their monasteries were cut into the cliff, but it wasn't until much later, in the fifth century CE, that the remaining twenty-five or so caves were cut. Some of the monasteries were given pillared halls, colonnades, and verandas, and some were cut on two levels. Many are richly decorated with scenes from the life of the Buddha. It has naturally become a place of pilgrimage for Western and Eastern Buddhists alike, as well as for tourists. Throughout Maharashtra there are some eight other rock-cut Buddhist caves, among which the most ancient are the caves of Bhaja, said to date back 2,000 years, which are situated at the top of the Western Ghats about halfway between Poona and Bombay.

We were fortunate enough to be able to acquire some land in the valley below the Bhaja caves, and here we built our first retreat centre. The initial building was quite a feat. The first person to be employed on the project was the water diviner. The hand-pumped well that was bored according to his directions has never run dry, and still provides cool, sweet, clear water for the whole retreat complex. Local rock was dynamited out of the earth and laboriously hammered into building blocks by young girls and women. Supplies and building materials, such as roof tiles, which had been transported by truck to the nearest village, were carried on heads for half a mile around the rice fields to the site.

Within a few months a basic grey stone building with red roof tiles and painted wooden shutters had been erected. Now there is a cluster of large buildings that together constitute Saddharma Pradip. Despite this expansion the accommodation is still very basic, with virtually no furniture (you bring your own bedding and sit on the floor), and still no road (a delightful walk across the fields instead).

Since its opening Saddharma Pradip has seen almost continuous retreats of between 8 and 150 people at any one time, some for men, some for women, and a few mixed. Sometimes special events are held for children. The retreats may last a day, a weekend, a week, or even a month at a time. Buddhists come from all over Maharashtra and from other Indian states too, and a few even come from the West.

Sitting on the steps in front of Saddharma Pradip one looks out across the paddy fields, which are barren and dusty in the hot season as though nothing could possibly grow there, but suddenly become lush and vivid green in the rains. In the far distance, rising out of the plain, another group of Buddhist caves cut into the hillside, the caves of Karla, can just be distinguished. Saddharma Pradip itself nestles into jungle-covered hills on top of which loom two ancient forts. Most striking of all are the caves of Bhaja. Cut into a sheer wall of rock and facing west, they gravely look down on Saddharma Pradip. Sometimes when I sat on those steps during a retreat looking up at the caves, I would become more acutely aware than at any other time of the remarkable revolution that was happening with the revival of Buddhism in India. And it was on this site that the first two Indian women went forth and were ordained as members of TBM (the Indian wing of the Western Buddhist Order) in January 1987.

When Sangharakshita founded the Western Buddhist Order in 1968, he did not identify the spiritual life solely with the monastic life and the formidable burden of numerous rules or precepts that generally accompanies it, many of which have little meaning in modern society. He saw a person's commitment, traditionally referred to as 'Going for Refuge', as essential, or primary; one's lifestyle, the expression of that commitment, was secondary, though not unimportant. Thus he refused to recognize the perceived inherent spiritual superiority of the celibate nun or monk over someone leading a family life. Nor did Sangharakshita uphold the classical idea of the subordination of female disciples to male disciples. At present, issues concerning the position of women in Buddhism are being discussed throughout the Buddhist world, for traditionally the *bhikshuni* (nun) sangha is subordinated to the *bhikshu* (monk) sangha, and this subordination is not considered appropriate or advisable by many twentieth-century Buddhists.

Until recently, when someone was deemed to be effectively Going for Refuge, and thus ready to be ordained a member of the Western Buddhist Order, Sangharakshita would perform the ordination ceremony. However, during the last few years he has handed on the responsibility to senior Dharmacharis or Dharmacharinis to act on his behalf. When the first two women in India were ready to take the step of Dharmacharini ordination, Sangharakshita was unable to go to India himself, so he requested that two Dharmacharinis from England, together with myself, should act on his behalf. It was the first time that women were to ordain women within the Order. I was a little apprehensive.

Srimala and Ratnasuri were the two women who were to join me from England. Srimala, originally Jane Goody, another of Lokamitra's sisters, was living as a single parent in Norfolk with her two teenage daughters, had been involved with the FWBO since its early days, and had had much to do with helping the expansion of the women's wing of the movement. She is about my age, and from a not dissimilar background.

Ratnasuri is an older woman who had served with the ATS during the war. Originally christened Beryl, she worked for many years in a chocolate factory in Norwich, brought up two sons and, shortly after her separation from a near-alcoholic husband, went along to her first Buddhism class in 1976. Her friends in the chocolate factory thought her mad when she told them of her interest in meditation and yoga. By this time she was living on her own and making a fresh start, but she says that as far back as the end of the war she had known that she wanted to do something with her life: 'I'd been a cabbage for long enough. I knew I had to grow and do something with myself – either that or I wouldn't have lived.' She now lives at Taraloka, a women's retreat centre in

Shropshire, having moved there as one of its founder members in 1985. She is an *anagarika* (literally 'cityless one'), which means that she has taken a vow to abstain from non-chastity. She has cropped her hair short, and for special occasions, including her visit to India, wears saffron robes. Both Srimala and Ratnasuri were old friends of mine and I was very excited about their arrival.

Despite having to deal with jet lag, culture shock, hot food, noise, dust, and heat, they were both remarkably robust and willing. During their first few days in Poona we went on shopping expeditions to buy suitable clothes for Srimala and sandals for Ratnasuri. Nobody batted an eyelid at Ratnasuri striding along Poona's classy Mahatma Gandhi Road in orange robes; I couldn't help thinking that she would have caused a mild sensation doing the same in her local high street in England.

The three of us had received several invitations for every meal and snack possible within a day and we were also trying to sort out the programme for the forthcoming retreats. There was a lot to do and much excitement all round, so it was with some relief that the three of us eventually made our way out of Poona towards the idyllic valley of Saddharma Pradip. We took the train from Poona, via Dapodi, through the suburbs and out into the countryside. An hour and a half later we stepped down from the train at Malavali in the still early morning, and drank cups of hot sweet tea out of stained and chipped white saucers at the platform tea-bar. Leaving our bags at the stationmaster's house (his was a Buddhist family with whom on many occasions I had left my luggage) to be brought on to the retreat centre later in the day by bullock cart or bicycle, we began the forty-minute walk over the fields to the retreat centre.

The sun was already streaming down into our faces from a deep blue sky. Being January, this was the cold season, when nights and early mornings are cold enough to warrant a sweater and even socks, but the days are like summer in the Mediterranean. The air is at its freshest, the visual clarity at its sharpest, and the sky at its deepest azure. The first part of the walk took us along a well-worn track with part bare, part scrub-covered hills rising steeply to our left, and the valley of harvested paddy fields and a meagre copse of eucalyptus trees opening out to our right. We skirted a wall behind which old and lofty trees grew in abundance up the hillside and headed along the track to Bhaja village.

The village itself, though tiny, had a school to which came not only the village children but children from outlying hill settlements. The front rooms of a few of the huts served as shops selling basic provisions. Many of the inhabitants knew who we were, and as we passed through children came up to us and shouted 'Jai Bhim!' before running off again, bubbling with mirth. A herd of water buffalo sauntered down the track towards us, their dark grey bodies glistening in the sunlight and their great horns swaying in front of them like immobile antennae. A bullock cart piled high with rice straw rumbled past on its wooden wheels. A couple of boys rushed up to us saying, 'You want to go caves? You want guide?'

'No, thank you, we're going to the ashram,' we replied. Most visitors who pass through the village are going to visit the Bhaja caves; any others are bound for Saddharma Pradip, or 'the ashram', as it is called by the locals. The huts in the village are mostly made from mud and straw, and may well have been standing for many decades. They blend into the landscape as though they have always stood on that spot and it is not difficult to imagine a very similar village in the same place 2,000 years ago, a settlement where the monks from the caves could go begging on their almsround, and have their bowls filled with scraps of food.

As I was writing this book I received a letter from my Indian friend Vimalasuri. Virabhadra, now a registrar in a leading London hospital, was visiting my home in Cambridge and translated it for me. We sat securely sheltered from the frost outside in front of my purring gas fire as he read this devastating news aloud:

'The monsoon has been very heavy this year. There was a landslide at Bhaja village, and thirty-eight people were killed. Our friends at Saddharma Pradip went and helped.'

Thirty-eight men, women, and children had been buried alive, and the news probably warranted a few lines in a local newspaper. Yet the catastrophe will linger on in Bhaja village for several generations.

From the village we carried on along narrow dykes that served as footpaths around the stubble of the rice fields, and past the village well. Women chattered and laughed as they drew their water in buckets and poured it into two, three, or four brass pots which they balanced on their heads and carried, almost running, barefoot over the hot dusty earth back to their homes. One of the women looked our way and called us to come and join her. We waved back and passed on. Sometimes the paths crossed dried river beds, channels where during the monsoon one would wade knee-deep – or even thigh-deep – in water. Now to our left we could see the Bhaja caves, in shade at this time of day. The sun gradually comes round to light up the great stupa in the main chaitya hall by evening. The buildings of Saddharma Pradip now came into sight, at the foot of a semicircle of wood and scrub-covered hills.

Land crabs scuttled along in front of us and dived down holes as we approached. The shed skin of a snake lay in our path: discarded, papery scales in a perfect unbroken tube. An occasional herdsman passed by, nodding in greeting, and women came along carrying branches and sticks they had lopped off the remaining trees high up the mountain, unknowingly adding to the ecological devastation caused by deforestation. They carried them in enormous bundles on their heads, the wood sticking out four or five feet in front and behind, perspiration dripping from their brows. We stood to one side and admired their extraordinary balletic poise and elegance as they glided past us on their way to sell the wood in local villages and towns.

We paused in the shade of a single mango tree and drank the water we had carried in a bottle from Poona. We should have taken an earlier train. Ratnasuri took my umbrella to protect her from the sun. Eyeing the figure beside me with her grey cropped hair, her saffron robes, and her trainers, striding out beneath a black umbrella into the dusty landscape, I wondered what her chocolate factory friends would have made of her if they could have seen her now. At last we reached a battered blue and yellow sign which read in Marathi 'Saddharma Pradip Meditation Centre'. We mounted some crumbling stone steps and passed a group of newly-planted guava trees. The doors were open. Buddhapriya was sitting on the steps in front of the entrance, chatting to a local herdsman and chewing a stalk of grass. He jumped up grinning widely.

'Jai Bhim, Jai Bhim, Jai Bhim!' Putting his hands together in salutation, he bowed before each of us in turn. We grinned back at him, put our own sweaty palms together, and replied, 'Jai Bhim!'

Buddhapriya is a man in his early sixties, one of the first Indian Dharmacharis. I got to know him when I first arrived in Poona. He had relatives living in Bhaja village and some of the nearby settlements, and was known and liked by an enormous number of people in the area. It was through his efforts and contacts that we acquired the land for Saddharma Pradip. The retired headmaster of a primary school, he now works full-time for the Buddhist movement, and at this particular time he was joint caretaker of the retreat centre. Within minutes he had primed and pumped a kerosene stove, brewing a cup of black sweet tea for us.

Going for Refuge

The ordination of women by women is not a traditional practice. Ever since the time of the Buddha, nuns had one ceremony performed by a senior nun, but their ordination was not considered complete until it had also been conferred by a monk. In our case Dharmacharinis would perform the entire ordination. Sangharakshita had put his trust in us. He knew that we were not perfect, nor even necessarily very spiritually advanced, but he also knew that we were making a constant and resolute effort to make progress in our lives.

The two women coming on the retreat to be ordained had been born Untouchables. Shobha Labhane came to Buddhism from politics, though she had considered herself a Buddhist since the conversions in 1956. She had managed to get a good education. In 1982 there was agitation for the Marathwada University in Aurangabad to be renamed 'Dr Ambedkar University', after its founder. It led to some dreadful communal violence and Shobha spent a week in prison for her part in a protest against the failure of the authorities to punish Caste Hindus for the raping of women and destruction of property in Buddhist villages in her area. In prison she discovered that she had a natural ability to lead. She taught some of the women to meditate (she had recently been on one of our retreats), and encouraged them to sing songs about Dr Ambedkar. They even refused to eat the prison food, and took over the cooking. Eventually she became disillusioned with politics, and turned to Buddhism as a path of self-development. She is married with four daughters.

Nirmala Karat was brought up in a family which was so poor that her mother broke stones on the road to earn a living. None the less, her mother had such a commitment to education that Nirmala was the only Untouchable girl in her school. Later, married and living in a Bombay slum, she began to search for a Buddhist teacher. Although she met many bhikkhus from Sri Lanka, it wasn't until she came into contact with TBMSG that she felt she was shown a coherent path to follow.

Before the ordination retreat started, Srimala, Ratnasuri, and I spent three days at Bhaja on our own, preparing ourselves for the week ahead and in particular for the ordinations which were to take place at the end of the retreat. The practical preparations included familiarizing ourselves with the ordination ceremony and learning the Pali and Hindi verses. I also needed to teach Srimala and Ratnasuri how to sit on the floor and eat with their fingers, how to walk, sit, and bow to the shrine wearing a sari, or in Ratnasuri's case robes. Every day we openly shared our thoughts and feelings with each other. We had a common apprehension about the task we were about to perform, but speaking plainly and declaring ourselves honestly in this way we arrived at a strong affirmation and understanding of one other. We meditated together, and went for walks in the cool of evening around the valley.

Soon the retreatants were arriving, and we sat where Buddhapriya had sat awaiting our arrival and watched them come in twos and threes over the fields in their colourful saris. Those who had been invited were all women who were seriously practising Buddhists and who had been involved in TBMSG for, in some cases, a number of years. Amongst them was Manorama, my interpreter.

During the week we meditated, studied, performed puja, and just spent time together, sometimes in silence. We studied the *Karaniya Metta Sutta*, the Buddha's words on 'metta' or loving-kindness. To make the passage more easily accessible to the all-female retreat, we substituted the feminine for the masculine form of the original translation, so that the sutta read as follows:

> *This must be done by one who kens her good,*
> *Who grasps the meaning*
> *Of 'The Place of Peace'.*
> *Able and upright, yea, and truly straight,*
> *Soft-spoken and mild-mannered, must she be,*
> *And void of all the vain conceit of self.*
> *She should be well content, soon satisfied,*
> *With wants but few, of frugal appetites,*
> *With faculties of sense restrained and stilled,*
> *Discreet in all her ways, not insolent,*
> *Nor greedy after gifts; nor should she do*
> *Any ignoble act which others,*
> *Wiser, beholding might rebuke her for.*
> *Now, may all living things, or weak or strong,*
> *Omitting none, tall, middle-sized, or short,*

> *Subtle or gross of form, seen or unseen,*
> *Those dwelling near or dwelling far away,*
> *Born or unborn – may every living thing*
> *Abound in bliss. Let none deceive or think*
> *Scorn of another, in whatever way.*
> *But as a mother watches o'er her child,*
> *Her only child, so long as she doth breathe,*
> *So let her practise unto all that live*
> *An all-embracing mind. And let a woman*
> *Practise unbounded love for all the world,*
> *Above, below, across, in every way,*
> *Love unobstructed, void of enmity.*
> *Standing or moving, sitting, lying down,*
> *In whatsoever way that woman may be,*
> *Provided she be slothless, let her found*
> *Firmly this mindfulness of boundless love.*
> *For this is what we call 'The State Sublime'.*
> *So shall a woman, by leaving far behind*
> *All wrongful views, by walking righteously,*
> *Attain to gnostic vision and crush out*
> *All lust for sensual pleasures. Such in truth*
> *Shall come to birth no more in any womb.*

Each morning we sat outside in a circle going through the sutta line by line, each one of us trying to relate the meaning to our own, albeit limited, experience of metta, finding and discussing ways of helping ourselves and each other to move towards a fuller understanding and expression of it. Each day we had longer and longer periods of silence, to allow the study and meditation, the awareness of ourselves and others, to sink to deeper levels of our being.

The ordination ceremony takes place in two stages, a private ceremony being followed, usually the next day, by a public ceremony. The former symbolizes one's intention to put the ideals and practice of Buddhism at the centre of one's life even if nobody else in the world were to do likewise. It represents an individual commitment which each person takes on for himself or herself and is responsible for following through. The ceremony is performed privately, the ordinand alone with just his or her preceptor, and during it the ordinand is given a new, Buddhist name which marks his or her spiritual rebirth as a Buddhist and which usually symbolizes some positive quality that he or she has to some degree, and can develop further. The public ceremony represents the recognition of one's commitment by the Sangha, the community of other individuals who have also gone for Refuge, who welcome the new Order member into the Order. In the context of this ceremony the new name is announced.

On the day of the private ordinations a quiet excitement suffused the retreat. The retreatants spent the afternoon in silence decorating the main shrine, while Srimala, Ratnasuri, and I made a small shrine for the private ordinations. The rooms at Saddharma Pradip are high, echoing, and rather impersonal, so in one room we built a tent using blue and white saris. It was just high enough to stand up in, and just large enough for two people to sit in comfortably. Inside we made a small and simple shrine with white cloths, a statue of Shakyamuni Buddha (the historical Buddha, the 'Sage of the Shakyans'), a picture of Sangharakshita, flowers, and many little candles. In a bowl in the centre we lit sandalwood incense. Nobody else saw this shrine until after the ceremony.

Just before the start of the private ordinations, as the women were making their way to the large shrine-room and settling themselves on their cushions, I went outside, and stood on the mound in front of Saddharma Pradip where an eight-spoked Dharmachakra (a traditional symbol of the Dharma), made from chunks of locally-found white quartz, lay on the ochre earth. I gazed up at the caves of Bhaja. The evening sun setting over the western hills was throwing a rosy radiance on the rocks, and almost as though on fire the stone stupa shone down into our tranquil valley from the great chaitya hall. In that moment I was struck by a charge of history, carried by a wave that came from the Buddha himself 2,500 years ago through the monks or nuns who had once lived and practised in those very caves, beneath that very stupa; from all the great sages down to my own teacher, and to this present moment, when two Indian women were about to commit themselves to the Buddha, Dharma, and Sangha. In that moment I experienced the revival of Buddhism as a mighty, boundless, and potent force, and realized how much I and other Buddhists had a part to play, not only in the revival of Buddhism in India, but in making the Dharma available throughout the world. I felt humbled yet extraordinarily calm as I felt the force of this majestic tradition.

I joined the retreatants in the main shrine-room and in unison we bowed three times to the shrine. We then began a meditation to cultivate metta towards ourselves and all living creatures, but particularly at this time towards Shobha and Nirmala who sat in their sky-blue saris at the front of the shrine-room. Srimala was to conduct the private ordination ceremony of Shobha, and I that of Nirmala. Ratnasuri was to perform the public ceremony the following day. The shrine-room was very silent as we started the Metta Bhavana meditation.

After about ten minutes Srimala left the shrine-room to go to the private shrine, shortly followed by Shobha. The private ceremony over, they returned to the main shrine and it was my turn to leave. The corridor was lit with night-lights, and on top of a shoe rack at the far end of the corridor we had placed a thangka of Shakyamuni on a red cloth lit with candles. I passed it and entered the separate room, then ducked down into the tent. Shobha's candle offering was still alight, and her stick of incense burning sweetly. I lit the rest of the candles. Bowing three times to the Buddha image, I composed myself on the cushion placed next to the shrine. In the following five minutes, as I sat there alone, I thought of many things, but inevitably the strongest recollection was that of my own ordination, seven years before almost to the day. And now I felt the presence of my own teacher and preceptor, Sangharakshita, in the tent there with me. Just as I had sat in front of him seven years ago to receive my own ordination, and his presence had seemed almost superhuman, so it felt now. I had no doubt that his good wishes were with us.

Nirmala entered the room and shut the door, then came into the tent, and the ceremony began. Contrary to my expectations it felt the most natural thing in the world to be doing, and no other thought passed through my mind than the significance of what was happening. The sense of harmony and unity between Nirmala and me in those minutes was unique and inexpressible. The Refuges and Ten Precepts were recited (Order members take five extra precepts as well as the traditional five), three traditional offerings of a flower, a candle, and incense were placed on the shrine by Nirmala, a mantra was chanted, and I told her her new name, chosen by Sangharakshita. Beaming, she left the tent and returned to the main shrine. I reflected for a while and then, leaving the two candles and two sticks of incense burning, and leaving the two fresh white flowers to fade and wither, I too withdrew from the tent and returned to join the others still meditating in the main room. We all went to bed in silence, leaving the two new Order members to meditate alone for a while.

For the public ordinations next day, an awning had been set up outside where the ceremonies were to take place, giving a bit of shade. Final touches were being put to the mass of flowers on the shrine as the first trickle of people were arriving in a snake-like procession over the fields, not only from nearby Poona, but from Bombay, Aurangabad, and as far away as Nagpur, a day and a half's journey away. Ratnasuri led the ceremony with great joy. Around the neck of each woman she placed a white kesa (a kesa is a kind of sash worn around the neck, adopted from the Japanese tradition). Then she announced their new names. Shobha had become Jnanasuri, meaning heroine of knowledge, and Nirmala became Vimalasuri, which means pure and stainless heroine. A mighty shout of 'Sadhu!' ('Hurray!') reverberated around the valley.

I recalled my reflections of the evening before. For two women to join an Order which in India had until this point consisted only of men was a huge step forward. These two women were stepping out of a conditioning which acted strongly against their development as individuals. Born as women, born as Untouchables in a caste-ridden society, with all that that entailed, they were now truly being reborn as heroines.

After the ceremony everyone dispersed around the fields to eat their tiffin. By early evening they were all gone, save a few stragglers and the five of us Dharmacharinis. Srimala and Ratnasuri had brought with them presents from well-wishers in England: perfumed candles, cards, malas, paintings of Buddhas and Bodhisattvas, crystal gems that threw rainbows in the sunlight, each wrapped in coloured paper, and bearing a message of welcome and joy from across the globe, celebrating the step Jnanasuri and Vimalasuri had taken. The two of them opened each present carefully, gasping with delight at each object, holding it this way and that, and showing it to the rest of us. We spent five more days together at Saddharma Pradip, before going our separate ways, Vimalasuri back to the slums of Bombay, Jnanasuri to Aurangabad, and Srimala and Ratnasuri returning with me to Poona and eventually to England.

A Delightful Friendship
I first met Vimalasuri soon after I arrived in India, when she was still known by her married name, Nirmala Karat. Living in Bombay, it was

Vajraketu who met her first. On several occasions he had said to me, 'You must meet Nirmala Karat; you'll love her. She's so full of positivity; she just bubbles with energy and life.' Likewise he had said to her, 'You must meet Padmasuri.' We eventually met on a retreat in Bombay on which I was leading a study group for women. Of the eighty to a hundred people attending that retreat, only ten were women. I immediately knew which one was Nirmala; short, chubby, eyes glinting with vitality, awestruck like a child, she came straight up to me, held her hands together, and said 'Padmasuri, Jai Bhim!' 'Jai Bhim! Mrs Karat,' I replied. Wonder and amazement that I should know her name spread across her smiling face. Sudatta, her nine-year-old son, was standing beside her. Confidently he looked up at me and said in perfect English, 'My mother had been waiting a long time to see you. She is very pleased.' As Nirmala spoke no English, Sudatta acted as interpreter between us on that retreat.

In those early days our meetings were infrequent, as I was very busy with the medical project in Poona, and only rarely visited Bombay. I did on a couple of occasions take time out to go and visit her in Bombay, in a district called Andheri, a vast sprawling slum area not far from the airport. Her home was near the massive concrete water pipeline which runs overground carrying drinking water to the city; this was reflected in her address:

Plot No.—,
The Pipeline,
Andheri,
Bombay.

Her tiny hut fronted on a filthy open sewer which carried thick black fluid, excrement, and chemical waste from nearby factories. It ran several feet deep and some six feet wide down a small ravine right in front of her hut, and only a narrow footpath separated it from her front door. Foot-bridges had been slung over the ravine at regular intervals to provide access to the houses and to the public latrine on the other side. Nirmala lived here with her husband, her son Sudatta, and her younger daughters Vandana and Vaisali.

Over the following months and years our acquaintance grew into a strong friendship, and during that time I began to piece together the things she told me about her life. I particularly remember an evening several years later, by which time the family had moved from Andheri to live in New Bombay in a concrete jungle of cheaply-built apartment blocks where they owned a one-room flat with running water, electricity, and an inside latrine. Despite the rather soulless surroundings it was quite luxurious compared with their hut in Andheri. Her husband was doing a late shift at the electronics factory where he worked, and the children were playing outside. She and I lay on the bed together and she began to pour out her life story.

She spoke with great passion, the emotional tone of her voice and facial expressions filling the gaps when my vocabulary failed. Her grandmother on her father's side had been a very beautiful woman, but proud, for which she was cruelly persecuted by her in-laws. After her first child died, she ran away from her home and ended up in a village temple where the priest arranged another marriage for her. With this husband she had a son, Prakash, Nirmala's father. Prakash's marriage took place when he was a teenager and his wife was only seven years old. They had nine children who died, plus Nirmala and one surviving son. Prakash was 'a very lazy man' who didn't like work, but he moved to Bombay and worked in a mill, occasionally sending money home to his wife who stayed in the village with the two children. When Nirmala was five her father returned to the village and she remembers him worshipping various Hindu gods, but rarely working. Unable to depend on him to feed the family, her mother used to work on the roads to earn a few rupees by smashing up rocks with an iron mallet for the foundations. 'Padmasuri, I felt so sorry for her. She'd had such a hard life; all those children who had died; she looked so old, much older than her years. Her hands were blistered and gnarled. I felt sorry for her, and often at night when all was dark I used to cry for her.' As Nirmala told me this, tears welled up in her eyes. Vaisali and Vandana came upstairs and she told them to go out and play a while longer. They snatched a banana apiece and went outside.

In the holidays Nirmala used to help her mother on the roads: 'Though she didn't think it right for a small girl to work, I think she also admired me. I also spent a lot of time collecting fresh cow-dung, beating it between my hands into cakes, and leaving it in the sun to dry for use as fuel. Vaisali and Vandana will never have to do that sort of work. They are getting a good education, so they should be able to earn money working in offices, not on the roads.' Nirmala's parents also thought education important and sent her to the village school. There were only four girls in a class of twenty, and she was the only ex-Untouchable. She befriended the other three girls in the class, who were all Brahmins. When, after school, they came to play with Nirmala near her house, they ate her mother's food and drank the water she gave them; but when she went to their homes, their parents made her stand outside and hold out her cupped hands for water. One day Nirmala gave red meat scraps to the Brahmin girls as a joke, because they were not allowed to eat cows, which are sacred. One of their parents found out and she got into terrible trouble. She was in the second standard at school and seven years old when Dr Ambedkar died. Nirmala vividly remembers her mother wailing and banging her head against the wall, but not understanding why. Not long afterwards her father took the *Dharma-diksha* (conversion to Buddhism) in Bombay, and when he returned he destroyed all the pictures of Hindu gods, though her mother kept a picture of Lakshmi, the goddess of wealth, by the cooking stove. In their place he hung a picture of Dr Ambedkar, and later one of the Buddha.

When Nirmala's brother got married the whole family moved to Bombay and her brother started looking out for a suitable husband for her. He did not have to look far because a Mr Karat, who used to follow her to school, wanted to marry her. There was a lot of contention over this idea, but eventually she agreed, even though many of his relations were not happy with the match. They were married and she moved into the Karat family home. It was so small that there was not enough room for them all to sleep inside. There were eight adults and two children living in a room about nine feet square, so Nirmala and her husband used to sleep outside, even in the rains. Inevitably she had a miscarriage, then hepatitis, and was very ill indeed. I once visited this house, occupied now only by her brother-in-law, his wife, and their one daughter. It opens straight off the street with the traffic roaring past; no pavement divides the road from the row of huts. She showed me the tiny ledge where she and her husband used to sleep. Before they moved out to the ledge she and Mr Karat used to sleep underneath the only bed, on which the eldest brother and his wife and child slept, while the middle brother and his wife and child slept in one corner, and her mother and father-in-law slept against a wall.

'But worse than the physical conditions was the way I was maltreated by other members of the family. I became desperate to the point of wanting to commit suicide.' Being the youngest son's wife, hers was the lowest place in the family hierarchy, and that, coupled with the fact that theirs was a 'love marriage' as opposed to an arranged marriage, made her status an unenviable one. Her husband was not cruel to her, but they rarely, if ever, saw each other alone, and as he was out most of the day working, he probably never understood what was going on.

Her father-in-law, she told me, was the only one who really seemed to care for her, and on many occasions he took her along to see a Buddhist monk in a local temple. After this introduction, she would escape from the house whenever she had the chance and go to see the monk. Eventually Nirmala and her husband got their own hut in a large slum area and left the family home. Though the hut was filthy and squalid, she was much happier, and they managed to save enough money to buy a sewing machine so that she could do some tailoring work to bring in extra income. Later she got involved in a Buddhist political group and with their guidance started a Mahila Mandala. Indira Gandhi once came into their locality and, as a supporter of the Congress Party, Nirmala was delegated to meet and garland her. She has a picture of this meeting framed and hanging on the wall of her home.

'I was mixing political work with Buddhism: nobody could tell me the difference, so I began to think Buddhism meant politics. Yet, beginning to see that so many politicians were corrupt, I became frustrated, for I knew this wasn't what Dr Ambedkar had taught.'

Another frustration in her life was that apart from a miscarriage early in marriage, she had not conceived. Thinking she must have done something evil, she became fearful lest Mr Karat should find another wife. All this time she carried on seeing the monk, and began to tell him of her worries and fears. He told her that it would benefit her to fast every full-moon day. She did so, and within weeks discovered she was pregnant after seven years of marriage. Naturally she ascribed this miracle to the monk's blessing.

For five years after they moved out of the joint family home her brothers and sisters-in-law would not speak to her and she became an outcast from her own family. 'I couldn't see what I'd done wrong. I tried so hard to please them, yet everything I did was wrong. In the end I stopped worrying about it, and began to feel free again. The only family member I continued to see was my father-in-law. He came to visit me the day before he died. I was even blamed for his death by other members of the family. What did they think I'd done? Poisoned him or something?

I loved him, Padmasuri; he was a hundred times better than any of the others, and I knew he loved me. I was heart-broken by his death, and to have their blame on top of my grief was more than I could bear.'

Deep down she knew that Buddhism was the one thing which would make her happy, but she could not find a teacher. Having moved, she was too far away to go and visit the monk, and by this time she had three children, little freedom of movement, and almost no money. She told me amusing stories about Indian and Sri Lankan monks, who despite – or perhaps because of – wearing the traditional Buddhist saffron robes, expected to be revered without doing anything to merit it. Many had become as corrupt as the politicians, and none was even able to teach her how to meditate, let alone how to practise the Buddhist path.

'I have such a great respect for Dr Ambedkar; it was he who pulled us out of the mire of caste stigma, it was he who gave us dignity and confidence. I was lucky, for I did not suffer in the way that my ancestors suffered in the past as Untouchables, but I also knew that his conversion to Buddhism was the only real hope for our people. After the conversions, though, nobody really knew what Buddhism was. My father-in-law had extraordinary faith – he had lived through terrible humiliations of caste prejudice – and he always said to me, "Nirmala, you must practise Buddhism." But he only knew how to say, "Homage to the Buddha, homage to the Dharma, homage to the Sangha." I only wish he had lived to attend a Dharma shibeer.'

Eventually, through her continued searching, she found her way on to a retreat led by an Indian Dharmachari. She talks of her first retreat as the greatest turning point in her life. Instead of attending it alone she gathered a group of people together from her locality and took them along with her. When she met Vajraketu she was amazed that foreigners would mix so freely with them. For the first time she began to understand a little of the Buddha's teaching and to see that it is not to be practised only by monks, as she had always believed, but is a way of life for anyone who chooses to follow it, whatever their circumstances.

It was not long after this initial retreat that she and I met and began to develop our friendship. Until I had a better grasp of her language our meetings were frequently frustrated by the limits in our verbal communication – speaking through a interpreter does not make for a spontaneous 'feast of reason and flow of soul', but we soon learned to act out our communication through mime, and this is still an integral part of our interaction, giving us hours of fun and enjoyment.

Her determination to keep trying to put theory into practice is remarkable. Her inner life has quite dramatically changed over the years I've known her. Although her children are still young and at school, and although she has little education or sophistication, she will not be fettered by the householder's life. She will not see any obstacle as a permanent block to realizing her ideals, but rather as a challenge. To crown it all, she has had a thoroughly positive influence on her extended family, many of whom have great admiration for the way she is leading her life.

The longest periods of time we spent together were on retreats, or when she visited me in Poona, or I saw her in Bombay. Wherever it was, our best conversations were those that lasted well into the night when the family was asleep, and our hearts could open up. Often lying on a shared mattress under a mosquito net we would discuss ourselves, our lives, our thoughts, feelings, and aspirations. What we held in common was far greater than the differences of background, culture, education, and other external trappings that go to make up our concept of 'ourselves'.

We travelled together to many a town or village on every type of Indian conveyance: train, bus, rickshaw, bullock cart. We ate together from the same plate, we wore each other's saris and bangles, carried each other's luggage; she would beat my clothes clean on the rocks, laughing at my feeble attempts, while I picked out stones from the uncooked rice (something I could do well); she kneaded and rolled the chapatti dough while I cooked the chapattis. We worked together in harmony. I marvelled at my good fortune; what a privileged position this was, to be able to make such a friendship with someone from a culture so different from my own – and not just a superficial fleeting friendship with someone I would never meet again and soon forget, but a friendship that has the possibility of lasting a lifetime.

Vimalasuri is someone who never holds back secrets and is not diffident about herself, her background, her life. She wants nothing of me other than my friendship, and just by being the way she is, she demands it. She knows her weaknesses, but also her strengths and her potential, so that over the years she has become an enormous inspiration not only for me, but also for many of the Buddhist women who come from backgrounds similar to her own. After her ordination, despite not seeing each other sometimes for weeks on end, our lives became intertwined to the degree that we began to form psychic links with one another. One day when I was at a large gathering of Order members, during a session of mantra chanting dedicated to the invocation of the Bodhisattva of compassion, Avalokiteshvara, I was filled with an overwhelming feeling of warmth and friendship towards Vimalasuri, and I found myself choked with tears. I had a sense that she was suffering, that she was in some sort of trouble, but I could not fathom out why this should be, so I opened my eyes and looked across the candlelit shrine-room to where Vimalasuri sat. Tears were streaming down her face. Afterwards I asked her what had been going through her mind during the chanting. A little taken aback, she told me that she had been carried away with a deep sensation of loss and sadness linked to the time when her father had been killed in a road accident. He had adored her, but because of feuds between his family and hers they had not spoken for many months before his death. What she was experiencing was an intense sense of regret.

On another occasion I awoke early one morning feeling angry and frustrated at myself for being so dull-witted in my attempts to pick up Marathi. There seemed to be so much I wanted to speak about, yet sometimes it all seemed such an effort. I just lay there wishing Vimalasuri could speak English. Lying next to me she awoke, turned over towards me, and never having spoken a word of English before, said in the most pure and beautiful Oxford English, 'Good morning, Padmasuri!' I burst out laughing and asked her to repeat it again and again. And once during a siesta one hot afternoon on retreat I lay fantasizing about Vimalasuri visiting England some time in the future. I was imagining all the places I might take her to and the people she would meet, and trying to imagine her responses to it all. I visualized taking her to my parents' very English cottage in Wiltshire, sitting on their sofa, eating with knife and fork at their dining table. I imagined her watching colour TV in front of a log fire, soaking in a bubble bath of steaming water, walking around the garden admiring the flowers, riding in a car, going on an outing to the local stately home.... As I elaborated on the scenario in my mind she was quietly talking with another woman about something far removed from my thoughts of the moment. As their conversation came to a pause, she turned to me and said 'Padmasuri, I've decided to give up chewing tobacco. I shall save the rupees I would otherwise have spent, and one day I'll be able to come to England, visit your friends, visit your family, and see how you live over there.'

There were of course moments when we clashed too, but these differences were soon blown to the wind. If there was one person who might have persuaded me to stay in India it was she.

I end this book with Vimalasuri because she stands for what I value most of the eight years I spent in India. I wasn't in India just to offer my nursing skills. Nor was I there to patronize those less fortunate than myself or to be a representative of a charity giving conventional aid from a rich country to a poor country. And I wasn't there as a missionary to convert people to Buddhism, for most of those with whom I worked were already Buddhists. Dr Ambedkar had already given them a new vision of social and spiritual development based on the highest human values of individual dignity, self-respect, and self-determination. If I was able to help any of his followers to begin to realize something of that vision in their own lives this was achieved through the contact I made with individuals, through learning their language and sharing their lives, their joys, and their traumas, through the making and deepening of friendships. The theme of this book, if it were to be described in a single word, is friendship.

I am not the first person to celebrate friendship. Its importance was clearly stated 2,500 years ago by the Buddha, when his close disciple, Ananda, joyfully proclaimed to him one day a new and great realization. 'Lord Buddha, Lord Buddha!' one can imagine him almost singing. 'I have realized that friendship is half of the spiritual life.' The Buddha did not congratulate him for his insight, however. Solemnly he replied, 'Say not so, Ananda, say not so. Friendship is not half of the spiritual life. Friendship is the whole of the spiritual life!'

The Windhorse symbolizes the energy of the enlightened mind carrying the Three Jewels – the Buddha, the Dharma, and the Sangha – to all sentient beings.

Buddhism is one of the fastest growing spiritual traditions in the Western world. Throughout its 2,500-year history, it has always succeeded in adapting its mode of expression to suit whatever culture it has encountered.

Windhorse Publications aims to continue this tradition as Buddhism comes to the West. Today's Westerners are heirs to the entire Buddhist tradition, free to draw instruction and inspiration from all the many schools and branches. Windhorse publishes works by authors who not only understand the Buddhist tradition but are also familiar with Western culture and the Western mind.

For orders and catalogues contact

WINDHORSE PUBLICATIONS
11 PARK ROAD
BIRMINGHAM
B13 8AB
UK

WINDHORSE PUBLICATIONS INC
14 HEARTWOOD CIRCLE
NEWMARKET
NEW HAMPSHIRE
NH 03857   USA

Windhorse Publications is an arm of the Friends of the Western Buddhist Order, which has more than forty centres on four continents. Through these centres, members of the Western Buddhist Order offer regular programmes of events for the general public and for more experienced students. These include meditation classes, public talks, study on Buddhist themes and texts, and 'bodywork' classes such as t'ai chi, yoga, and massage. The FWBO also runs several retreat centres and the Karuna Trust, a fund-raising charity that supports social welfare projects in the slums and villages of India.

Many FWBO centres have residential spiritual communities and ethical businesses associated with them. Arts activities are encouraged too, as is the development of strong bonds of friendship between people who share the same ideals. In this way the FWBO is developing a unique approach to Buddhism, not simply as a set of techniques, less still as an exotic cultural interest, but as a creatively directed way of life for people living in the modern world.

If you would like more information about the FWBO please write to the

LONDON BUDDHIST CENTRE   ARYALOKA
51 ROMAN ROAD   HEARTWOOD CIRCLE
LONDON   NEWMARKET
E2 0HU   NEW HAMPSHIRE
UK   NH 03857   USA

The Karuna Trust is a Buddhist-inspired charity supporting long-term development work with India's former 'Untouchable' communities. Since 1980 Karuna has helped to create health, education, skills training, and cultural projects which promote dignity and self-reliance. All projects are run by local people through Karuna's partner in India, Bahujan Hitay. The projects are bringing lasting improvements to the lives of thousands of people and are open to anyone in need, regardless of background or beliefs.

Karuna relies for its work on donations raised from individuals in the UK. If you would like to find out more, or make a donation to support these projects, please write to:

THE KARUNA TRUST
ST MARK'S STUDIOS
CHILLINGWORTH ROAD
LONDON
N7 8QJ
UK

OR TELEPHONE 0171-700 3434

also from windhorse

TERRY PILCHICK (NAGABODHI)
Jai Bhim!
DISPATCHES FROM A PEACEFUL REVOLUTION

In the 1940s and 50s, Bhimrao Ramji Ambedkar – champion of India's 60,000,000 'Untouchables' – could have launched a violent struggle for freedom. Instead he asked his people to find dignity, strength, and prosperity by converting to Buddhism.
There are now millions of new Buddhists in India; they still meet and part with the words 'Jai Bhim!' – 'Victory to Bhimrao Ambedkar'.

Travelling around the Buddhist localities, meeting and living with Ambedkar's modern followers, Terry Pilchick gained an intimate impression of the unique revolution they are building. In a colourful, moving account, he allows us to witness the revolution for ourselves.

256 pages
ISBN 0 904766 36 5
£5.95/$12.50

SANGHARAKSHITA
Ambedkar and Buddhism

The remarkable and stirring story of Dr Bhimrao Ramji Ambedkar, lawyer, politician, and educationalist, who, in 1956, started the most important social revolution occurring in India today: the conversion from Hinduism to Buddhism of millions of Indians wishing to escape the degradation of the caste system.

Sangharakshita knew Ambedkar personally, and has himself played an important part in the Mass Conversion Movement that Ambedkar set in motion. In this book he explores the historical, religious, and social background to that movement, and assesses the considerable contribution made by Ambedkar to the spiritual tradition in which he placed his trust.

192 pages
ISBN 0 904766 28 4
£5.95/$11.95

SANGHARAKSHITA

FACING MOUNT KANCHENJUNGA

AN ENGLISH BUDDHIST IN THE EASTERN HIMALAYAS

In 1950 Kalimpong was a lively trading town where India runs into Nepal, Bhutan, Sikkim, and Tibet. Like a magnet, it attracted a bewildering array of guests and settlers: ex-colonials, Christian missionaries, princes in exile, pioneer Buddhologists, incarnate lamas from the Land of Snows – and Sangharakshita, the young English monk who was trying to establish a Buddhist movement for local youngsters.

In a delightful volume of memoirs, glowing with affection and humour, the author shares the incidents, encounters, and insights of his early years in Kalimpong. Behind the events we witness the transformation of a rather eccentric young man into a unique and confident individual, completely at home in his adopted world, and increasingly effective as an interpreter of Buddhism for a new age.

512 pages, with photographs
ISBN 0 904766 52 7
£11.95/$24.00

SANGHARAKSHITA

IN THE SIGN OF THE GOLDEN WHEEL

INDIAN MEMOIRS OF AN ENGLISH BUDDHIST

This engaging volume of memoirs recounts the unique experiences of an English Buddhist monk working in the mid-1950s to revive Buddhism in the land of its birth.

We follow Sangharakshita in his quest – from his hermitage in Kalimpong in the Himalayas to collaboration with a film star in Bombay, a visit from the Dalai Lama, and involvement in the spectacular festivals celebrating 2,500 years of Buddhism.

Brimming with life and colour, this book is a notable addition to the canon of travel literature as we follow the spiritual adventures of an unorthodox and extraordinary Englishman.

384 pages, with photographs
ISBN 1 899579 14 1
£14.99/$29.95

KAMALASHILA

MEDITATION

THE BUDDHIST WAY OF TRANQUILLITY AND INSIGHT

A comprehensive guide to the methods and theory of Buddhist meditation, written in an informal, accessible style. It provides a complete introduction to the basic techniques, as well as detailed advice for more experienced meditators seeking to deepen their practice.

The author is a long-standing member of the Western Buddhist Order, and has been teaching meditation since 1975. In 1979 he helped to establish a semi-monastic community in North Wales, which has now grown into a public retreat centre. For more than a decade he and his colleagues developed approaches to meditation that are firmly grounded in Buddhist tradition but readily accessible to people with a modern Western background. Their experience – as meditators, as students of the traditional texts, and as teachers – is distilled in this book.

304 pages, with charts and illustrations
ISBN 1 899579 05 2
£12.99/$25.95

SANGHARAKSHITA

BUDDHISM FOR TODAY – AND TOMORROW

To lead a Buddhist life we need, above all, four things: a vision of the kind of person we could become; practical methods to help us transform ourselves in the light of that vision; friendship to support and encourage us on the path; and a society or culture that supports us in our aspirations.

This book is a succinct introduction to a Buddhist movement that exists precisely to make these things available. The author, Sangharakshita, brought the experience of twenty years' practice of Buddhism in India back to his native Britain, to found the Friends of the Western Buddhist Order in 1967.

This heartfelt statement of his vision is recommended reading for anyone who aspires to live a Buddhist life in the world today – and tomorrow.

64 pages
ISBN 0 904766 83 7
£4.99/$8.95